Evermore Shall Be So

Commentaries by Ficino on Plato's Writings
a four-volume series

Gardens of Philosophy
Evermore Shall Be So
When Philosophers Rule
All Things Natural

Evermore Shall Be So

FICINO ON PLATO'S *PARMENIDES*

ARTHUR FARNDELL

SHEPHEARD-WALWYN (PUBLISHERS) LTD

First published in 2008 by
Shepheard-Walwyn (Publishers) Ltd
15 Alder Road
London SW14 8ER

British Library Cataloguing in Publication Data
A catalogue record of this book
is available from the British Library

ISBN: 978-0-85683-256-7

Typeset by Alacrity,
Sandford, Somerset
Printed and bound through
s|s|media limited, Wallington, Surrey

CONTENTS

ACKNOWLEDGEMENTS

THE TRANSLATOR is very happy to give the first accolade to his wife, Phyllis, who as 'an help meet for him' has been with this work from its inception to its completion. Her encouragement and her intuitive guidance have proved invaluable.

John Meltzer has supported the work throughout; Adrian Bertoluzzi and Christophe Poncet have kindly supplied Latin texts; Nathan David has again magnanimously granted permission for jacket designs based on two of his beautiful sculptures; Emma Bomfim has courageously transposed handwriting into meticulous typing; Jean Desebrock has imparted intelligence and artistry to the appearance of the book; and Anthony Werner has deftly waved his publishing wand over the whole project.

Clement Salaman, John Meltzer, Andrew Sisson, and Ian Murray have given generously of their time and attention to join the translator and his wife in reading the work and in making pertinent observations.

Each of these fine people is hereby acknowledged and thanked.

Arthur Farndell

TRANSLATOR'S INTRODUCTION
to Ficino's *Parmenides*

MULTIFARIOUS are the introductions that could be written to the commentary made by Marsilio Ficino to Plato's *Parmenides*. The translator has chosen to focus on the two themes that particularly struck him as he read and re-read Ficino's text. The first is the care shown by Parmenides in the training he imparts to Socrates. The second is Ficino's presentation of Plato's text as a work of practical spirituality.

The care shown by Parmenides

IN HIS DEDICATION of the commentary to Niccolò Valori, Ficino remarks that 'Parmenides, though older, does not contradict Socrates'. In Chapter 15 some correction does occur in dealing with the doubts expressed by Socrates: 'Parmenides does not correct the first doubt, but he does correct the second.' It is the next chapter that clearly depicts the care evinced by the elder philosopher, whom Ficino here presents in the likeness of a midwife:

> Just as Socrates, the son of a midwife, performs the office of a midwife in different places towards boys and youths and proclaims this before others, so the aged Parmenides, like a dutiful midwife, exhorts and helps the youthful Socrates to give birth to the wonderful, almost divine, opinions with which he is pregnant and which he is trying to bring forth.
> Moreover, he does not reject or destroy the children that are born lacking beauty, but rather he takes them up and cherishes them in a wonderful way. He strengthens the weak, straightens the crooked, gives shape to the shapeless, and perfects the imperfect. No one, therefore, will think that Parmenides the Pythagorean, the friend of Ideas in the manner of his fellows, and the pursuer of Being, which is detached from sensory perception, and of the One Itself, which is above Being,

condemns opinions of this kind; but every follower of Plato will remember that Socrates is being very carefully trained by Parmenides in dialectic, in order that he may be much more heedful when considering the divine mysteries, that he may proceed with greater care, and that he may reach the end of his journey in greater safety.

The portrayal of Parmenides as a midwife appears again in Chapter 26, where he is also compared to a teacher:

That Parmenides does not pursue Socrates at every point like a disputant and rebuke him, but in the manner of a midwife encourages, assists, cherishes, guides and corrects him, is plain to observe, because this young man does not gradually wane but gains strength at every step, being led towards better things ... Therefore, being now guided by Parmenides as by a teacher, he puts forward a true and definite view of Ideas.

The third comparison of Parmenides to a midwife occurs in Chapter 34, where Ficino says:

When Parmenides pursues, in relation to Socrates, the dedicated function of midwife which he introduced at the beginning, stimulating the inner powers of the young man to a most precise consideration of Ideas and showing on numerous occasions that very serious errors arise from imprecise answers and responses, and that it is a difficult task, and one that requires an excellent mind, to prove that Ideas exist, to show how they exist, to truly resolve doubts as they arise, and to teach with clear reason the person who is listening, all of these things make Socrates very careful and precise.

In Chapter 18 Ficino portrays Parmenides as being a particularly careful tutor when Ideas are being considered:

When Parmenides, therefore, is going to instruct Socrates, or rather encourage him, to contemplate that true way of participation by which Ideas are perceived by what is below them, he rejects, one by one, the ways which are not lawful ... Thus Socrates is advised to consider a non-physical, indeed divine, way of understanding, for we are considering either the power of an Idea or the property of an Idea ... Moreover, in comparing an Idea to the light of day he speaks rightly, but in thinking that light spreads through air like heat and is like a sail spread over the heads of many men, and in thinking that this is how an Idea is present in many objects, he is refuted by Parmenides, who says that, if this were the case, an Idea would not be totally present in anything but would be present in some parts of the objects through some of its own parts; and in this way he compels the young man to answer with greater care.

In the following chapter Ficino indicates that Socrates, for his part, is a ready student:

> Step by step Socrates is instructed in these matters so that he may consider a partaking of the Ideas which is higher than any physical principle. To this instruction Socrates readily assents, being inclined towards it by nature.

The measured restraint practised by Parmenides throughout the training imparted to Socrates is clearly in evidence in Chapter 21 of Ficino's commentary:

> As a Pythagorean with due regard for Ideas, Parmenides does not cross Socrates when the latter supposes that, on account of assemblages of items coming together within something definite in response to a cause related to form, type, nature, and perfection, there is a single Idea for each and every assemblage within a type.
> He does, however, temper Socrates' enthusiasm, in order to avoid the possible inference that any collection of items has to be related to a specific Idea, even if these items seem to come together by some accidental or passing circumstance, by some deficiency, artificiality, or name; for if this were the case, there would be an unnatural number of causes for many of the occurrences within nature, and the number of Ideas would be infinite ... This is how Socrates is advised not to imagine a new Idea for every apparent combination.

The restraint continues to be evident in the following chapter, where Ficino, after comparing Socrates to 'a young man without sufficient training', says:

> Finally, Parmenides does not in fact reprove Socrates for seeking refuge in such notions, but he does reprove him for appearing to stay there. He therefore takes pains, through this reference to new notions which relates to the naturally implanted types, to call him back next not only to these types but also to the divine types.

However, from this point onwards the training of the young man's mind does seem to become somewhat stricter:

> For this reason Parmenides, intending to lead Socrates on to a fuller explanation of these things, will henceforth insist upon many reasonings.
>   (Chapter 26)

> ... when Socrates was being tested by Parmenides.
>   (Chapter 27)

Parmenides advises the young man ... to proceed more carefully henceforth.   (Chapter 27)

Parmenides therefore advises Socrates, in relation to the divine Ideas, to
acknowledge both the pre-eminence of their nature and their ability to
impart their power.   (Chapter 28)

In brief, Socrates had to answer Parmenides by saying that the ideal lordship and the ideal service are not related to us but to each other, I mean
through their first indissoluble relationship.   (Chapter 30)

For this reason Socrates is now carefully trained, so that he learns to
resolve doubts about Ideas, which, if unresolved, would detract from
divine providence.   (Chapter 32)

Even in the later chapters of the commentary Ficino reminds us of
the unremitting dedication shown by Parmenides in his instruction
of Socrates. In Chapter 87 he says that 'Parmenides hones the young
man's mind ever more keenly', and in Chapter 90 we find:

Parmenides, when preparing to train the mind of the noble young man
along these lines, obliges him repeatedly, by means of the tightest
constraints, either to withdraw from the false or else to make use of these
abstractions, in which, as the man whom you know also says, there is
no falsehood ... Parmenides tacitly reminds us of these things, partly
instructing the mind of the young man by means of some logical
stratagem and partly sowing some hidden teaching here and there.

Finally, in Chapter 93, Ficino again draws our attention to the same
theme:

Notice how Parmenides, at times when philosophic tenets are being torn
to shreds, trains the young man to be careful in his replies and judicious
in his discrimination.

What effect did this training at the hands of Parmenides have upon
Socrates? Ficino gives the answer in Chapter 37 by referring to a
response given by Socrates in the *Theaetetus*:

In the *Theaetetus*, when Socrates was asked to refute those who posited
a single motionless being, he did not undertake to do so himself but
gave this answer: Although I honour Melissus and others, who say
that there is one self-consistent totality, for it may seem immodest of me
to cross them, yet I honour them less than I do Parmenides alone, for
Parmenides, to use Homer's words, strikes me as one who is sagacious

and worthy of great honour. I once conversed with him when he was advanced in years and I was but a youth, and he struck me as having a wisdom that was profound and noble in all respects. This is why I fear that we do not have the slightest understanding of his sayings and expressions, and what he himself implied by his words is, I fear, even more of a closed book to us.

Practical Spirituality

FICINO SEES MAN as made in the image of God, and he recognises that the full realisation of human nature is nothing less than to become God. In his commentary to Parmenides, the dialogue which he says embraces all theology, Ficino presents this realisation as an ascending movement, which starts from the material forms of the universe, rises through the hierarchy of creation, and ends in God. In Chapter 41 Ficino tells us that 'Plato rises to the Supreme by two paths: by the path of analogies in the *Republic* and by the path of negations in *Parmenides*.' This is a process that is available to every human being. In Chapter 31 Ficino says:

> But we do at times cognise, through the forms which are objects for us or which are innate in us, the intellectual Ideas which shine clearly in our minds subsequent to the first Idea and through which, being illumined particularly by the higher minds, we finally ascend, as far as we may, after the expiation described in the *Phaedrus*, to the first Ideas, which are rightly named the intelligible types, ourselves being raised above the human condition.

Our capability is portrayed in Chapter 34:

> With this process of reasoning and with very many others given in the *Theology*, we have shown conclusively that the patterns and models of all things are naturally implanted within our mind ... This is why, as Parmenides says, we shall find no true substance to which we may properly turn the eye of the mind, for it is not right to move towards higher things, except through the world within, or to hold the contents of the inner world as worthy of respect when they are taken from the worthless outer world ... Man himself, however, as universally defined, should embrace each and every thing totally.

In Chapter 35 Ficino re-states the aim and gives directions for achieving it:

> Since the hierarchy of creation strives, step by step, towards perfection, and since the order of the universe takes its origin from the most perfect principle, we must finally reach the most perfect forms, that is, the ideal and intelligible types, which are totally devoid of all the limitations of material forms ... For anyone who would consider matter is obliged to lay aside every form, and this runs counter, of course, to the usual operation of consciousness; and anyone who would contemplate Ideas is compelled to discard all the mists and wisps of material forms, an action quite contrary to the normal mode of human consciousness. In this way, Ideas are finally attained by the simple gaze of steady intelligence, a gaze utterly dissociated from all considerations of material things.

In Chapter 44 Ficino continues his words of practical guidance in the process of contemplation:

> Being about to perceive the single best principle of the universe, we are obliged, first of all, to lay aside whatever is most at variance with it, that is, evil and multiplicity, and to use all our powers to be called back to our unparalleled and best quality, back to the simple and peaceful contemplation of sublime intelligence.
>
> And so, according to the measure of the divine light shining within the first intellect and within Ideas, we look up to that in exactly the same way as we look up on a clear night to the stars in the firmament, employing all our powers to contemplate that intellect through our own intelligence and to contemplate Ideas through the ideal forms innate within our own intelligence ... If we progress by long perseverance in such contemplation, the new and incredibly wonderful light of the Good itself at last flashes upon us from on high, just as the radiance of the sun illumines astronomers who have been observing the stars until daybreak, the radiance which miraculously removes the stars at once from their eyes, just as the light of the Good itself, if it is to be perceived, obliges us to put in second place its intelligence as forms, as well as the intellect itself and Ideas and all intelligible things.
>
> Just as we look up at the sun with half-closed eyes, so we look up at, or rather worship, the light of the Good with half-closed intelligence. For it is not permissible or right ever to direct the gaze of the intelligence upon that which is above the intelligible ... Finally, if it can in any way be right to describe the Good itself, look around at all the perfections in the creation, which are to be sought for their own sakes. Their wellspring is therefore the Good itself, which resides as the centre in all

things that are sought, in part producing perfections to be sought after within desirable things, and in part, with these perfections as baits, enticing all that seek to come to itself.

In Chapter 45 we are told that 'mind, perfected through the Good, now possesses truth, joy, and fulfilment.'

For Ficino the whole process is a live reality, and to dispel any thought that it might be otherwise he exclaims in Chapter 50, 'This One, therefore, is not a name invented by some logician, but it is the very principle of the universe.' And in Chapter 53 he continues to describe a movement which he has clearly followed himself:

> But shall we, in the manner of Proclus, rise from the intelligible which is within the intellect to the intelligible which is outside the intellect? Indeed, wherever the intelligible resides within any intellect – not the intelligible in all respects, but some intelligible, and not, in fact, identical with the substance of mind – there we shall search for a more exalted intelligible.
>
> But after we have reached the first intellect, where the intelligible is so complete and so deep within the intellect as to be the very essence of this intellect, we shall yearn for no intelligible beyond this.
>
> However, since the unity here is not simple unity itself, but a unity which is essential, intellectual, and intelligible, and which has formal number as its companion, we shall proceed from here to the simple One Itself, from which, as from a watchtower, we shall contemplate the divine unities, the gods, flowing forth in their hierarchy.

Ficino's use of the language of the mystics intensifies as the commentary proceeds:

> Indeed, a movement of change within the soul occurs when the soul, as if now changed, undergoes the emotion, the life, the form, and the action of things that are higher or of things that are lower. There is a direct, inward, rational movement from the higher to the lower, an outward change of place, and a quickening of the body.   (Chapter 63)

The language used by Ficino reaches a new pitch of intensity in Chapter 78:

> If it is not perceived by knowledge and intelligence, much less will it be perceived by the lower faculties of imagination, belief, and the senses. This is what Plato maintains in his Epistle to the Syracusans, where he says that the Self can in no way be taught or declared, but that at length the light of the One suddenly flashes on those minds that are fully

turned towards the One Itself through unity and silence, that is, through the absence of the usual activity ... And so, by this marvellous sense and yearning, all things are turned towards the First, even though they do not cognise the First; and the soul likewise, even prior to a clear notion and choice made by her own counsel, seeks the One Itself by her natural sense and inclination through a single impression made by it upon her ... Parmenides thinks that the One Itself is not directly attainable even by intelligence, the guide of knowledge, since intelligence takes many forms and it is through forms that it is conveyed to beings. But after the clarity and the flash of intelligence, another light now shines from above – the light by which our own unity is miraculously united with the One Itself ... Finally, in his Epistle to the distinguished Hermias and his companions, Plato gives evidence that the supreme God can in some way be perceived, for he says that if, through the right practice of philosophy, we seek God, the Guide and Father of all, we shall eventually cognise Him clearly, as it is given to the blessed to cognise Him ... The words of Proclus are very satisfying: By the name of the One it is not the One within itself that is being expressed but that which is deep within us from the One, the one hidden concept of the One; for within all beings there is an innate yearning for the first principle as the end of all. And so, before the yearning there is a hidden sense (if I may call it that) of That.

The following chapter (79) focuses on the need for inner silence and trust in God:

We therefore ask: 'Where in Plato's writings does the process of dialectic rise step by step through all negations and up to the first cause of all beings and intelligibles?' For if it is not in this dialogue it is definitely nowhere ... For this reason Parmenides is right to advise us to put our trust not in negations so much as in a silence that is peaceful, divine, and loving ... The prophet David, too, says, 'Silence praises Thee, O God.' ... We have travelled thus far along these roads, indeed through places where there are no roads, with Proclus and Syrianus as our guides or at least as sign-posts for us. But beyond this, where there is no one to guide us, we must move forward with God as our guide and trust henceforth in inspiration alone.

Since it would be difficult to find better guides for our own spiritual journey, let us joyfully move forward with Proclus and Syrianus, with Parmenides and Socrates, and, of course, with Plato and Ficino.

AN OVERVIEW
of Ficino's *Parmenides* Commentary

Dedication to Niccolò Valori

'Plato ... has embraced all theology within *Parmenides* [Plato ... universam in Parmenide complexus est theologiam].'

'He seems to have drawn this celestial work, in a divine way, from the deep recesses of the divine mind and from the innermost sanctuary of philosophy [videtur et ex divinae mentis adytis intimoque Philosophiae sacrario caeleste hoc opus divinitus deprompsisse]. Anyone approaching his sacred writings [Ad cuius sacram lectionem quisque accedet] should prepare himself with sobriety of soul and freedom of mind before daring to handle the mysteries of the celestial work [prius sobrietate animi mentisque libertate se preparet, quam attrectare mysteria caelestis operis audeat]. For here the divine Plato [Hic enim divinus Plato], speaking of the One Itself, discusses with great subtlety how the One Itself is the principle of all things [de ipso uno subtilissime disputat quemadmodum ipsum unum rerum omnium principium est]: how it is above all [super omnia], and all things come from it [omniaque ab illo]; how it is outside all and within all [Quo pacto ipsum extra omnia sit, et in omnibus]; and how all come out of it [omniaque ex illo], through it, and to it [per illud atque ad illud].'

'*Parmenides* ... unfolds the whole principle of Ideas [Parmenides integram idearum explicat rationem].'

Parmenides 'introduces nine hypotheses [suppositiones] ..., five on the basis that the One exists and four on the basis that the One does not exist.'

Ficino gives a brief statement on the nature of each hypothesis, and he points out that Parmenides' main intention is to affirm that 'there is a single principle [principium] of all things, and if that is in place everything is in place, but if it be removed everything perishes.'

The first hypothesis 'discusses the one supreme God [de uno supremoque Deo disserit].'

The second 'discusses the individual orders of the divinities [de singulis Deorum ordinibus].'

The third 'discusses divine souls [de divinis animis].'

The fourth 'discusses those which come into being in the region which surrounds matter [de iis, quae circa materiam fiunt].'

The fifth 'discusses primal matter [de materia prima].'

The Preface of Marsilio Ficino to his Commentary on *Parmenides*

'Under the guise of a dialectical and, as it were, logical game aimed at training the intelligence [sub ludo quodam dialectico et quasi logico exercitaturo videlicet ingenium], Plato points towards divine teachings and many aspects of theology [ad divina dogmata passim theologica multa significat.]'

'The subject matter of this *Parmenides* is particularly theological [Materia ... Parmenidis huius potissimum theologica est] and its form particularly logical [forma vero praecipue logica].'

Chapter 1: Setting the scene for the dialogue

A request is made for a previous discussion involving Parmenides, Zeno, and Socrates to be recounted.

Chapter 2: How the whole of being is one, but the One Itself is above being [Quomodo omne ens sit unum, ipsum vero unum super ens]

'The universe, or the all [universum sive omne] is appreciated in these three ways [tribus his modis accipitur]: individually, collectively, as a whole [singulatim, congregatim, summatim].'

'Beyond that unity which partakes perfectly of the intelligible world [praeter unitatem illam intelligibili mundo perfecte participatam] he (Parmenides) postulates a supreme unity [eminentissimam excogitat unitatem] higher than the one universal being [universo ente uno excelsiorem], for the nature of being is different from the nature of unity [alia enim ipsius entis, alia unitatis ipsius ratio est].'

'Therefore the one being [Unum igitur ens] is not the simple One Itself [non est ipsum simpliciter unum] but is in all respects a composite [sed quoquomodo compositum] mixed with multiplicity [multitudinique permixtum].'

Chapter 3: All multiplicity partakes of Unity [Omnis multitudo est particeps unitatis]

Zeno, Parmenides' disciple, confirms his master's proposition with another, 'whereby he shows that beings are not many [ens non esse multa], that is, not only many [id est, solum multa], but beyond their multiplicity [sed praeter multitudinem] they partake of unity [esse participes unitatis].'

Chapter 4: The Existence and Nature of Ideas [Ideas esse, et quales]

'Human nature depends on the Idea of man [ab idea hominis humana natura (dependet)].'

'Now the cause which is unmoving and universal at the same time [Causa vero immobilis simul universalisque] is necessarily the intellect [necessario est intellectus] and the intellectual Idea [et intellectualis idea].'

'Again, there are many Ideas [Ideae rursus multae sunt], as least as many as the types of natural phenomena [quod saltem rerum species naturalium], and each one is called a unity [et unaquaeque unitas appellatur], I mean, not simply unity [unitas inquam non simpliciter], but a unity [imo quaedam].'

'For this reason [quamobrem] there exists above ideal unities [super ideales unitates extat] the One that is simply itself [ipsum simpliciter unum], governing the full expansion of all species [per quaslibet multitudines latissime regnans].'

Chapter 5: In what respects Ideas differ among themselves and in what respects they agree [Quomodo ideae inter se differant et conveniant]

'Since Ideas are eternal and intellectual in their extreme purity [Ideae cum sint aeternae et ad puritatis summum intellectuales], they produce within the same sequence beneath them unmoving and pure effects prior to moving and impure effects [effectus procreant in eadem sub ipsis serie stabiles atque puros, priusquam mobiles et impuros].'

Chapter 6: For what there are Ideas, and for what there are no Ideas: there are as many Ideas as there are rational souls [Quorum sint ideae. Quorum non sint. Quot sunt rationales animae, totidem earum sunt ideae]

'There is a single Idea for the whole of a single type [unius communiter speciei una est idea].'

Chapter 7: There is no Idea for matter [Nulla est idea materiae]

Chapter 8: There are no Ideas for individual items [Singularium non sunt ideae]

Chapter 18: An Idea is not partaken of in a physical way, so that neither the whole nor any part of it is received [Idea non participatur corporeo more: ita ut vel tota vel pars eius aliqua capiatur]

'Nothing in our world [Nulla quidem rerum nostrarum] apprehends the whole power of an Idea [totam capit ideae virtutem]: that eternal, effective, and totally indivisible essence, perfect life, and perfect intelligence [scilicet aeternam illam efficaciam individuam prorsus essentiam, vitam intelligentiamque perfectam].'

Chapter 19: Ideal largeness, ideal equality, and ideal smallness are not partaken of by any nature divisible into parts [Ipsa magnitudo aequalitas, parvitas ideales non participantur conditione quadam in partes divisibili]

'Let us consider ideal equality [consideramus idealem aequalitatem]: an intellectual ratio [scilicet rationem quandam intellectualem] which is both a model and a unifier [tam exemplarem, quam conciliatricem] of universal harmony [universae congruitatis] and of harmonic proportion [et proportionis harmonicae] and of any kind of equality [aequalitatisque cuiuslibet].'

Chapter 20: Neither by nature nor by circumstance do Ideas meet with material things [Ideas non convenire cum materialibus neque natura neque conditione]

'It is clearly the case [plane constat] that Ideas are remote from [illas procul ab] all differentiation, all place, all movement, and all time [omni divisione, loco, motu, tempore esse], being indivisible, unmoving, eternal, and present everywhere [impartibiles, immobiles, aeternas, ubique praesentes]: so present [ita praesentes] that each quality of an Idea [ut cuiuslibet ideae proprietas quaedam] extends to the uttermost ends of creation [ad ultimas perveniat mundi formas].'

'However, it is important now to remember [Meminisse vero nunc oportet] that forms in the physical world [formas in materia] are not produced directly from Ideas, but are made through the seed-powers of nature derived from Ideas [non proxime ab ideis, sed per vires seminales naturae illinc infusas effici].'

Chapter 21: We should not suppose that every assemblage of multifarious items suggests that there is a single Idea for those items [Non debemus ex qualibet multorum communione, unam illorum ideam excogitare]

Chapter 22: From types which are created by the soul we must rise to types which are naturally present in the soul, and then rise from those to types which are divine [Oportet a speciebus quae fiunt ab anima ad species ascendere quae naturaliter insunt animae. Ab his insuper ad divinas]

'We use reason aright to take physical things back to their non-physical causes [resque corporeas ad incorporeas causas recta ratione reducimus].'

Chapter 23: The first types of creation, which are also the principal subjects of the intellect, are prior to the intelligences [Primae rerum species, quae etiam sunt principalia intellectus obiecta intelligentias antecedunt]

'Just as true sense [quemadmodum verus sensus] focuses on something perceptible [circa sensibile quiddam versatur] which actually exists [quod et revera existit], which is prior to sense [et antecedit sensum], and which is united with sense at the time of perception [ac denique cum sensu iam sentiente coniungitur], so true intelligence [sic intelligentia vera], which he now calls *notion* [quam nunc nominat notionem], is directed towards something that is intelligible to it [ad intelligibile suum dirigitur], that really exists and is prior to it [revera existens atque praecedens], and is more united with *notion* [et magis cum notione coniunctum] than the perceptible is with sense [quam cum sensu sensibile].'

Chapter 24: Ideas are intelligible things rather than intelligences, and these intelligible things are prior to intelligences [Ideae non tam intelligentiae quam intelligibilia sunt. Atque haec intelligentias antecedunt]

'This universe has taken its rise not so much from the intellect or the intelligence as from intelligible things, namely, the first essence, which is full of intelligible types and powers [universum hoc non tam ab intellectu vel intelligentia quam ab intelligibilibus, id est, ab essentia prima intelligibilium specierum virtutumque plena].'

Chapter 25: The quality of an Idea somehow remains one throughout an entire sequence, while the power of an Idea varies [Proprietas idealis una quodammodo est in tota serie. Virtus autem varia]

Chapter 26: Ideas are not simple notions but natural types which possess model power and effective power [Ideae non sunt simplices notiones quaedam, sed species naturales, vim exemplarem efficientemque habentes]

'The nature of the Idea is not conveyed to our world [neque ipsa ideae natura ad haec nostra transfertur], nor, conversely, do the things of our world in any way meet Ideas [neque haec igitur in re ulla conveniunt cum ideis], but merely reflect them [sed solum illas referunt], just as the image in a mirror reflects the face [quemadmodum specularis imago vultum].'

Chapter 27: Natural forms are rightly said to be similar to Ideas, but Ideas must not be described as similar to natural forms [Naturales formae dicuntur quidem ideis similes. Ideae vero harum similes appellari non debent]

Chapter 28: Contrary to the opinion of the Stoics and the Aristotelians, Ideas and all things divine are separate from nature and have a power that can be imparted to everything [Contra stoicos atque peripateticos, quod ideae divinaque omnia et natura segregata sunt et virtutem habent cunctis communicabilem]

'The first Good acts and cares with the greatest possible providence [primum denique ipsumque bonum quam maxime facit et providet].'

Chapter 29: The ways in which Ideas cannot be known by us, and the ways in which they can be known [Quomodo ideae a nobis cognosci non possint. Item quomodo possint]

'But when we say in this discussion that the first types are within themselves, you should understand [Tu vero inter haec ubi primas species esse dicimus in seipsis, intellige] that they are not within the first intellect [non esse in primo intellectu] like parts within a whole [velut partes in toto], or like qualities within an object [vel qualitates aliquas in subiecto], but like numbers within unity [sed quemadmodum in unitate numeri], like the beginnings of lines within a centre [in centro capita linearum], like the rays and colours within the light of the sun [in solis luce, radii, vel colores].'

Chapter 30: The ways in which Ideas are not related, or may be related, to the things of our world, and vice versa. Also concerning lordship and service and relationships in the realm of Ideas [Quomodo ideae non referantur vel referantur ad nostra, et haec ad illas. Ac de dominatione illic et servitute, et relationibus idearum]

Chapter 31: How pure knowledge relates to pure truth, while human knowledge relates to human truth. How Ideas

may be unknown or known [Quomodo ipsa simpliciter
scientia ad ipsam simpliciter veritatem refertur. Scientia
humana, ad humanam. Quomodo ideae ignotae vel notae]

Chapter 32: Concerning the way of divine consideration and providence [De modo divinae cognitionis atque providentiae]

'By being aware that He Himself is the origin of all [cognoscendo se ipsum principium omnium], He immediately cognises all and makes all [omnia statim et cognoscit et facit].'

Chapter 33: On divine lordship and consciousness, and on the six orders of Ideas or forms [De dominatione et cognitione divina, atque de sex ordinibus idearum vel formarum]

'For it is not by intelligence [Non enim intelligentia] but by some more mysterious act [sed occultiore quodam actu] that we are able to appreciate the first principle of the universe [frui primo universi principio possumus].'

Chapter 34: If there be no Ideas in the presence of God and no ideal patterns within us, then Dialectic will perish, and so will all Philosophy. There will be no proof, definition, division, or explanation [Nisi sint et ideae penes deum et ideales in nobis formulae, peribit dialectica omnisque philosophia. Non erit demonstratio vel definitio, vel divisio, vel resolutio]

'We have shown conclusively [confirmavimus] that the patterns and models of all things [formulas regulasque rerum] are naturally implanted within our mind [esse menti etiam nostrae naturaliter insitas].'

Chapter 35: On the practice of Dialectic through the intellectual forms and with the intelligible types as the aim [De dialectica exercitatione per formas intellectuales, ad species intelligibiles]

Parmenides 'will begin [exordietur] from the One [ab uno] as the cause of Ideas and of divine matters [tanquam causa idearum atque divinorum], showing throughout the debate [significans in toto disputationis cursu] that this One [ipsum unum] produces all beings step by step [producere entia omnia gradatim].'

In this way Ideas [Illas igitur] are finally attained [attingit tandem] by the simple gaze of steady intelligence [stabilis intelligentiae simplex intuitus], a gaze utterly dissociated from all considerations of material things [ab omnibus materialium cogitationibus penitus segregatus].'

Chapter 36: The rules of Dialectic which pre-suppose being or non-being, and the number of ways in which non-being is described [Regulae dialecticae supponentes esse vel non esse, et quot modis dicitur non ens]

'Parmenides maintains that the most powerful form of reasoning is [Potissimam argumentandi formam esse vult] that which proceeds from hypothesis [quae ex suppositione procedit] and examines carefully [perpendens], with many steps [multis gradibus] what follows [quid sequatur] if something is affirmed and what follows if it is denied [affirmato quolibet vel negato], for this form of reasoning [forma enim eiusmodi] does not depend on any human contrivances [non machinis quibusdam confidit humanis], but relies on a rational succession of natural and divine things [sed ipsa rerum naturalium divinarumque consequenti serie nititur] and has the hierarchy of the universe as its teacher of truth [praeceptoremque veritatis habet ipsum ordinem universi].'

Chapter 37: The subsequent discussion is said to be difficult, because it is not only logical but also theological [Futura disputatio dicitur ardua, quia non solum logica est sed etiam theologica]

Chapter 38: On the hypotheses of Parmenides; and on the Good, which, according to the words of Plato, is higher than being and higher than intellect [De suppositionibus Parmenidis. Et de uno bonoque quod ente et intellectu superius, per verba Platonis]

'It is shown in the *Philebus* [In Philebo probatur] that from the One [ab ipso uno], which is the beginning of creation [rerum principio], two are immediately produced [statim produci binarium]: the principles of beings [scilicet principia entium], or the two elements known as limit and limitlessness [vel elementa duo, terminum scilicet infinitatemque] … From these two [ex quibus] all beings are directly compounded [omnia prorsus entia componantur], but before the compounding of other beings [sed ante aliorum entium compositionem] the first to be compounded and mixed from these two [primum ex his confici mixtum] is the first being [scilicet ens primum], which contains universal being within itself [in se continens ens universum].'

Ficino draws support also from the sixth book of the *Republic*: 'The Good Itself [ipsum bonum] is not the intellect or the intelligible [neque tamen est intellectus vel intelligibile] or the truth or essence [vel veritas vel essentia], but is higher than all these in excellence and power [sed his omnibus dignitate et potestate superius].'

Further support is taken from the *Sophist*: 'It is clear that in the first being [probatur in primo ente] there are all those things [omnia esse] which are necessarily required for the perfection of being [quae ad perfectionem entis necessario requiruntur].'

'Finally, he shows in the *Sophist* [probatur denique in Sophiste] ... that the first universal being [ipsum primum et universum ens] is subject to the One [patitur unum], both in its parts [tum in partibus suis] and as a whole [tum in toto].'

Chapter 39: Next, how Plato proceeds to the First. Its name. The Idea of the Good [Item quomodo Plato procedit ad primum. De nomine eius. De idea boni]

'Throughout his writings Plato reduces perceptible multiplicities to intelligible unities, that is, to Ideas [Plato ... ubique sensibiles passim multitudines ad intelligibiles redigit unitates, id est, ideas]: for his intention is to relate each single multiplicity [scilicet unamquamque multitudinem invicem cognaturum] to a single Idea [ad ideam unam], and then to relate the intelligible unities to the simple One Itself [ad ipsum simpliciter unum], which excels the intelligible world by at least as much [quod ita saltem intelligibilia superat] as the intelligible world excels the perceptible world [quemadmodum ab his sensibilia superantur].'

Chapter 40: Next, Plato's two paths to the First; and the two names of the First [Rursus duae Platonis ad primum viae. Duo nomina primi]

'Plato rises to the Supreme by two paths [Plato per duas ad summum vias ascendit]: by the path of analogies in the *Republic* [per comparationes quidem in Republica] and by the path of negations in *Parmenides* [per negationes autem in Parmenide]. Both the analogies and the negations [Utraeque pariter tam comparationes quam negationes] affirm that God is set apart from all beings and from all intelligibles [declarant Deum esse tum ab omnibus entibus et intelligibilibus segregatum], and that He is also the beginning of creation [tum etiam principium universi].'

'He defines God as the sole beginning of everything, totally simple and totally supreme [Deum principium omnium unicum, simplicissimum, eminentissimum esse designat].'

Chapter 41: Some Platonic discussions follow which show that the One is the beginning of all things, and that the One Itself, the Good, is above being. The First Discussion [Secuntur discursus Platonici probantes unum esse principium omnium, et esse ipsum unum bonumque superius ente. Primus discursus]

Chapter 42: The Second Discussion on the same subject [Secundus ad idem discursus]

> 'The One indwells all things both individually and collectively [omnibus et singulatim et summatim inest unum]; and with the very multitude [et in ipsa multitudine] which seems opposed to the One [quae uni videtur opposita], the One Itself makes the multitude [unum ipsum conficit multitudinem], for what is a multitude but one repeated over and over again [quid enim aliud multitudo est nisi aliquod saepius repetitum]?'

> 'This One, therefore [Hoc igitur unum], which is absolutely common to all [omnibus communissimum], derives its existence from the simple One which is the most common of all [ab ipso tandem existit simpliciter uno omnium communissimo].'

Chapter 43: The Third Discussion on the same subject. Also on the simplicity of the first and the last [Tertius ad idem discursus. Ac de simplicitate primi et ultimi]

> 'In the hierarchy of the universe [In ordine universi] there is the first and there is the last [ad primum pervenitur et ultimum], and each of these is of necessity [utrumque necessario est] one and simple [unum atque simplex], devoid of multiplicity [multitudinis expers].'

> 'Certainly matter is in the highest degree one in its ability to receive form [Est certe materia maximum unum scilicet formabile], just as the first being [sicut ens primum] is in the highest degree one in its power to impart form [maxime unum est formale]. But neither of these is the simple One Itself [Neutrum vero est ipsum simpliciter unum].'

Chapter 44: The Fourth Discussion on the same subject; and on the contemplation of the Good [Quartus ad idem discursus, et de contemplatione boni]

> 'For these reasons [Propterea] we consider the One Itself and the Good to be absolutely identical [ipsum unum bonumque idem prorsus esse coniicimus].'

Chapter 45: The Fifth Discussion on the same subject; and on the naming of the First [Quintus ad idem discursus, et de appellatione primi]

Chapter 51: Plutarch's analysis of the hypotheses of Parmenides [Dispositio propositionum Parmenidis apud Plutarchum]

'That this dialogue was held to be divine among the ancients is attested by Plutarch [Dialogum hunc divinum apud veteres iudicatum, testis est Plutarchus].'

Chapter 52: The meaning of the negations and of the affirmations within the hypotheses. Which ones are dealt with and in which order [Quid significent in suppositionibus negationes. Quid affirmationes. Quae et quo ordine tractentur in eis]

'Since the first hypothesis [Quoniam vero suppositio prima] focuses attention upon the simple One Itself [colit ipsum simpliciter unum], which is higher than being [ente superius], it negates all the conditions of beings with respect to the One [ideo omnes ab eo entium conditiones negat], which is detached from all things [est enim ab omnibus absolutum], being their final principle [tanquam principium finale], a principle which is especially – even predominantly – efficient [praecipue et eminenter efficiens].'

'The first hypothesis [suppositio prima], if we are allowed to believe the ancients [si antiquis licet credere], deals with the way in which the first God creates and orders the respective hierarchies of gods [tractat quomodo primus Deus singulos deorum ordines procreat atque disponit]; the second hypothesis treats of the divine hierarchies [Secunda vero de divinis ordinibus], how they have come forth from the One [quomodo processerunt ab uno], and of each essence [et de qualibet essentia] that is conjoined by God to every unity [unicuique Deo unitati videlicet coniugata]; the third hypothesis [Tertia] deals with those souls [de animabus] which do not possess substantial divinity [Deitatem quidem ipsam substantialem non habentibus] but do have a manifest likeness to the gods [sed similitudinem ad deos expressam]; the fourth hypothesis treats of material forms [Quarta de formis materialibus], how they proceed from the gods [quomodo proficiscuntur a diis], and which ones depend on which respective order of gods [et quae proprie ab unoquoque deorum ordine pendent]; the fifth hypothesis deals with primal matter [Quinta de materia prima], how it is not composed of formal unities [quomodo formalium unitatum non est compos] but depends on the unity that is above essence [sed desuper ab unitate superessentiali dependet], for the action of the first One extends right through to final materialisation [nam usque ad materiam ultimam unius primi actio provenit], which in all manner of ways sets limits to the unlimited nature of the One through particular participation in unity [interminatam illius naturam, per quandam unitatis participationem quoquomodo determinans].'

The First Hypothesis (Chapters 53-79)

Chapter 53: The Aim, the Truth, and the Arrangement of
the First Hypothesis [Intentio, veritas, ordo suppositionis
primae]

Chapter 54: When the characteristics of beings are negated
with respect to the One, this indicates that the One
surpasses and creates all these [Ubi entium proprietates
de uno negantur, significatur ipsum haec omnia antecellere
atque procreare]

> 'Affirmations concerning almighty God [Affirmationes circa summum
> Deum] are very misleading and dangerous [fallaces admodum peri-
> culosaeque sunt], for in our everyday affirmations we usually think of a
> particular type and characteristic to name and define something [solemus
> enim in quotidianis affirmationibus nostris certam quandam speciem
> proprietatemque concipere, et appellare aliquid alteri atque definire]. But
> to do this in relation to the First is unlawful [Hoc autem agere circa
> primum, nefas].

Chapter 55: On the one being. On the simple One Itself.
On the aim of Parmenides both here and in his verses.
The aim and conclusion of his negations [De uno ente.
De ipso simpliciter uno. De intentione Parmenidis hic et
in poemate. Intentio et Epilogus negationum]

> 'Perhaps it would now be useful to repeat briefly [Operaepretium forte
> fuerit repetere breviter in praesentia] what we have said many times before
> [quod saepe iam diximus]: the principle of unity [rationem unitatis] is
> different from the principle of being [a ratione entis esse diversam].'

Chapter 56: On the universal being and its properties; and
why these are negated with respect to the First. Which
multiplicity is negated, and why it is negated [De universo
ente et proprietatibus eius. Et quomodo negantur de primo.
Et quae multitudo negatur et quare negatur]

Chapter 57: Through the negation of all multiplicity, parts
and totality are negated with respect to the One: number is
prior to essence, and all multiplicity partakes of unity. The
first essence, life, and mind are identical [Per negationem
multitudinis negantur de uno partes et totum. Numerus est
ante essentiam. Omnis multitudo particeps unitatis. Idem
est prima essentia, vita, mens]

Chapter 58: An opinion affirming the abstracts of abstracts with respect to God. Again, negations and relations about God are safer [Opinio affirmans abstractorum abstracta de deo. Item tutiores sunt negationes relationesque circa deum]

Chapter 59: If the One has no parts, it follows that it has no beginning, no end, no middle [Si unum non habet partes consequenter nec habet principium vel finem aut medium]

Chapter 60: In what way the One Itself is called the limitless and the limit of all [Quomodo ipsum unum dicatur infinitum, omniumque finis]

Chapter 61: How shape is negated with respect to the One, as well as straight lines and circular lines [Quomodo negatur de uno figura et rectum atque rotundum]

'Indeed, movement is the beginning of differentiation [Processus quidem discretionis principium est].'

Chapter 62: The One Itself is nowhere, because it is neither within itself nor within something else. How discrete things are said to exist of themselves or to be produced from themselves [Ipsum unum nusquam est. Quia nec est in se ipso nec in alio. Item quomodo separata dicuntur ex se ipsis existere vel produci]

Chapter 63: How the One is said to neither move nor rest; and how movement and rest are in everything except the First [Quomodo unum neque moveri neque stare dicatur et quomodo sit motus et status in omnibus praeter primum]

'In our *Theology* [In Theologia nostra] we have shown [probavimus] that in everything after the First [in omni re post primum] there is a differentiation of these four [quatuor haec inter se differre]: essence, being, power, and action [essentiam, et esse, et virtutem, et actionem].'

And so the Good Itself, the One Itself [Ipsum itaque bonum unumque], creates and perfects all things, not through something else, but by its own unity and goodness [non per aliud, sed ipsa unitate bonitateque facit et perficit omnia].'

'The principle of equality is different from the principle of the One [Alia aequalitatis alia unius ratio est], for the One is absolute [unum enim est absolutum], while equality is relative [Aequalitas relativa], since equal is related to equal [aequale enim ad aequale refertur].'

Chapter 73: In relation to itself and to other things, the One cannot be younger or older or of the same age [Unum neque iunius neque senius neque coetaneum vel ad se vel ad alia esse potest]

Chapter 74: The One Itself is above eternity and time and movement. It cannot, on any basis, be said to be within time [Ipsum unum super aeternitatem et tempus et motum est. Nec ulla ratione esse in tempore dici potest]

Chapter 75: A rule for relatives, with some confirmation of what has gone before [Relativorum regula cum confirmatione quadam superiorum]

Chapter 76: Since the One is above time, it transcends the conditions of time and of things temporal [Cum unum sit supra tempus, consequenter conditiones temporis temporaliumque excedit]

Chapter 77: The One Itself does not partake of essence; it is neither essence itself nor being itself, but is far higher [Ipsum unum nec est essentiae particeps, nec ipsa essentia nec ipsum esse. Sed longe superius]

Chapter 78: How essence, or being, is negated with respect to the One; and why the One cannot be known or named [Qua conditione negatur essentia vel esse de uno. Item quare cognosci vel nominari non possit]

Chapter 79: On the unshakeable nature of the first hypothesis. The One is higher than being [De firmitate suppositionis primae. Et quod unum ente superius]

The Second Hypothesis (Chapters 80-95)

Chapter 80: The aim of the second hypothesis [Secundae suppositionis intentio]

Chapter 81: In the same being there is the principle of the One and there is also the principle of being. The whole has parts and infinite multiplicity [Quomodo in uno ente alia sit ratio unius alia entis sit, totum partes habeat et multitudinem infinitam]

Chapter 82: Within the one being all the numbers are held by means of two and three. The numbers are prior to the development of the one being into many beings [In uno ente per binarium et ternarium omnes numeri continentur. Qui numeri distributionem entis unius in entia multa praecedunt]

Chapter 83: How essence, together with the One, is distributed in the intelligible world, and how multiplicity is either limited or unlimited [Quomodo in mundo intelligibili dividatur essentia simul et unum, multitudoque finita vel infinita sit]

Chapter 84: Within the intelligible world the multiplicity of parts is subsumed in a double form of the whole; it has limits and a mean, as well as forms [Quomodo in mundo intelligibili partium multitudo sub gemina totius forma concluditur. Quomodo terminos mediumque habet atque figuras]

Chapter 85: The one being is within itself and within something other than itself [Quomodo unum ens in se ipso sit et in alio]

Chapter 86: The one being is always unmoving, and yet it moves [Quomodo unum ens stet semper atque moveatur]

Chapter 87: The one being is the same as itself and different from itself. Again, it is the same as other things and different from them [Unum ens est sibimet idem atque alterum. Item caeteris idem atque alterum]

Chapter 88: The one being is similar to itself and to others; it is also dissimilar to itself and to others [Unum ens et ad se ipsum et ad alia simile est atque dissimile]

'In the *Philebus* it is shown [In Philebo probatur] that within all things subsequent to the First [in omnibus post primum] there are simultaneously
the One and multiplicity [esse unum simul atque multitudinem]. It follows
that within all things [Igitur in omnibus] there are the same and the different [est idem et alterum], the convergent and the divergent [convenientia
atque differentia], and therefore similarity together with dissimilarity
[igitur similitudo simul et dissimilitudo quaedam].'

Chapter 89: How the one being touches and is touched; but it neither touches nor is touched insofar as it belongs to itself and to other things [Quomodo unum ens tangit et tangitur. Neque tangit, neque tangitur, quantum ad se et ad alia pertinet]

Chapter 90: The one being is both equal to itself and unequal to itself; it is also equal to others and unequal to others [Quomodo unum ens sit aequale, vel inaequale sibi, vel aliis]

'Now anyone who does not know how to make use of such rigorous exercises [Qui autem discretiones eiusmodi uti nescit] is not a Platonist [non
est Platonicus] and never uses the intellect [nec unquam utitur intellectu].'

'Moreover, as we have indicated from the outset [Praeterea quemadmodum
significavimus ab initio], he (Parmenides) conducts the whole discussion
[totam disputationem agit] as an exercise in logic [ut logicam exercita-
tionem quandam]. But in this form of dialectic [Sub hac vero Dialectica
forma] he often commingles mystical teachings too [mistica quoque
dogmata frequenter admiscet], not in a continuous unbroken sequence
[non ubique prorsus continuata], but sporadically [sed alicubi sparsa], as
befits an exercise in logic [quatenus admittit exercitatio logica].'

Chapter 91: The one being, in relation to itself and to all else, is numerically the same. It is also both more and less [Quomodo unum ens sit numero par: et plus et minus ad se ipsum atque caetera]

Chapter 92: How the one being, in relation both to itself and to everything else, may be described as older and younger and of the same age [Quomodo unum ens dicatur senius et iunius atque coetaneum ad se ipsum atque caetera]

'Remember, too [Memento rursus], as we have advised you to do from the
beginning [quemadmodum admonuimus ab initio], that Parmenides is

here taking up the divine soul, in addition to the intellectual nature and the animate nature [Parmenidem hic ultra naturam intellectualem, animalem iam assumere animamque divinam].'

Chapter 93: How older becoming is distinguished from younger becoming, and also how older being is distinguished from younger being. Concluding words on the one being [Quomodo distinguitur senius iuniusve fieri, rursus senius iuniusve esse. Ac de uno ente conclusio]

Chapter 94: A summary or review of the second hypothesis. On distinguishing the divinities [Summa vel Epilogus suppositionis secundae. De distinctionibus divinorum]

Chapter 95: The distinctions made in the summary or review. On the one being; on multiplicity; on limitless number; and on the orders of the divinities [Summae huius vel Epilogi distinctiones. De uno ente multitudine, numero, infinito, ordinibus deorum]

The Third Hypothesis

Chapter 1: The aim of the hypothesis. How the soul may be called being and also non-being. On movement and time within the soul. On its eternal quality. How it manifests all things through some change in itself [Tertia suppositio. Intentio suppositionis. Quomodo anima ens dicatur atque non ens. De motu et tempore in anima. Item de quodam eius aeterno. Rursus quomodo commutatione quadam sui ipsius omnia repraesentet]

'Just as the soul consists of opposites [quemadmodum anima componitur oppositis], as we have shown in the *Timaeus* [ut probavimus in Timaeo], so the third hypothesis [ita suppositio tertia], which examines the soul [tractans animam], is a mixture of affirmations and negations [ex affirmationibus negationibusque miscetur].'

The Third Hypothesis

Chapter 2: Why the celestial soul moves and makes an orbit around the steadfast mind. How many movements of the soul there are. The number of movements and the

stillness within time. Concerning the mean between movements [Qua ratione caelestis anima circa mentem stabilem moveatur, agatque circuitum. Quot sint motus animae. Quod motus et quies in tempore; et de medio inter motus]

The Third Hypothesis

Chapter 3: A summary of the third hypothesis: or concluding words on the One, multiplicity, being, non-being, movement, stillness, moment, time, and oppositeness. The movement towards movement and towards stillness [Summa suppositionis tertiae vel Epilogus. De uno, multitudine, ente, non ente, motu, statu, momento, tempore, oppositione. Motus ad motum atque statum]

The Fourth Hypothesis

Chapter 1: The aim of the fourth hypothesis. The whole before the parts. The whole after the parts. Divine matters. Natural matters. The relation of the parts to the whole [Suppositio quarta. Quartae suppositionis intentio. Totum ante partes. Totum post partes. Res divinae. Res naturales. Relatio partium ad totum]

'The three previous hypotheses, as we have said elsewhere [Tres, ut alibi diximus, praecedentes suppositiones], contemplate the One Itself rather than all else [unum ipsum potius quam alia contemplare], and they relate the One to itself first of all, and then relate it to all else [illud ad se in primis, deinde ad caetera quoque comparaverunt].'

The Fourth Hypothesis

Chapter 2: On multiplicity and its relation to the One. On the unlimited and on limit. On the elements of beings. On other things that are mutually opposed [De multitudine, quomodo se habeat ad unum. De infinito et termino entium elementis. De caeteris inter se oppositis]

The Fifth Hypothesis

Chapter 1: The aim of the fifth hypothesis. On the One. On things separate from the One. Whether the One is in accord with them. On omniform being. On formless

matter [Suppositio quinta. Quintae suppositionis intentio.
De uno. De aliis ab uno. Utrum unum cum his conveniat.
De omniformi ente. De informi materia]

The Fifth Hypothesis

Chapter 2: Confirmation of the above, and how matter has no formal conditions within itself. Also, where it comes from, how it is formed, and how it moves [Confirmatio superiorum, et quomodo materia formales in se conditiones nullas habeat. Item unde sit, vel formetur vel moveatur]

The Sixth Hypothesis

Chapter 1: The aim of the sixth hypothesis. In what way Parmenides is poetical. More on being and non-being [Sexta suppositio. Sextae suppositionis intentio. Et quomodo Parmenides poeticus. Item de ente atque non ente]

'Parmenides not only expounded the mysteries of philosophy as a philosopher but also sang them in verse as a divine poet [Parmenides non philosophus tantum, sed etiam poeta divinus, carminibus philosophica mysteria cecinit]. And in this dialogue, too, he plays the part of the poet [Atque in hoc dialogo agit quoque poetam]. For, like a poet, he cultivates the number nine [Novenarium enim quasi poeta colit numerum], which, as it is said, is sacred to the Muses [musis (ut dicitur) consecratum]. By means of nine hypotheses [Per novem sane suppositiones], which are like the nine Muses [quasi per novem musas], the guides to knowledge [scientiae duces], he leads us to truth and to Apollo [ad veritatem Apollinemque nos ducit]; for while he is moving towards the simple One Itself [dum enim ad ipsum provehit simpliciter unum] he seems to be advancing towards Apollo [ad Apollinem promovere videtur], the name by which the followers of Pythagoras mystically designate the simple One Itself [Quo nomine Pythagorici sui solent ipsum simpliciter unum mystice designare]; for Apollo, as Plato and his followers teach, signifies the simple Absolute devoid of multiplicity [Quippe cum Apollon (ut Platonici quoque cum Platone docent) absolutorem significat simplicem a multitudine segregatum].'

'So far he has gone through five hypotheses that assume the One to be [Hactenus quinque suppositiones si unum sit peregit]. But from this point onwards [Deinceps vero] he adds four hypotheses that assume the One not to be [quattuor si unum non sit adiunget].'

'Finally, in this sixth hypothesis, he imagines the one being, the intellectual nature, not to be [Fingit denique in hac suppositione sexta unum ens, id est naturam intellectualem ita non esse]; but in such a way that it partly is and partly is not [ut partim quidem sit, partim vero non sit]. But in the seventh hypothesis [In septima vero] he is more at liberty to imagine that it absolutely is not [licentius fingit omnino non esse], for he is clearly in a position to understand the absurd conclusions that arise from both propositions [quid utrumque sequatur absurdi facile deprensurus].'

The Sixth Hypothesis

Chapter 2: How the One, which is called non-being, may also in some way be understood as being. How this kind of non-being is recognised. Concerning the soul [Quomodo unum dum dicitur non ens, possit etiam quodammodo ut ens intelligi. Et quomodo non ens eiusmodi cognoscatur, et de anima]

The Sixth Hypothesis

Chapter 3: How the One which is called non-being is the nature of the soul; why it is subject to movement; knowledge concerns this non-being; to it belong change, multiplicity, and characteristic features [Quomodo unum quod dicitur non ens sit natura animae, qua ratione mobilis est, de hoc non ente est scientia, huic competunt alteritas et multitudo, et signa significativa]

The Sixth Hypothesis

Chapter 4: Around this non-being One stand dissimilarity, similarity, inequality, equality, largeness, smallness, and, in some measure, essence. Also concerning the soul [Circa hoc unum non ens existunt dissimilitudo, similitudo, inaequalitas, aequalitas, magnitudo, parvitas. Essentia quodammodo et de anima]

The Sixth Hypothesis

Chapter 5: Around this non-being One exist being and not-being, movement, change, and annihilation, together with their opposites. More on the soul [Circa hoc unum non ens existunt esse atque non esse, motus, alteratio, interitus atque horum opposita et de anima]

The Seventh Hypothesis

The aim of the seventh hypothesis. Concerning the levels of the One, of being, and of non-being. How all things are negated with respect to the One and with respect to non-being [Suppositio septima. Septimae suppositionis intentio. De gradibus unius et entis atque non entis. Quomodo negantur omnia, de uno atque de non ente]

'In the seventh hypothesis [in suppositione septima] we consider the one being not only to have fallen of itself into a soul subject to movement [unum ens non solum in animam per se mobilem degeneratum excogitamus], and not only to have been cast into a flux that is dependent on something external [nec solum in fluxum ab alio dependentem praecipitatum], but also to have been finally released into total non-being [sed in ipsum omnino non ens denique resolutum]; strictly speaking, to have fallen into nothingness [Proprie forsan in nihilum iam prolapsum], but metaphorically to have been restored, as I might say, to the simple One Itself [metaphorice vero in ipsum simpliciter unum (ut ita dixerim) restitutum].'

'For my part [Ego equidem], I strive as far as I can to harmonise individual items and to deduce possibilities [singula ferme pro viribus accommodare studeo, et probabilia facere], so that, when he makes suppositions, his suppositions do not seem rash [saltem ne ubi fingit, temere fingere videatur]. For your part [Tu vero], learn to understand the reasonings on both sides in any subject [disce in materia qualibet et utrinque argumenta captare] and to distinguish the two meanings [et utrobique distinguere sensus], and thus avoid being obliged to admit impossibilities [ne impossibilia cogaris admittere].'

The Eighth Hypothesis

Chapter 1: The aim of the eighth hypothesis. If mind is removed and soul remains, soul will be deceptive and will abide in the realm of shadows [Octava suppositio. Octavae suppositionis intentio. Si mens auferatur supersitque anima, haec erit mendax et versabitur circa umbras]

The Eighth Hypothesis

Chapter 2: If you remove the One, all things will cease; they will be shadowy multitudes; the inconceivably infinite will merge with their opposites about the same; and faltering imagination will be ever deceitful [Si substuleris unum, res ipsae desinent. Umbratiles erunt turbae, innumerabiliter

infinitae, contingent apposita circa idem. Imaginatio ambigua semper erit mendax]

The Ninth Hypothesis: The aim of the ninth hypothesis [Suppositio nona. Nonae suppositionis intentio]

'After such words [Post haec eiusmodi] the conclusion of the whole book is reached [affertur totius libri conclusio]. If the simple One Itself [Si ipsum simpliciter unum], from which arises the one being and from which comes each particular everywhere [a quo est ens unum. Ex quo tandem est ubique quodlibet unum], be removed from the universe [ex universo tollatur], there will be absolutely nothing anywhere [nihil penitus usquam erit].'

The Commentary of Marsilio Ficino
to Plato's *Parmenides*

The subject matter of *Parmenides*:
On the one Principle of all things.
Written by Marsilio Ficino of Florence
and dedicated to Niccolò Valori,
that wise and excellent citizen

ALTHOUGH PLATO has sown the seeds of all wisdom throughout all his dialogues, he has gathered all the institutes of moral philosophy within the books of the *Republic*; he has embraced all knowledge of natural phenomena within the *Timaeus*, and all theology within *Parmenides* (a feat which, as Proclus says, might seem incredible to everybody else but which is indisputable to those who know Plato), and although in other matters he thus anticipated all other philosophers by a long period of time, in this last matter he seems to have surpassed himself and to have drawn this celestial work, in a divine way, from the deep recesses of the divine mind and from the innermost sanctuary of philosophy.

Anyone approaching his sacred writings should prepare himself with sobriety of soul and freedom of mind before daring to handle the mysteries of the celestial work. For here the divine Plato, speaking of the One Itself, discusses with great subtlety how the One Itself is the principle of all things, which is above all and from which come all; how it is outside all and within all; and how all come out of it, through it, and to it.

Step by step Plato rises above the intelligence of the One, towards that which is above essence. The One, indeed, is found in a triple order: in those things which flow and are subject to the senses and are named the perceptible; in those things, too, which are always the same and which are called the intelligible, perceptible no longer by the senses but by mind alone; not in those things only, but also above the senses and the perceptible, above the intellect and the intelligible, the One itself exists.

And so, in this dialogue, Zeno of Elea, a disciple of Parmenides the Pythagorean, first demonstrates that the One is in the perceptible,

3

showing that if there were many, not in any way partaking of the nature of the One, very many errors would follow. Secondly, Socrates, without refuting Zeno, but simply lifting him higher, takes him to the consideration of the One and of the unities which are inherent in the intelligible, to avoid delaying in this one which is inherent in the perceptible. From this, therefore, they come to the investigation of Ideas, in which the unities of all things consist.

Finally, Parmenides himself, though older, does not contradict Socrates, but ends the contemplation which he has begun and unfolds the whole principle of Ideas. He introduces four questions about Ideas. The first is whether they exist. The second is to whom the Ideas belong and to whom they do not belong. The third is what kind of Ideas they are and what power they have. The fourth is how those things which are below partake of them.

From here he himself now arises to the One, which exists above the intelligible and above the Ideas, and he introduces nine hypotheses about this, five on the basis that the One exists and four on the basis that the One does not exist, asking what follows from each of these standpoints. But these hypotheses arise from the three-fold division of the One and from the two-fold division of non-being. Indeed, the three-fold One is found above being, within being, and beneath being. But non-being itself is subject to a double consideration: for some think either that it does not exist at all, or that it partly exists and partly does not exist.

Thus the first hypothesis is: if the One exists above being, what follows around it in relation to itself and to other things? The second: if the One is with being, that is, the one being, what is its relationship to itself and to other things? The third: if the One is placed beneath being, what happens to it in relation to itself and to other things? The fourth: if the One stands above being, how are other things related to themselves and to the One? The fifth: if there is that One which is located with being, what happens to other things in relation to themselves and to that One? The sixth: if there is not one being which partly is and partly is not, how is it related to itself and to other things? The seventh: if there is not one being which in no way exists, how is it related to itself and to other things? The eighth: if there is not that one which partly is and partly is not, what happens to other things in relation to themselves and to it? The ninth: if this one is not, so that it does not exist at all, what do other things suffer in relation to themselves and, finally, in relation to it?

4

In all these hypotheses the general intention of Parmenides is to affirm this above all: there is a single principle of all things, and if that is in place everything is in place, but if it be removed everything perishes. Thus in the first five hypotheses he conveys five steps of creation in a single assumed order of creation. However, in the following four hypotheses he examines how many absurdities and errors and evils follow if the One itself be removed.

Of the five earlier hypotheses the first discusses the one supreme God, how He creates and arranges the orders of the divinities that follow. The second discusses the individual orders of the divinities and how they proceed from God Himself. The third discusses divine souls; the fourth discusses those which come into being in the region which surrounds matter and how they are produced by the highest causes. The fifth discusses primal matter, how it is free from differentiation by its own nature, and how it is dependent on the original One. It should also be noted that when One is mentioned in this dialogue it can, as in the system of the Pythagoreans, indicate any single substance that is totally detached from matter, such as God, mind, and soul. But when the terms *other* and *other things* are used, they may be understood both as matter and as those things which come into being within matter.

Having, therefore, stated and heeded these things first, let us move to the dialogue itself.

The Preface of Marsilio Ficino to his Commentary on *Parmenides*

The subject matter of *Parmenides* is intensely theological, but its form is dialectical.

IT WAS the custom of Pythagoras, Socrates, and Plato to cover the divine mysteries with figures and veils in all their works; to modestly cloak their wisdom, in contrast to the ostentation of the Sophists; to jest seriously and to play most zealously.

And so in *Parmenides*, under the guise of a dialectical and, as it were, logical game aimed at training the intelligence, Plato points towards divine teachings and many aspects of theology. It was also the custom of the Pythagoreans and of Plato to harmoniously blend many substances together, partly through the law of nature and partly through grace. In the *Phaedrus* he combines oratory and poetry with theology, and in the *Timaeus* he mixes mathematics with natural science, and he often joins the art of discussing with the divine or even with the moral. In the same way he joins the analytical art and the definitive art with the divine in the *Philebus* and *Politicus* and the *Sophist*; and in *Parmenides* he joins demonstrative art with the divine.

In order to avoid seeming like a pedagogue teaching boys, as he could appear to be if he transmitted only the bare logical rudiments, he thinks that, just as the demonstrative art excels the analytical art and the definitive art as their end, so it is transmitted in a more divine substance. So Aristotle, indeed, mixed the highest dialectic – for I prefer to say dialectic rather than dialection – with the divine, imitating Plato as I think, who in the *Republic* calls theology by the name of dialectic. Therefore the subject matter of this *Parmenides* is particularly theological and its form particularly logical.

We have explained in the beginning that this is certainly how Proclus and his followers considered the arrangement and order of the book, but I shall show step by step in what follows what I myself think about this and how far I follow them.

Chapter 1:
Setting the scene for the dialogue

CEPHALUS and his companions ask Adeimantus and Glaucon, the brothers of Plato, born to the same father and mother, to persuade Antiphon, their brother – born to their mother but not to their father – to relate to them that discussion which he had received from Pythodorus, who had previously been present when the Pythagoreans, Parmenides and Zeno, were reasoning together with Socrates.

Chapter 2:
How the whole of being is one, but the One Itself is above being

WITH VERY many arguments Parmenides confirmed in his poem that the universe, or the whole of being, is one, but the universe, or the all, is appreciated in these three ways: individually, collectively, as a whole.

Thus, according to the first way, any being whatsoever – this one by itself, as well as that one, and that one yonder – is something that is one within itself, distinct from all others by its particular quality. Now, according to the second way, the whole expanse of beings, taken together, is one, so that in all possible respects all things come together in being, having been brought forth from the same beginning and having finally been brought back to the same common end, and harmonising with each other in movement, in actions performed, and in actions suffered. Finally, according to the third way, the first among beings is both one and all: it is one because just as natural beings are ascribed to one nature, and bodily phenomena to one body, so all beings, in the end, are simply ascribed to a single being; and it is all because, just as the powers of all natures and of all bodies are contained in the first nature and the first body, so all beings are comprehended within the one primal being, which we call the intelligible world.

But the false statements of certain Aristotelians are not to be accepted, whereby we might mistrust Parmenides when he says that the whole of being is one, and that the whole brings forth multiplicity from the universal, for otherwise when Plato speaks in the *Theaetetus* of the one unmoving being, he would not be honouring Parmenides, but rather attacking him.

For Plato, together with the Pythagoreans, places multiplicity – the variety of opposing types and ideas, and the complete origin of numbers – in the primal being, but he maintains that at the same time that primal being, together with number, is so fully one that no further one beyond the first can be contemplated. Thus far Parmenides understands the One through participation, naming the One three times. In the first way and the second way the participation in unity is imperfect, but in the third way it is perfect. However, beyond that unity which partakes perfectly of the intelligible world he postulates a supreme unity higher than the one universal being, for the nature of being is different from the nature of unity, since multiplicity and composition are not opposed to the nature of being but are opposed to the nature of unity. Moreover, non-being is opposed to the former, while the non-One is opposed to the latter. But to say non-being is not the same as saying non-One, since the non-One does not necessarily signify nothing but signifies diverse multiplicity. Therefore the one being is not the simple One Itself, but is in all respects a composite mixed with multiplicity.

Just as from heat mixed with cold or from light mixed with darkness reason and nature teach that heat in its purity is to be attained and light in its purity is to be attained, and from incorporeal substance conjoined to the body incorporeal substance divorced from the body is to be attained; again, from temporal being which in some way is mixed with non-being eternal being is to be attained; in the same way, from unity conjoined with essence unity totally liberated from essence is to be attained. Indeed, whatever is simpler than essence for any reason is necessarily superior to it. This is the name Parmenides gives to the beginning and end of all things on account of its supreme simplicity and power signified by unity.

Chapter 3:
All multiplicity partakes of unity

THE PROPOSITION of Parmenides, whereby it is asserted that the whole of being is one, that is, partakes of the One, is confirmed by his disciple Zeno with another proposition, whereby he shows that beings are not many, that is, not only many, but beyond their multiplicity they partake of unity. For unless there were some participation in unity within such a great number of diverse beings, they would be totally dissimilar one to another, nor would they agree with each other in order or in any other way, which everyone can clearly see is untrue. Again, they would be dissimilar one to another, and for the same reason they would also be similar, which is a foolish thing to say, since they would have this in common, that just as *this* is totally different from *that*, so in turn *that* is totally different from *this*, both returning like for like, as the saying goes.

Therefore, insofar as they lacked the One they would be dissimilar, for similarity consists in a kind of union, and for the same reason they would be similar, since between them they would have this in common, namely that we were imagining them to lack the One. Again, they would be neither similar nor dissimilar. They would not be similar if they were deprived of the one author of all similarity, nor would they be dissimilar while agreeing in this very deprivation. These absurdities will undoubtedly follow, as well as very many others which we have mentioned elsewhere and which we shall mention again, if anyone imagines that the multiplicity of creation be devoid of unity. These absurdities will also follow if there are many first principles of creation, for if these principles partake of one and the same, they themselves will not be located beneath that one as beneath a principle, and if they have no One in common, they will be neither principles in general nor similar one to another, nor again totally dissimilar, since they suffer the common absence of the One, and, for the same reason again, they will ultimately be shown to be both dissimilar and similar.

Chapter 4:
The existence and nature of Ideas

THIS DISCUSSION by Zeno about multiplicity as a partaker of union Socrates transfers to Ideas, with himself as the constant friend of Ideas now holding debate with the Pythagoreans, as Plato, in the *Sophist*, bears witness to the lovers of Ideas. In the *Theology* and in Plotinus I have pursued more fully the reasons which corroborate the Ideas. Socrates now strives to offer a proof of this kind.

Any special assemblage of individuals comes together through a particular characteristic and nature, as, for example, many men through their single humanity. But that one which is common depends neither on the many – for which reason there are the many and the various – nor on any one of the many – for which reason there is something special and different – nor does it exist through itself and of itself, since it does not abide within itself but resides within the assemblage. Nor is it the One, pure and perfect, since it partakes of multiplicity. Nor is its nature perfect, being mixed with hostile elements and being subject to change.

Thus the nature within these many depends ultimately on the one perfect nature which is far superior to these many; and so human nature depends on the Idea of man; fiery nature, too, depends on the Idea of fire; and, indeed, the human race, if it be eternal, is so only because it depends on an unmoving cause. Again, if it be universal, it is so, not from a particular cause, but from a universal cause alone. Now the cause which is unmoving and universal at the same time is necessarily the intellect and the intellectual Idea.

Socrates thinks that the definitions and sciences of natural phenomena belong to these very Ideas, simply because what is defined and known is absolute and cannot be otherwise, and because what is truly intelligible moves the intellect from within, just as what is truly perceptible moves the senses from without. Again, there are many Ideas, at least as many as the types of natural phenomena, and each one is called a unity – I mean, not simply unity, but a unity. Indeed, the Idea of man is not the absolute One Itself, but a particular one, that is, the human one, nor does it hold sway over any of the assemblages in creation but only over the assemblage of men. Likewise, the remaining Ideas are limited to their own particular species. For this reason there exists above ideal unities the One that is simply itself, governing the full expansion of all species.

It is true that the Ideas are not only beneath the One Itself, as we have said, the Father of the primal intelligence, but they are also within a particular one, that is, the primal intellect and the primal form; for just as natural forms, however diverse, exist within one substance, so ideal forms exist within one and the same mental form, which, being uniform, depends totally on something higher which is utterly simple and which is also, as I might put it, uniform.

Since material forms are within evil, they partly fight against one another and partly blend together, while Ideas, being under the Good itself, are directly within the best and they neither blend together nor oppose each other. There fire does not unite with water, human nature does not unite with brute nature, nor are they kept separate through any violence, just as the divine virtues of what we see as opposing qualities, together with opposing movements, can co-exist harmlessly in the celestial nature.

Therefore Socrates calls some Ideas mutually opposing, not because they disagree among themselves, but because they produce opposites in our world and because God Himself sees and moves opposites through these Ideas. If you wish to perceive more clearly the Ideas which are there, consider within nature herself the seed-causes of the natural creation. Again, observe in art the forms of man-made objects. The seed-causes in nature, however, have the power to act, but not the power to cognise, while the very forms in art are actually the causes of cognising and judging, although they do nothing of themselves unless the motive power is also present, being instruments that may be equally engaged or disengaged. But since that divine intellect wonderfully unites within itself these gifts which are disunited in our world, the Ideas governed by that intellect are the principles both of contemplation and of action. Again, since that intellect perfects the universe, not by reasoning, not by chance, but by its own intellectual nature, and makes it in its own image, it necessarily possesses within itself the powers and forms of all things: powers and forms that are distinct through their intellectual cause as well as through their natural cause.

But there are thought to be other Ideas which are very common, such as essence, sameness, change, immobility, and movement; and yet other Ideas which are very particular, such as man and horse; and yet others which are mid-way, such as the beautiful, the just, the large, the small, the similar, the dissimilar. Socrates therefore thinks that many things share in a single Idea and also that they are mingled together through partaking in a number of Ideas. Yet no Idea is united with another, even though they all exist through the intelligence of the one divine mind. In some ways, indeed, the intellects themselves, as well as the intellectual and rational souls, are united with their own Ideas, and in other ways corporeal matters and lives are united with bodies. For the former are like the offspring or children of Ideas, though falling away from them to some extent, while the latter are merely images, having no ideal nature within themselves, yet mirroring the likeness of the Ideas.

Chapter 5:
In what respects Ideas differ among themselves and in what respects they agree

IT SHOULD NOT be thought that the Ideas which we are considering differ no whit one from another; for if that were the case, there would be but a single Idea, and that which is second in the hierarchy of creation would be utterly simple, just like the first, and any distinction in what follows would perhaps happen by chance.

On the other hand, it should not be thought that the Ideas are so different one from another that not one of them has anything belonging to the others; for if that were the case, that first world would be more diversified than the second, and the first offspring of divine unity would perhaps have no unity within it, nor would there be any unity or any order within all that follows.

Each and every Idea, therefore, has its own nature and power, truly distinct from all the others, but at the same time it receives something from the others and, in turn, transmits something to them. They are also joined to each other by a marvellous presence and communion, while at the same time remaining wonderfully distinct through their own quality. Joined, I say, but not confused, and distinct but not separated. For when we consider three things in the physical world – matter, dimensions, and physical qualities – we understand that matter is the origin of change and confusion, and that dimensions are the cause of distance, while qualities are the cause of repulsion. Hence it comes about that bodies and bodily forms stand apart from each other and repel each other on account of their dimensions and qualities and cannot be easily reconciled into one, and it also comes about that they finally mingle and merge with each other on account of their matter, if it be compressed by some force.

Those ideal forms, however, not being subject to conditions, are always deep within indivisible sameness, preserving the maximum inter-communication and at the same time being distinct from each other through their quality, so that none of them can lose or return their own purity or quality through their dealings with the others.

Since the radiant appearances of visible objects are further from matter than are the qualities of sound, smell, taste, and touch, the Ideas are related in exactly the same way. For they are all within indivisible sameness, and they all exist together at the same time; nor are they in any way confused one with another. Sounds are not quite so free from confusion, smells are less free, and all else not at all free.

Moving now from here to the soul, you will understand that the seed-causes within enlivening nature and the technical causes within art, as well as the causes within knowledge itself, are very similar to the Ideas, maintaining a wonderful distinctiveness along with indivisible communion. However, we have noted above that nature conjoins with intellect and devises both the intellectual nature and the natural intelligence, in which any cause, whether it be a power or a form, being a concept, is a kind of contemplation and a kind of nature. Furthermore, if it is nature it is equally a concept also; any Idea of this sort is the foundation both of cognition and of generation.

Accordingly, there is therefore both immobility and movement: immobility, by which all immobile things are known and come into being; and movement, whereby all moving things are known and come into being. From this, and in a similar way, there arise sameness and difference and the remaining types. Immobility itself is not movement itself and never becomes anything other than immobility, and because it is immobility it cannot under any consideration be judged as moving, and yet it gives the impulse to movement itself, for all the Ideas impart something to each other in some way; and insofar as it imparts movement itself – the movement within Ideas – it plays some part in the effects of movement itself. Again, sameness is not difference, and because it is sameness it is not both same and different. However, through participation in difference it is different from the others; and all else must be judged in the same way.

Since Ideas are eternal and intellectual in their extreme purity, they produce within the same sequence beneath them unmoving and pure effects prior to moving and impure effects. Thus beneath the Ideas of the elements there are immaterial elements in the heavens prior to the material elements which are under heaven: a heavenly lion, horse, and tree are celestial before being elemental; and beneath the ideal man there is firstly the heavenly man and then the man of air and the man of earth. And just as any intellect embraces everything through intellectual and intelligible reason, intellects are completely circular and pure; and in the same way every sphere embraces everything through bodily nature as well as through one of its own properties.

Chapter 6:
For what there are Ideas, and for what there are no Ideas: there are as many Ideas as there are rational souls

ALTHOUGH RATIONAL souls, as Proclus says, cannot be distinguished one from another either through matter itself or through material conditions – for they stand apart from matter – they are distinguished through their qualities of form and type. Therefore there are as many Ideas of rational souls as there are souls and types. However, although irrational souls depend on moving causes, that is, on the lower gods and on the rational souls, and are therefore changeable in their essence and are distributed among bodies as if each one were mortal, they have a single everlasting type, which has received unbroken continuity from an unmoving cause, that is, from an Idea. And for this reason there is a single Idea for the whole of a single type. Moreover, the types of natures and of bodies within the world are matched in number by the Ideas within the establisher of these types.

Chapter 7:
There is no Idea for matter

BUT THERE is no Idea for matter, which totally lacks all type. Since an Idea is a type, but a type cannot be a model for anything devoid of all type, formless matter has its divine cause among the gods but it does not have a model; on the other hand, if the matter proper to heaven appropriates to itself a particular and inalienable type – which is probable – so that it is perfect above imperfect matter, then it has its own model, if we follow the view of Proclus.

Chapter 8:
There are no Ideas for individual items

HOWEVER, THERE are no Ideas proper to individual bodies, and for this reason they are individual. For an Idea is a totally unmoving cause, and what arises from a cause of this kind is unchangeable in its essence, while individual bodies are not so. Again, if there are Ideas for individual items, which are subject to change, each being succeeded by another, and innumerable in their acts, two absurd conclusions follow: the first is that an Idea will be a model when the image is present but will not be a model when the image is absent; the second is that there will be innumerable Ideas and that that intelligible multiplicity which is closest to unity will have no limit and will be far from one.

However, there is a difference between a model and a cause, for that intelligible model is a cause, and yet not every cause is a model. Therefore, although individual items do not become a particular model, they are produced in accordance with a cause, or rather causes, and these causes are their own particular ones: the different movements of the world, the particular natures, and the differences of time and place.

Chapter 9:
There are no Ideas for parts

THERE IS accordingly an Idea for the whole of fire, but no Idea for its parts. There is an Idea for the whole of the human body, but there are no particular Ideas for the head, the hand, or the foot. For, in relation to that intelligible multiplicity which is as close as possible to unity, One is prior to multiplicity, and the indivisible is prior to the divided, and the whole is prior to the parts, and these are subsumed within the cause of those. However, in relation to enlivening nature, which is not united, there are particular causes for individual limbs: the eye, the finger, the foot, and the hand.

Chapter 10:
How there are Ideas for the accidental

IF ALL those qualities which we have elsewhere called accidental belong to some types or kinds of substances and inevitably fill and perfect the essences there, undoubtedly they are all subsumed as models within the Ideas of those types; but if they perhaps belong to no types, yet have distant contingent causes scattered among individual items, these causes too, in the realm of Ideas, do not have models but proximate causes, not only within the constitution of bodies but also within those natures in which there are additionally the seed-causes of such things.

Chapter 11:
There are no Ideas for skills

IN THE tenth book of the *Republic* Plato seems to declare that there are Ideas for skills, not because the divine intellect, or our intellect, naturally has the Ideas of bed and table, but because our intellect, through divine power, has a capacity for skills, and through this capacity it devises within itself what appear to be Ideas for skills. In the words of Plato, Socrates adduced all this for the sake of a particular example.

Indeed, the ideal causes are naturally within everyone's intellect, be it divine or human, and proceed as if through an intermediate living nature, which has been formed from them, into matter, in which they produce living beings. The products of skills, on the other hand, do not proceed from the intellect through an intermediate nature and are not alive. They therefore have no natural Idea anywhere.

These conclusions, as well as the earlier ones, Xenocrates confirms, as Proclus testifies, defining Ideas in the following way: Ideas are the model causes of those things which always exist in accordance with nature. He said *model* because the final cause is higher, being the Good itself, while the efficient cause is in some way lower, being the maker of the intellect, looking up to the ideal model, which is also efficient. He added *of those things which exist in accordance with nature* because there are no Ideas for those things which come into being outside nature or through art. He added *always* because there are no Ideas for individual items which are subject to change.

This is sufficient on the definition given by Xenocrates. Let us proceed to what remains.

Chapter 12:
There are Ideas for only the speculative branches of knowledge

THERE IS no Idea for the branches of knowledge which lead the soul down to material things and which are concerned with human affairs. But the power of these branches lies initially in the daemons: medicine in Phoebus, agriculture in Ceres, bronze-working in Vulcan, weaving in Minerva. This power is secondarily within us, but it is in them for a different reason and is much more excellent in them.

On the other hand, there are Ideas in some measure for the contemplative branches of knowledge which, as a group, call the soul back to the intelligible. In the same way, there are Ideas for the moral virtues: not for the civil virtues, I say, but for those more excellent virtues which purge the soul and lead it to the intelligible.

Chapter 13:
There are no Ideas for evils

EVILS HAVE no ideal model in the presence of God. If it were otherwise, that model would be either evil or good. But it is not evil, because there is no evil within the best; and it is not good, for it would produce good from its nature, but not evil. Finally, if there be an Idea for evil in the presence of God, then God creates evils, for an Idea, being beyond its model, is also the efficient cause. Indeed, God would be evil if He had His own Idea of evil, for God Himself is every Idea. But when Plato says that the architect of the world wanted to make everything as similar as possible to Himself, yet nothing evil but everything supremely good, he is clearly proclaiming that there exists no model for evils in the presence of God.

Chapter 14:
There are no Ideas for vile things

IN THE presence of the Creator there are no Ideas except for those things which He Himself makes and perfects. Therefore there are no Ideas for things that are vile, that is, things that are degenerate and detrimental and evil, which happen through the meeting of separate causes or through our actions and passions.

There is no distinct Idea for hairs, but for the whole body together, and not for isolated parts or details. He acknowledges, however, that it will suffer deprivations and hideous ills through the Ideas for forms and good things.

There is no Idea for mud, but there is an Idea for water and for earth. Mud, however, is not any type that is naturally perfected for a particular purpose, a type that usually belongs to an Idea, but it happens either by chance or through human skill.

Chapter 15:
Even those things which are not expressed through Ideas are related to providence and to a divine cause

SOCRATES, considering the deficiencies of those things which a little while ago were affirmed to be the basest, falls into two doubts. The first doubt is whether these things have come into being outside of

Ideas. The second doubt is whether they have perhaps happened outside even all divine cause and providence.

Parmenides does not correct the first doubt, but he does correct the second, recognising that, within a world which is ordered so wisely, so beautifully and so well, there is nothing so deformed or so base that it may not be brought back to the universal beauty and partake of some good.

No one doubts that even the small parts of an animal have been designed for a particular end and are necessary for the whole, or that formless matter is necessary for this divine workmanship. Therefore everything of this sort is undoubtedly embraced by providence and depends at all events on the first cause, the Good itself, whose office it is to impart unity, goodness, and essence to all things, while the office of the intellect, through the Ideas, is to adorn all things with forms.

These things, therefore, which are deformed and formless, even if they come about outside of that most beauteous model, do not move beyond the full awareness of that mind or beyond the action of the Good itself. The seed-causes, divine in every possible way, of the limbs of an animated body reside within living nature, and those things which are allotted forms by our art receive their essence from the divine intellect, just as those things which take their varied forms from the divine intellect have their primal substance from the Good itself.

Chapter 16:
Parmenides corrects or modifies the replies of Socrates, but does not destroy them

JUST AS Socrates, the son of a midwife, performs the office of a midwife in different places towards boys and youths and proclaims this before others, so the aged Parmenides, like a dutiful midwife, exhorts and helps the youthful Socrates to give birth to the wonderful, almost divine, opinions with which he is pregnant and which he is trying to bring forth.

Moreover, he does not reject or destroy the children that are born lacking beauty, but rather he takes them up and cherishes them in a wonderful way. He strengthens the weak, straightens the crooked, gives shape to the shapeless, and perfects the imperfect. No one, therefore, will think that Parmenides the Pythagorean, the friend of Ideas in the manner of his fellows, and the pursuer of being, which is detached from sensory perception, and of the One Itself, which is above being, condemns opinions of this kind; but every follower of Plato will remember that Socrates is being very carefully trained by Parmenides in dialectic, in order that he may be much more heedful when considering the divine mysteries, that he may proceed with greater care, and that he may reach the end of his journey in greater safety.

Chapter 17:
How the things of our world partake of Ideas, being the images of Ideas, without their having any identical or common cause

ALTHOUGH THE way in which matter becomes a partaker of Ideas cannot be compared at all with the ways that are usual for us, it is right to make a threefold comparison as far as is possible. For Plato, partly in the *Timaeus* and partly in the *Sophist*, indicates the number three, and therefore the followers of Plato are right to pursue the number three: it is certainly good to consider both the power of the universal Architect and the plasticity and everlasting simplicity of matter, as well as the flimsiness and insubstantiality, so to speak, of natural things if they are compared with divine things. Therefore, if you say that the way matter participates in Ideas is like the impressions made on wax tablets by a seal, or like reflections appearing in water and a mirror, or like pictures; and if you make the comparison in the right way and within proper limits, then you agree with Plotinus and with the followers of Plato. Be that as it may, the ideal causes are in the intellect of the Maker and also in the world-soul and in universal nature. Again, through the functions of the supercelestial deities and the functions of celestial and supercelestial beings, the causes enter into matter.

If you consider the intellect and the supercelestial deities, you form some sort of picture; if you rightly reflect upon the world-soul and the celestial beings, you conceive an image; if you consider the universal nature and the supercelestial beings, you justly form a picture of matter itself, derived from the primal cause, from which many philosophers derive the first intellect. And so they say that the Good itself made both mind and matter eager for the Good and for union, and that mind is totally efficient and ready to shape, while matter is most easily and readily shaped. This is why forms come into being very easily and continually.

The things in our world which are called *these* or *those* are not so in truth and perfection, for they are mixed either with their opposites or with unfavourable conditions: thus warm things have some cold; equal things some inequality; light things some weight; beautiful things some deformity; and man something brutish. Yet at the same time, through his unique form, he is man, but through his multitude of parts he is clearly not man. In movement there is something which is not movement, and in time something which is not time.

What more? Indeed, fire itself, which in the general view accepts no admixture, contains something gross, something inert and dark. In the heavenly world, too, movement tolerates an opposing movement as well as stillness. Again, not everything that is in the sun is totally the sun itself, and the composition and size of heavenly bodies are not of themselves absolutely indissoluble, nor is movement of itself forever constant. In the *Theology* we have already spoken at great length on this subject.

And in the *Timaeus* and the seventh book of the *Republic* Plato clearly states that the Ideas are the true substances but that the things of our world are the images of the true things, that is, of Ideas. For this reason there is no unequivocal name common to the things of our world and the true things. But a man in this world and a man in that world are both called *man*. And it is the same in the case of a horse. In the same way, too, we have the depicted Socrates and the living Socrates, just as things in this world have their nature from the things in that world and are given this imaginary name from the things in that world.

For the first names are in the realm of the gods, names which they give both to the things in their world and to the things in our world. But the second names are in the minds of the wise, who, through the ideal concepts which are naturally known to them and which constitute [...] tly named divine things and then ours, which are made in [...] ss of those.

Chapter 18:
An Idea is not partaken of in a physical way, so that neither the whole nor any part of it is received

THIS BODY partakes of that body in a particular way; the body partakes of the soul in a different way; the soul partakes of the mind in another way; and our mind, or the universal mind, partakes of God in yet another way.

When Parmenides, therefore, is going to instruct Socrates, or rather encourage him, to contemplate that true way of participation by which Ideas are perceived by what is below them, he rejects, one by one, the ways which are not lawful. He examines in particular the physical nature of participation. If you receive something physical, either you take all of it, like a bait, or you take part of it, as you would with an element: if you drink water, you drink all of it or part of it. He therefore shows that Ideas cannot be received in a physical way like this, so that neither the whole of an Idea, nor even a portion, is apprehended.

Thus Socrates is advised to consider a non-physical, indeed divine, way of understanding, for we are considering either the power of an Idea or the property of an Idea. Nothing in our world apprehends the whole power of an Idea: that eternal, effective, and totally indivisible essence, perfect life and perfect intelligence. All the members of the same type apprehend equally the ideal property granted to that type; and so an Idea is totally within something, or partly within something, not in a physical way, but in some other way.

Again, since an Idea exists within itself, it can, through its presence, be fully present at the same time in many disparate objects, because of course it cannot coincide with a body, which needs a specific place, or with a physical attribute which is specific to a particular object.

Socrates, therefore, being naturally inclined to the contemplation of Ideas, rightly thinks that a whole Idea can be in every way simultaneously present in many objects, and he strives towards an incorporeal way of appreciating this presence, but he does not directly achieve this.

Moreover, in comparing an Idea to the light of day he speaks rightly, but in thinking that light spreads through air like heat and is like a sail spread over the heads of many men, and in thinking that this is how an Idea is present in many objects, he is refuted by Parmenides, who says that, if this were the case, an Idea would not be totally present in anything but would be present in some parts of the objects through some of its own parts; and in this way he compels the young man to answer with greater care.

Chapter 19:
Ideal largeness, ideal equality, and ideal smallness are not partaken of by any nature divisible into parts

DIVISION IS an action that is undergone, not by quality or by power, but by quantity. Therefore, after you have divided a uniform body you see that the parts of the whole are always unequal: they are always unequal one to another, although very similar in quality and power.

Ideal largeness, ideal equality, and ideal smallness seem to relate to quantity, for they necessarily carry with them the concept of quantity, yet they are not divisible in a physical way. Much less, therefore, are the remaining Ideas divisible; but if you wish to consider ideal largeness as divisible and able to be partaken of through its parts, like some mass whose parts are small and less than the whole, two absurd consequences follow at once.

The first is that the measure of largeness will consist of small and contrary items, as if fiery heat were composed of cold items. The second is that these many things which we usually call large because they participate in largeness, are now made into small parts through this dissection of largeness – for it is certainly through smallness of some kind, rather than through largeness, that things are wrongly called large – but that ideal largeness does not primarily discern mass alone, but it discerns excellence, excellence which is universal and by which incorporeal things exceed one another through their powers and easily outstrip bodily things through the same powers; that excellence by which, on earth, bodily things vie with each other not only through their powers but also through their dimensions. In that Idea there are not many parts, but there are powers.

In all the powers there is the same property, which is called largeness itself. This distributes some powers, one by one, to some subsequent things, which are thereby made large, and in the same way it distributes different powers to other subsequent things, which are also made large thereby. The ideal property, however, which it distributes is very similar: in fact, it is the same.

After ideal largeness let us consider ideal equality: an intellectual ratio which is both a model and a unifier of universal harmony and of harmonic proportion and of any kind of equality. This ideal ratio is found in all equal things according to the fullness of its own property, although not according to all its powers. If you imagine it as some mass divided into two unequal parts of the whole, when it is partaken of by two equal things, you will be compelled to make the absurd confession that equality itself makes things equal through some inequality, since it is necessarily divided into two unequal parts of the whole, so that other things are made equal one to another through partaking of it.

After equality Parmenides makes the young man work at smallness, not so much because he thinks that there is a particular Idea of smallness which is perhaps included within largeness, but rather to show generally that no Idea can be partaken of by being divided into parts like some mass. However, there are some who think that by the Idea of smallness is indicated whatever has been gathered into a whole, whether it be individual or whether it be unified. Let us now examine the argument. Let there be, if we are allowed to so imagine, an ideal smallness, and let it be divided into two parts, to be distributed to two objects so that these objects are made small by these two parts. Two errors will then follow.

The first error is that ideal smallness will become large when it is compared to the parts that are smaller than the whole itself. But we are now considering the principle of smallness in isolation, to which nothing is added from largeness, its opposite. The second error is that those things to which the divided parts are added after the division of ideal smallness will become either larger or smaller than they were before the addition. If they become larger, which also seems probable, you were imagining in vain that these things would become small on account of smallness. If they become smaller, which is what you yourself were seeking, it will be foolish to say that some things become smaller through addition.

Step by step Socrates is instructed in these matters so that he may consider a partaking of the Ideas which is higher than any physical principle. To this instruction Socrates readily assents, being inclined towards it by nature.

Chapter 20:
Neither by nature nor by circumstance
do Ideas meet with material things

FOR WHEN we consider that the Ideas just mentioned, as well as any others, can be present in an identical way to all that partake of them – larger or smaller, in the east or in the west, now or at some other time – we can easily conceive that Ideas are not attached to dimension, place, or time, but are totally detached from all these. And since, with all the changes wrought by time, the Ideas display particular forms in the generating of beings prepared for each moment and now appearing as objects, it is clearly the case that Ideas are remote from all differentiation, all place, all movement, and all time, being indivisible, unmoving, eternal, and present everywhere: so present that each quality of an Idea extends to the uttermost ends of creation. For the followers of Plato trace the lines of creation all the way from Ideas to here. Beneath the Idea of sun, the Idea of moon, and the Idea of lion there are, of course, celestial bodies of such kinds. Then there are the corresponding daemons, as well as the living beings and the corresponding minerals and stones.

Now since the qualities of Ideas and the qualities of celestial beings are found even in the final forms of creation, they exist with all the greater certainty within the forms that are intermediate; and thus it is clearly the case that, through this interweaving of the parts of creation, the highest parts resonate and harmonise with the lowest parts, and vice versa.

But we have spoken sufficiently on this in the third *Book of Life*.

However, it is important now to remember that forms in the physical world are not produced directly from Ideas, but are made through the seed-powers of nature derived from the Ideas; and that the physical forms are connected with these seeds, not in their nature – for they are non-physical seeds – but in very special and fluid circumstances. However, their contact with Ideas is not through nature or circumstance, but through relationship, dependence, and name; for, of course, specific forms of creation arise from specific Ideas, which they strongly follow and chiefly depict.

Nor, again, is there a third situation to inquire into, in which those things are declared to meet with Ideas, as if there were a third possibility in which the reflections or shadows of the soul met with their physical forms.

Chapter 21:
We should not suppose that every assemblage of multifarious items suggests that there is a single Idea for those items

AS A Pythagorean with due regard for Ideas, Parmenides does not cross Socrates when the latter supposes that, on account of assemblages of items coming together within something definite in response to a cause related to form, type, nature, and perfection, there is a single Idea for each and every assemblage within a type.

He does, however, temper Socrates' enthusiasm, in order to avoid the possible inference that any collection of items has to be related to a specific Idea, even if these items seem to come together by some accidental or passing circumstance, by some deficiency, artificiality, or name; for if this were the case, there would be an unnatural number of causes for many of the occurrences within nature, and the number of Ideas would be infinite.

You should understand, however, that Parmenides' reasonings on the many, the large, and on largeness itself also apply to many men and to the actual Idea of humanity; for in name these individuals join the Idea, since they actually come from it and are particularly related to it. Yet this is not the case in nature or in circumstance, and so the individuals do not join the Idea in some sort of third type by means of which there is a different way of moving to a higher Idea, and from that and those together to yet another Idea, and so on, endlessly.

This is how Socrates is advised not to imagine a new Idea for every apparent combination.

Chapter 22:
From types which are created by the soul
we must rise to types which are naturally
present in the soul, and then rise from
those to types which are divine

SOCRATES, therefore, to avoid the possibility of being forced to
postulate an infinite number of types of substance within the nature of
creation, like a young man without sufficient training, has recourse to
a common conception of individual items, a conception which is made
by our intelligence and which he calls *noema*, but which we designate
with the more convenient word *notion*. Now it is called *noema* from the
Greek word for *intellect*. This is really any kind of intelligence, although
by common custom we may also call it the *intelligible*, yet not the first
intelligible but a kind of intermediary between the two, a concept
explaining what is perceived and within which the intelligence ceases;
but above such concepts which are devised by us every day there are
naturally within our minds the *noemata* which have been divinely
implanted there, that is, certain intermediary types in addition,
between the intelligence and the intelligible, since at times our intelligence, through such types, recognises the Ideas themselves, which are
the principal intelligible things.

That these types are implanted within us we have proved with many
arguments in the *Theology*. Here we shall be content with a single one,
and a very brief one at that: as intellect is more eminent and closer to
reality than is sense, so intelligible things are closer to perfection and
reality than are perceptible things.

Now the intelligible things are those to which the intellect naturally
turns whenever it is unencumbered. These are the universal and
absolute causes of creation. Therefore, if perceptible things are substances within the hierarchy of creation, much more so are their causes;
but these causes cannot exist except within the power of some
intellect, nor are these causes the first of all those things that we were
considering just now, for such causes are changeable and come later
than our intelligence. The true intelligible things, however, are both
unchangeable and prior to intelligence. Therefore the first of such
causes are in the divine mind, but within us also there are causes which

are naturally implanted prior to the concepts which I have called accidental concepts.

Through these causes we bring forth conceptions, and hence we rise up to Ideas. That such causes are within the very depths of the soul we ourselves demonstrate most clearly when, intending to give an absolute definition of some things, we leave external isolated items, take refuge in the universal, and seek the innermost depths of the mind, where we are met by those intelligible things which are closest.

Now Ideas are distant intelligible things, while these intelligible things which are closest, being nearer to perfection, are not gathered together by perceptible things, which are imperfect, but are imparted by the first intelligible things; through their power, while we are looking at some particular object, we fully consider a type-cause which, being in something individual, is not universal, and we use reason aright to take physical things back to their non-physical causes.

Finally, Parmenides does not in fact reprove Socrates for seeking refuge in such notions, but he does reprove him for appearing to stay there. He therefore takes pains, through this reference to new notions which relates to the naturally implanted types, to call him back next not only to these types but also to the divine types.

Chapter 23:
The first types of creation, which are also the principal subjects of the intellect, are prior to the intelligences

BEGIN TO understand, therefore, the reasoning of Parmenides: just as true sense focuses on something perceptible which actually exists, which is prior to sense, and which is united with sense at the time of perception, so true intelligence, which he now calls *notion*, is directed towards something that is intelligible to it, that really exists and is prior to it, and is more united with *notion* than the perceptible is with sense.

Now the things that are intelligible are the type-causes of all things: they are universal, unchangeable, absolute. Therefore our *notion* always understands one thing, according to one type which always possesses within itself a true and unchangeable essence, and which imparts its own quality and name to the individual items comprised within the same type. But what is intelligible is not within the individual items, for if that were the case it would now be divided and subject to change; nor is it our own newly formed notion, for if it were it would be changeable and artificial, and there would be no true understanding. Again, it is not in particular that higher notion which is naturally implanted within our mind, for this higher *notion* imparts nothing to the things that are perceived and is not common to any of them. It is therefore what I was just now calling the intelligible: a type within that very intellect which frames all creation.

The offspring of this type are: a seed-cause imparted to nature for every type of burgeoning; a common property imparted to all the individual items within the same type; and the *notion* that is divinely implanted within us. But in all cases intelligible things are prior to the intelligences, just as perceptible things are prior to sense; for if they were not prior the result would certainly be that the intelligences, being now prior to intelligible things, would be unoccupied at that prior time, not being directed towards any object, yet soon ready to fabricate for themselves something to perceive.

Therefore, when we speak about Ideas, we ought not to consider Ideas as intelligences or actions, but as subjects, as the types and natural powers which accompany the essence of the primal intellect and upon which is focused the intelligence of that intellect – the intelligence which follows them in some fashion, yet which is miraculously unified with them.

These being the hidden meanings of what Parmenides says, he does not know how Socrates assents to them.

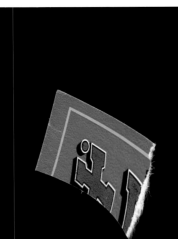

Chapter 24:
Ideas are intelligible things rather than intelligences, and these intelligible things are prior to intelligences

BUT BEFORE Socrates openly admits this, he seems in some way to suppose that the first types of creation are perhaps intelligences which are within our intellect or within a higher intellect. So Parmenides reasons first of all that just as all things which, through their own quality, partake of life or wisdom are alive or understand, so those things which partake of the intelligences comprehend.

However, all natural phenomena partake of the first types, and yet they do not all comprehend. Therefore the first types are not actually intelligences, but intelligible things, that is, the essential, actual, and true causes of all things, the models and efficient powers of all things, within the one Maker of all, in whom life and intellect exist beyond the fullness of these types. And although all the types *there* soon become alive and intellectual, not all the things produced *here* in accordance with those types are alive and comprehend, since *there* type and intellect and life are not exactly the same, but those things are imparted through the gift of life and intellect in addition to their type-form. But more on these things elsewhere.

Let us return to first principles. Intelligence is really an action and a sort of movement, while type is essence and power and aim. Therefore intelligence is not identical with the first type, which is perceived everywhere through intelligence. For the usual situation is that a single common intelligence is enough to understand many things.

Now the intelligible types by which those things are discerned through their form are especially in the higher intellects; for we often catch sight of very many forms with a single glance. But now within the first intellect, which discerns itself, what is intelligible is better than intelligence and better than the discerning intellect, for the intellect desires, the intelligence is the power of desire, and the intelligible is desirable.

The intelligible, therefore, is better, being more closely related to the Highest Good, and for this reason this universe has taken its rise not so much from the intellect or the intelligence as from intelligible things, namely, the first essence, which is full of intelligible types and powers. Therefore essences and types are everywhere, but intelligence and intellect are not imparted to all things everywhere.

Chapter 25:
The quality of an Idea somehow remains one throughout an entire sequence, while the power of an Idea varies

LET US now consider within any Idea both the quality of the Idea and the full power of the Maker. That quality, on account of its sameness, is given without variation to the entire sequence which follows it. The fullness of the power, however, on account of its diversity, is distributed with varying intensity, for, as we have said elsewhere, the powers which flourish in the lunar Idea have all descended somehow into the moon. But they do not all descend without variation into the lunar daemons; and again, they are fewer when they descend in a less regulated way to lunar men on earth. They are fewer still and even weaker when they reach animals, plants, metals, and then other things which are naturally subject to the moon.

In this way, therefore, that power of the Maker, under the regulation of wisdom, is distributed in different ways. But the lunar quality in the Idea, the quality through which that Idea differs from other Ideas and through which lunar natures differ from solar natures, is either unchanged in all the successive lunar steps or is certainly almost the same. Indeed, it is through this resemblance that any sequence is called single, and in this sequence the variation in steps follows the varying distribution of the powers, although the unity is still preserved.

Hence the Egyptians acknowledged the lunar Apis and the moon-fish, which imitate the moon in form and movements, as well as a precious stone which followed the moon not only in power and form but also in waxing and waning.

In brief, if that lunar quality of the Idea appears even at the ends of sequences, how much greater will its influence be earlier in the sequences.

Chapter 26:
Ideas are not simple notions but natural types which possess model power and effective power

THAT PARMENIDES does not pursue Socrates at every point like a disputant and rebuke him, but in the manner of a midwife encourages, assists, cherishes, guides and corrects him, is plain to observe, because this young man does not gradually wane but gains strength at every step, being led towards better things.

Therefore, being now guided by Parmenides as by a teacher, he puts forward a true and definite view of Ideas, saying that they abide within nature as models, while all other things are made like them and are nothing but the images of Ideas, and that there is no way they can share in the Ideas except by being made similar to them. He does not consider that new types are somehow our ideas within our world, nor does he think that Ideas are somehow scattered among the various intellects beyond our world, when he says that Ideas abide in nature: a nature, I say, which is single and full of life and intellect, a nature, indeed, which he calls Jove in the *Philebus*, where he says that the intelligence and soul of a king exist in the nature of Jove.

Moreover, when he here calls it nature, he is advising us to consider Ideas not as simply notions, but as essential types and natural powers. For if the natural forms and powers of the limbs are in the final natures of the souls, and if within the final nature of cosmic life there are the seed-powers of all things, seed-powers which have effective force, how much more are the efficient and natural types of creation within the essence of the divine mind. These, indeed, are present to the cosmic Maker not just as models for moulding these things, as Socrates clearly stated, but they also have the efficient force to make, preserve, and unify these things.

This latter part he seems to have expressed less strongly. For this reason Parmenides, intending to lead Socrates on to a fuller explanation of these things, will henceforth insist upon many reasonings. For although Socrates seems to have silently pointed to virtues of this kind, when he says that Ideas exist within nature as the eternal principles of creation, yet these principles are made by Ideas and are changed with the passage of time, he clearly postulated, as we have said, a single similar virtue which, being the only one now expressed, will henceforth give Parmenides opportunities for his reasonings.

But meanwhile remember, as I have advised you elsewhere, that these things which are separate in the soul from our point of view, are *there* joined in one, so that the intellectual Idea has effective power, as do the seed-powers within creative nature, and not merely model power, like artificial types within their maker or within some intellect, although the model function extends to the types of creation, while the effective power reaches to the individual items.

Finally, when Socrates says that these lower things have no relation with Ideas except as images, he seems to have given a satisfactory reply to his interrogator as to how Ideas are partaken of, namely, that neither the whole nor any part of an Idea is received at a physical level; the nature of the Idea is not conveyed to our world, nor, conversely, do the things of our world in any way meet Ideas, but merely reflect them, just as the image in a mirror reflects the face.

Chapter 27:
Natural forms are rightly said to be similar to Ideas, but Ideas must not be described as similar to natural forms

PARMENIDES does not deny that the first types of creation exist within nature, but he carefully investigates the way creation resembles those types. And so, when Socrates was being tested by Parmenides, he was rather too hasty to accept their mutual similarity. Parmenides rejected this characteristic of mutual similarity, for there is normally mutual partnership between two similar things which share in the same quality, as perceived by their maker, with the result that the relationship between them is: just as this is similar to that, so that is similar to this. Therefore, if these lower things, through this kind of relationship and reciprocal interchange, were similar to the ideal types, and the ideal types were, in turn, similar to them, it would undoubtedly follow that these things, together with the Ideas, would partake of yet a third type, and a ridiculous movement into infinity would proceed.

It was therefore reasonable for Socrates to reply that the manner of similarity was twofold; for this is similar to that either because both are from the same source or because this derives from that. In the first case there is an interchange, but not in the second case, where the model is one thing but similarity another: therefore, just as that which is similar to the model has neither the power nor the name of model in relation to the model, so that which is the model does not have its own characteristic of similarity in relation to this similarity. For this reason, therefore, these lower things are similar to the Ideas because they depend on them, but since the Ideas do not have any quality in common with them, the Ideas are not similar to them, but are simply models and principles. Therefore the way in which Ideas are partaken of is not through that similarity by which these share with those any common quality, but is because these forms are shaped by those Ideas and therefore reflect those Ideas.

Chapter 28:
Contrary to the opinion of the Stoics and the Aristotelians, Ideas and all things divine are separate from nature and have a power that can be imparted to everything

SINCE SOCRATES thought that the pursuit of Ideas was rather easy, and since he affirmed them simply on the basis of a quality and a limit common to many things, Parmenides advises the young man, for this very reason, to proceed more carefully henceforth and to consider first of all the very great difficulty in being able to understand what Ideas are, where they are initially, how they relate to themselves and to the things of our world, and through what steps and what kinds of powers they proceed to the things of our world. Ideas should not be rashly affirmed on the basis of a quality common to created things.

Indeed, in Plato's view it is certainly reasonable for an Idea to have two properties. The first is a distinctive substance, having no admixture or participation with nature and no tendency towards natural forms. The second is power and action which can be imparted throughout the universe, diffusing its own beneficial gifts in all directions. We therefore call the first quality pre-eminence, and the second quality providence that is available to all, but it is very difficult for us to observe both of these properties within the divine world. For the Stoics, indeed, deprived the Godhead of its pre-eminence and purity, since they considered that it provided and acted throughout the whole world, being diffused everywhere and darting hither and thither like a fiery spirit.

But certain Aristotelians seem to think that the divine substances do not produce perceptible objects or care for them, but exist in total isolation, and that it is through some desire that the celestial powers move towards perceptible objects.

We have refuted both these errors in our *Theology*. Against the Stoics we argue in many ways that that which has so many dealings with matter and movement cannot be the first. But against those Aristotelians we give abundant proof that separate substances – and especially the first substance – move, understand, and care for all that follow, and that the celestial souls and spheres seek God, love God, and imitate God for no reason other than that they are thereby perfected and are thereby brought to completion.

Moreover, to do nothing and to be unproductive pertains to the final step in creation, not to the first. Things in the middle realm act providentially, and this is even truer of those that are higher and better, and truest of all for those that are the first and the best. In short, the first Good acts and cares with the greatest possible providence. It is, in fact, quite ridiculous to say that heaven, with its ceaseless activity, imitates a God who is totally inactive. However, if it is good to be active, how can that which is first be inactive? If it is not good to be active, how can those things which follow imitate the best through activity?

Parmenides therefore advises Socrates, in relation to the divine Ideas, to acknowledge both the pre-eminence of their nature and their ability to impart their power, for previously he has clearly shown that the power of Ideas to impart themselves is pre-eminent and operates without the special manifestation and participation of nature, and he has pointed out the absurdities that would otherwise follow.

Through further absurdities, to which his arguments lead us, he shows next that it is impossible for that pre-eminence to be without all power to impart itself or to be devoid of all manifestation and all proportion. The first absurdity is that the Ideas would be completely unknowable to us. The second absurdity is that the Ideas would know nothing of our world and would not care for it. In both cases Parmenides makes the young man aware that in the consideration of Ideas he should not think of pre-eminence without participation or of participation divorced from pre-eminence.

Chapter 29:
The ways in which Ideas cannot be known by us, and the ways in which they can be known

IF SOMEONE is discussing Ideas with you, and if either of you considers that the simple pure excellence of Ideas is above human reach, your disputant will have no difficulty in proving from this that Ideas cannot be known by us. Yet if you doubt this, but are not naturally inclined towards divine matters or instructed in dialectics, physics, and mathematics, as well as being eager for this struggle and full of perseverance, you will find it difficult to argue against him or correct him.

Of course, if you have been trained in this way, as I imagine you have, you will give him this brief answer: The cognitive power of man, through its first direct action, connects with human, natural, and similar matters; and so these things can be known by us through our own mode of apprehension, that is, through a conclusion rightly drawn from cause to effect; divine matters, however, are not understood, either through our first direct perception or through a method of learning, but they are inferred by some reflective activity through human and natural matters as if through images and effects, and Ideas are inferred as the causes and models of human and natural matters; and the model, or at least the Ideas, can be apprehended, not through the normal process of reasoning which is the cause of knowledge, but, unusually, through simple perception that has been perfectly purified, rightly trained, and divinely illuminated. But perhaps the intellectual types that are naturally implanted within our intellects and within the higher intellects can be known for certain through our own endeavour.

The intelligible types, however, and the Ideas that are natural to the first intellect cannot be apprehended by our wisdom and by precise reason; and you will not be able to persuade your disputant that this matter is other than this. For you will never convince him that Ideas or first types are understood by our own power or by some power at our disposal. Again, you will not be able to obtain that knowledge of God by which God inwardly perceives that Ideas are related to the things of our world in such a way that through direct observation He views these things as the first objects. For, as a result, and by a truly reflective act, He cognises these things, through the Ideas themselves, as the effects and images of the Ideas.

Then, when Parmenides says that if the first types are within themselves it follows that they are not within us, Socrates has to concede that they are not within us as qualities are within objects, but that their clear images are infused into our minds, while their shadowy images appear in matter. For those first types are not sterile but fertile, much more fertile than natural qualities and celestial forms. Thus it is that we can conceive of clear tracks in the pursuit of Ideas, and that that first intellect – the fertile abundance of Ideas – through the causes of all that follows knows all these things and orders them providentially.

But when we say in this discussion that the first types are within themselves, you should understand that they are not within the first intellect like parts within a whole, or like qualities within an object, but like numbers within unity, like the beginnings of lines within a centre, like the rays and colours within the light of the sun, like the necessary propositions that follow from a perfect action in geometry, and like the seed-powers within creative nature once they have united their natural intelligence with their creative efficacy.

Chapter 30:
The ways in which Ideas are not related, or may be related, to the things of our world, and vice versa. Also concerning lordship and service, and relationships in the realm of Ideas

IF WE consider the things of our world as existing within themselves, and if we consider Ideas as existing within themselves, then Ideas are not related to the things of our world, and vice versa. However, if we contemplate this particular thing as something made and as an image, and if we contemplate an Idea as efficient and as a model, then through this set of conditions they are mutually related.

Again, when we consider lordship in the realm of Ideas, we must not connect it, through a comparable relationship, to the service that we know in our world, in the way that we normally adopt when speaking to each other, for a human lord is the lord of a human servant; but we must relate that ideal lordship, like a consort, to ideal service, and subsequently to the lordship in our world as a model and cause are related to an image and an effect. For if there is a maker of our lordship, and consequently of our service, we relate our service to the ideal service as to its cause, its model.

Accordingly, we must not place within Ideas themselves any chance relationships — such as when I say that, as you walk around, you are now on my right and now on my left — or, indeed, any natural relationships — such as when I compare my right hand to my left hand as one that works or moves more effectively to one that works or moves less effectively, or again, when we compare the creative to the created, the first working through its natural power and the second being born by a natural process.

Moreover, just as we relate intelligence to the intelligible, and a specific intelligence to a specific intelligible, on account of some natural manifestation and proportion, so Ideas seem to have a similar relationship one with another, but with this difference: whereas in our world the substances of the things that are related are diverse, in the realm of Ideas things are the same, for there the essence of the ideal parent and of the ideal offspring is one.

Although all Ideas are strongly joined together by the same substance of the intelligence and the intelligible, those Ideas are most strongly united which are companions through their mutual relationship. Indeed, the Idea of heat produces manifestations of heat which are necessarily separate from the Idea of cold, and at the same time it necessarily produces them in isolation from the Idea of wetness. But every time the Idea 'right' makes things on the right, it produces them in conjunction with the Idea 'left', which produces things on the left.

Now that ideal lordship is the true reason for mastery, and it is for this reason that what is everywhere naturally superior and better has pre-eminence over what is lower, and it provides for what is less good, using the works of the less good for its own work and adapting them to its own good. But ideal service is the true reason for obedience, by means of which what is less good naturally ministers to what is better. In the same way, higher Ideas take precedence over Ideas which are in some way lower. Moreover, the gods rule the daemons which are submissive by nature. The daemons naturally rule men, and wiser men naturally rule men who are not so wise.

In brief, Socrates had to answer Parmenides by saying that the ideal lordship and the ideal service are not related to us but to each other, I mean through their first indissoluble relationship; but they are related to us, too, by some subsequent kind of relationship, insofar as all lordship and all service depend on the first cause of true lordship and service as effects and images: it is through this cause that those things are related to the things of our world, and, consequently, the things of our world are related to those things.

Chapter 31:
How pure knowledge relates to pure truth, while human knowledge relates to human truth. How Ideas may be unknown or known

WITHIN THE primal intellect, ideal pure knowledge is nothing but intelligence and a sure understanding of itself and of all things. Again, it is the ideal truth, that is, the primal and complete essence and nature of the Good itself, shining with light, the light by which intelligence looks at and discerns its own intelligible; and this universal intelligible, which we have called truth, offers itself to the intelligence and penetrates it in order to be thoroughly understood.

From this there are also many similar branches of knowledge within subsequent intellects, as well as very similar kinds of truth; and all intelligences are related to their respective intelligibles: divine to divine, human to human, and so on. This happens by virtue of the first direct cognition, for, as we have said earlier, it is through result and reflection that the gods know the things of our world and we, especially through the purifying effect of love and through some illumination, perceive the divine world, just as Plato describes in the *Phaedrus*, as he conducts the purified souls, seized by frenzy, towards the lofty visions of the gods. But it is recorded elsewhere how, through the forms and types that are innate in us – the forms and types of lower things – we come to know Ideas as if through images and models.

No one, however, should say, as some do, that God does not reach the things of our world through His knowledge, for since He perfectly enfolds within Himself the causes of all things, comprehending Himself most precisely, in the same way He embraces all things. This is especially true since, if the first knowledge is the knowledge of all knowledges, on which all knowledges, by reason of being knowledges, depend, certainly by cognition it produces them all, and by making them it cognises them all. If all knowledges are known to themselves, then as a result all knowables (as I may call them) are joined to knowledges. But it is wrong to say that God does not have knowledge, just as it is wrong to say that what gives life lacks life. For I say that whatever is good within knowledge and life cannot be absent from the first good.

In short, the first Ideas are separated from our soul by the maximum number of steps possible, and they are not within us by means of any explicit character; nor are they around us, that is to say, there is nowhere where they are presented to us through an absolute image, and therefore we do not embrace them with absolute certainty – indeed, neither the angelic intellects nor our own intellects can define them with that perfection with which God Himself defines them. For just as within the divine intellect there are the Ideas of all other things, so there is, too, the Idea of knowledge itself, which through union holds and views the Ideas as its own objects. But that ideal knowledge itself of which we have just spoken is not, as it were, within us or specifically within the angels themselves; and since it is much less within us, we do not understand the Ideas which are comprehensible by this kind of knowledge. But we do at times cognise, through the forms which are objects for us or which are innate in us, the intellectual Ideas which shine clearly in our minds subsequent to the first Idea and through which, being illumined particularly by the higher minds, we finally ascend, as far as we may, after the expiation described in the *Phaedrus*, to the first Ideas, which are rightly named the intelligible types, ourselves being raised above the human condition.

Chapter 32:
Concerning the way of divine consideration and providence

WHEN PARMENIDES, through the concessions made by the young man, shows the consequence to be that we do not cognise Ideas and that Ideas do not cognise us, he adds at the same time that those men are seriously in error who are obliged to admit, by any arguments, that we are totally ignorant of divine matters, especially since it has been handed down from the ancients that the substance of the rational soul is divine. But he says that it is a more serious error to deny that the gods above have the care of human affairs, to the good state of which providence necessarily pertains. For this reason Socrates is now carefully trained, so that he learns to resolve doubts about Ideas which, if unresolved, would detract from divine providence.

In this discussion, however, remember that God has a kind of knowledge which has nothing at all in common with our knowledge, and also that God has a lordship which has nothing in common with our lordship. Therefore, as long as we conceive of some cause of knowing or of lordship which is our own or in any way similar to our own, we are able to admit that God does not know as we do or in any way comparable to ours, and that God has dominion over us. This was agreed to be far from error; but if you say that God is totally devoid of universal consciousness and lordship, then you will move far from the view held by Plato.

For the time being I pass over those men who – because they fail to see the order of fortune – have denied providence; but it is necessary, at least briefly, to speak against certain philosophers who, since they know that God is the furthest removed from all the characteristics of material and moving things, immediately argue that God cannot have any consciousness of these material things, for if consciousness has to concur with the thing cognised, divine consciousness has no concurrence with the material, changeable things beneath the moon. Indeed, if it is true, as these philosophers say it is, that the power of cognition must concur with what is to be cognised, perhaps it is true within our consciousness. For since we are not, through our consciousness, the makers of created things, perhaps there is no reason why we should perceive them, unless it be through some proportion. But since divine knowledge is the first cause of created things, God will be aware of created things, not because He concurs with the nature of things but because He is conscious that He is the cause of things.

By being aware that He Himself is the origin of all, He immediately cognises all and makes all; but not even within our own consciousness is there the truth of consciousness. There must be a way to match the way of created things, since even the efficient causes do their work in their own way and not according to the nature of the work. For man, when born, is one effect, but what comes from man is different, and what comes from the sun is different again. Indeed, from man it is particular, even when he is seeking counsel and anxious, while from the sun it is universal and for this reason does not lack counsel. Much more does everything arise effortlessly from the first cause. But of this elsewhere.

Let us now inquire whether an action moving into matter does not force the cause to produce its own particular effects. Much less does an action – that is, consciousness – remaining within the agent, that is, the cogniser, cognise what needs to be cognised, because everything that is conscious cognises and judges not simply for the quality of the thing cognised but for the nature, the form, and the intrinsic worth of the conscious power.

From this it is clear that a man who is presented to us is judged in one way by the outer senses, in another way by the imagination, in a third way by reason, and in yet another way by the intellect. For sense perceives only what is present and incidental, while imagination looks for what is absent, and in some way apprehends, composes, and divides the substance: it assembles only those things which the five senses deal with individually. Reason, however, makes all these things and, besides, transfers itself, by reasoning, to the universal reasoning type and nature. Finally, the intellect immediately sees with a single glance those things which reason examines from all sides with multifarious reasonings, just as sight immediately perceives a spherical object as round, while touch perceives it by frequent contact.

Indeed, the higher nature and power perceive and perform whatever the lower perceive and perform, and the higher nature and power understand better, and do so, moreover, without the actual use of the lower, often dealing with those things to which the lower cannot aspire.

For this reason, just as the lower power deals with the same object of perception in a particular way, while the higher power deals with the same object in a different and better way; and just as the five senses touch one by one, the imagination touches all together, and what is perceived so far as is possible by the individual physical nature is conceived by reason according to the intrinsic worth of its own nature and incorporeal judgement, while the intellect, being now almost divine, often understands with a single motionless apprehension those things which reason comprehends through many ways and movements, as well as many things to which reason does not attain; in the same way the first intellect knows all things, and others besides, far otherwise and far more felicitously than do reason and the human mind. And the intellect does not follow the circumstances of the things cognised, but follows its own nature through its cognition: its nature, I say, which is uniform, indivisible, and unchanging. Thus it apprehends many things with a single form, and it grasps material things in a non-material way, composite things in a simple way, changeable things in an unchanging way, and of necessity it grasps, once and for all, certain things which it is our fate to meet every day.

This is what Boethius and Proclus confirm; and if we may be allowed to use the examples given by Proclus, please picture to yourself a ship driven about by winds and waves. Now suppose that your imagination is so powerful that, while you are picturing the sea, a sea flows therefrom. Picture a ship, and let the ship be built accordingly. Imagine many winds and waves and buffetings, and let them all at once arise in accordance with your imagination. If this is what happens, you will not be obliged to entertain conjectures about these things that are to be examined; nor will you be distracted, but by fashioning them in this way you will make them simply, easily, and once and for all, and you will similarly acknowledge that the divine intelligence is for producing and simultaneously observing the lower things. Proclus thinks that he is able to do so. For this reason we have said that our judgement is preserved in the *Theology*, and, moreover, for Plotinus, since the divine intellect is the founder of the universe, and since it diffuses its power very widely through everything, it has, of course, the most expansive form, which has the ability to represent and make everything simultaneously; and just as the perfect effect pertains to it, so does perfect apprehension, but each of them is perfect, not only that which comes to universal things and to general things and commingled things, but also that which attains everywhere to the specific and distinct, and so, ultimately, to the most precise. If it were otherwise, both the operation and the cognition would be imperfect.

It therefore cognises, just as it causes, universals as well as particulars that are distinct from its own forms and properties, and thus it provides for particular things, because the following four qualities flow through everything: power, action, consciousness, providence. Undoubtedly it is perfectly aware of the nature and power of its own goodness and of all its own Ideas; thus it knows in how many ways and by how many steps and to what extent it can proceed and be partaken of, and therefore it understands the lowest things, I say, with a clearer awareness than is available to our senses and to our opinion. The consciousness which pervades all causes is more certain than the consciousness which does not pervade causes or does not pervade all causes, especially if it embraces the ideal essence and life and every ideal sense, but perceives all things intellectually, and through the intellectual sense, therefore, it clearly perceives what is discernible to us.

Hence it seems appropriate to repeat the statement of Proclus against certain Aristotelians, to the effect that if the first intellect understands itself perfectly as the maker of all and as the goal of all, since it is called the cause in relation to the effect, and the goal in relation to the manifest creation, it necessarily and perfectly cognises all its effects as well as all the things that seek it, not merely generally or in a confused way but by clear reason, for just as by precise reason it becomes aware of itself as the cause of all and as the goal of all, so undoubtedly and by clear reason it fully acknowledges all that come into being from it and that seek it again.

However, that knowledge, being in its purest form through right understanding, as we have said earlier, is divided into the purest objects, that is, the first Ideas and types. At this first level, indeed, it can be imagined that the things of our world are not perceived. For to perceive them subsequently through some result by observed Ideas, and through the right insight of knowledge, we have as objects nothing beyond these lower things, and consequently it is as if we have intimations of the higher things.

Chapter 33:
On divine lordship and consciousness; and on the six orders of Ideas or forms

IF ANYONE denies that God knows our world because there are many base and evil things here and the intellect is perhaps defiled by a consideration of such things, he should know that God does not have regard to these things as He surveys them, but He has regard to Himself as He looks within, for in His presence all things are perfectly beautiful.

Indeed, even with us nothing is simply evil, but is evil or base for this particular person or that particular person, though good and beautiful for others and for the universe. Again, those things which are opposed in our minds are united with each other in God and are often reduced to a single form and principle, so that, as a result, He recognises even what is evil and base as having the form of the good and the beautiful. For the human mind often has intimations of evil beneath the form of the good, and awareness of evil is just as good to the intelligence as is awareness of the good. Yet it is not through such an apprehension, which carries no weight with him, that Parmenides draws Socrates into doubt, but rather because anyone who contemplates only the sublime nature of the divine beings gives no thought to the fact that goodness can be transmitted.

Moreover, by removing from the divine beings all power of transmission, he is at the same time removing their awareness of human affairs and the providence they exercise over the human condition, which is an absurd thing to say, just as if you were to deny that God governs the lower world; and Parmenides is right to connect divine lordship with consciousness, thereby advising Socrates never to deny that God does know our world, just as he should never concede that God has no dominion over us, for with God action and understanding are so united that, just as the immensely powerful action of the supreme cause proceeds imperiously to its final effects, so does sure awareness care for even the lowest objects in creation.

Nor was Parmenides taking the discussion off the point when he added that, since the gods exist – insomuch as he knew that if the pure intellect lacked all divinity it would, in its natural state, acknowledge certain universals, and that Ideas, being likewise deprived of divinity, would move only to universals and types, because both the intellect and the Ideas extend their power through all things by means of action and knowledge – this is the particular reason why they partake of that higher principle of goodness and unity which pervades all things throughout their length and breadth; but in this discussion, when Parmenides attributed to God knowledge that is supreme and most exact, understand that this is why such knowledge will indubitably take cognisance of individual things. And when you hear some things relating to privation and negation, understand the negation not as some defect but rather as an excess.

For this is the advice that Dionysius the Areopagite often gives us, and the advice that Parmenides perhaps gives when he adds that the things of the divine world will be completely unknown to us and that if any Ideas exist in the first principle, they will be distinct one from another for relative reasons only and not for absolute reasons, and they will in no way be intelligible to us or to any other beings, since they will exist beyond all the limits of intelligence itself. For it is not by intelligence but by some more mysterious act that we are able to appreciate the first principle of the universe.

After these Ideas there follow the Ideas which are now simply intelligible, yet comprehensible to us with difficulty and at long last. These are the causes of all things within the first intellect – or, as our writers would say, within the first angelic level – causes distinct one from another through absolute principles. Thirdly, there are the intellectual Ideas within the successive intellects that have no dealings with bodily matters.

Fourthly, there are the living Ideas, implanted within the very minds and thoughts of divine, or even human, souls. Fifthly, there are the natural Ideas and types within quickening nature, that is, the seed-causes of bodily forms within the nature of the natural soul and within the natures of the higher souls and of our souls. Sixthly, there are the forms within matter, which, depending as it were upon all that is higher to them, have something from each preceding world: from the divine world, something mysterious and divine, as well as unity and goodness; from the intelligible world, a particular kind of eternality and the distinctiveness necessary for living beings, as well as a quite distinctive beauty, together with action and movement; from the natural world, their point of manifestation and their final differentiation. And this progression may be called, on account of the manifest differentiation of the world, the five orders of types below the first order, the orders that Timaeus, perhaps, speaks of in the writings of Plato.

To put it briefly, in the first order, beneath a single form, are all Ideas; in the second the Ideas are many forms, but within the smallest number there is the most extensive power to create and to realise; in the third order, a fuller differentiation of types; in the fourth, an even greater differentiation into very specific types; in the fifth, the seed-powers of the parts and limbs of the body; in the sixth, there are the chance happenings which occur outside the natural order.

Chapter 34:
If there be no Ideas in the presence of God and no ideal patterns within us, then dialectic will perish, and so will all philosophy. There will be no proof, definition, division, or explanation

WHEN PARMENIDES pursues, in relation to Socrates, the dedicated function of midwife which he introduced at the beginning, stimulating the inner powers of the young man to a most precise consideration of Ideas and showing on numerous occasions that very serious errors arise from imprecise answers and responses, and that it is a difficult task, and one that requires an excellent mind, to prove that Ideas exist, to show how they exist, to truly resolve doubts as they arise, and to teach with clear reason the person who is listening, all of these things make Socrates very careful and precise.

At the same time, however, with the aim of advising the young man not to deny Ideas in this investigation but to make an effort to affirm Ideas, he states clearly that if there be truly no Ideas existing within themselves in the presence of God and naturally implanted within our minds by means of their true patterns, then true intelligence will perish, since there will be no true objects to which it may properly be directed, and there will be no knowledge of dialectic and no philosophy.

We have often said that there must be some relationship between the cognitive power and the object it can cognise. In addition, the truer and higher the intellect is than sense, the higher and truer is the object of the intellect itself than the object of sense. Therefore universal and unconditioned form and reason are necessarily judged to be truer and more perfect than an individual material form. Hence, just as sense is turned to what is external, so the intellect turns to what is within, provided that it originates through the faculty of invention and judgement. Therefore, just as the object of sense is external, so the proper object of the mind is within. With this process of reasoning and with very many others given in the *Theology*, we have shown conclusively that the patterns and models of all things are naturally implanted within our mind.

Since these patterns and models are subject to movement in such a way that they pass from a latent state into the act of contemplation, we have also likewise proved that they, being not yet fully perfect as it were, cannot exist of themselves, but nor are they produced from external forms, which are lower than they, lest perchance the lowest object of sense were to produce the lofty object of the mind, which is higher than sense. Our patterns, therefore, being subject to movement through their own nature, depend not on perceptible forms, which are always moved by an agency outside themselves, but on Ideas, which are not moved in the least but always exist within the same impulse of intelligence.

And just as the multitude of perceptible forms is often reduced to a single seed-cause flourishing within nature, so the host of intellectual forms within us is reduced to the unity and immovability of the intelligible Ideas. For this reason, if there be no Ideas, neither will there be forms of this kind within us. Indeed, they are the first objects of our mind, the closest to our mind, and akin to our mind.

This is why, as Parmenides says, we shall find no true substance to which we may properly turn the eye of the mind, for it is not right to move towards higher things, except through the world within, or to hold the contents of the inner world as worthy of respect when they are taken from the worthless outer world. Nor should it be imagined, when we are trying to judge the true nature or even divinity of things, that the true eye of the mind turns towards new concepts which we have arbitrarily constructed, for concepts of this kind are imaginings, worse then external things, greatly at variance with the divine types, and totally alien to the substance and nature of the creation and to truth itself. Through them, in short, we would observe nothing except some details and sense-objects.

Here, as is often the case, we should join our Proclus in reasoning as follows: The fundamental principles of proof would be destroyed if there were no ideal types within our intellect or within the divine intellect. For proofs proceed through those things which are the principles of what is demonstrable, things which, not only in our view but also in accord with nature, are simply prior and more potent. The principles of proof, however, are not particular but are always universal. Being universal, they are prior to particulars and more potent in the hierarchy of principles.

In fact, definition, which is a principle of proof, will not exist, or will certainly be null and void, if there be no such types. For definition belongs, not to chance happening or to something quite specific, but to something natural and to a type that is equally common to many things, when that which is common is therefore defined by us as being governed by an immutable cause, but not within individual changeable things that belong to the realm of sense, especially since universal nature, if it be considered within individuals – for example, humanity in this person and in that person – embraces neither, but is the origin-ator in both cases. Man himself, however, as universally defined, should embrace each and every thing totally. But such extensiveness belongs not to the straits of material things but to absolute types. These types are within the divine intellect, and by divine providence they are indubitably within our own intellect.

The absolute, essential, and necessary principle of justice is also within each one of us. By means of this principle we can show what is just and what is unjust, and we can define justice. However, since principles of this kind are within our minds, which are many, and universally work together in accordance with unity, it must therefore be the case that these principles depend on a single lofty Idea of justice beneath which the things of our world, through such principles, accord with it. In a similar way we define all types, – man, lion, and horse – not a type which is deduced from a new concept and which is change-able and in no way relates to essence and nature, but rather the ideal truth which is expressed within ourselves and manifested outside ourselves through its effect.

In fact, division, too, which is the principle of definition, would likewise be destroyed if the ideal types were removed. For when we distinguish a general cause by means of some type-differences, we do not divide our newly deduced concepts, which do not pertain to the natural causes of creation, and we do not divide anything perceptible which is indiscriminately individual and changeable, but it is by dividing that we direct our attention to the ideal types that are expressed within us. For this reason, if all the ideal types are rejected at a stroke, the result is that division, too, is rejected, as are definition and proof and, in fact, true explanation, which proceeds from the complex to the simple. But these four contain all dialectic, and so all dialectic will simultaneously come to an end. Philosophy, which is the precise use of the tools of dialectic, will also perish, especially since perfect philosophy, not being contained within perfect causes, strives everywhere towards causes that are perfect, causes that are utterly simple, unshakeable, and absolute. None of these exist, in fact, without an essence that is intellectual, intelligible, and ideal. Most importantly, the ideal types that are implanted within us relate to dialectic, while the divine types relate to philosophy.

In short, if we follow Plato's teaching as given in his letter to the Syracusans, we shall conclude that through division, definition, and proof, we come to recognise correctly the ideal patterns that are expressed within all intellects subsequent to the first intellect. These patterns are called intellectual, and it is through somehow considering them that we rightly descend to the natures of material things. But we shall also conclude that the intelligible Ideas, which are the first types within the first mind, being furthest from complexity and movement, cannot be recognised immediately through those steps of dialectic which involve complexity and movement, but after discourses of this kind, which lead the purest aspect of our mind closer to the ideal patterns, we now see the first Ideas by means of that simple intelligence to which we are brought by the power to explain, rather than by the power to define or divide, or by proof.

Chapter 35:
On the practice of dialectic through the intellectual forms and with the intelligible types as the aim

SINCE PARMENIDES, from this time onwards, intends to train Socrates himself in dialectic so thoroughly that he will not err concerning divine matters, but will know how to resolve doubts on divine matters, he will, of course, give Socrates henceforth the structure of dialectic on the divine substance itself, for in this way he will be better informed. But he will begin from the One as the cause of Ideas and of divine matters, showing throughout the debate that this One produces all beings step by step, as well as the common qualities of beings. Yet neither in the *Philebus* nor in the *Republic* is Plato willing to introduce the host of young men to dialectic, for this might make them rather arrogant.

Through Parmenides, however, he very strongly encourages Socrates' mind, which is divine by nature, to embrace, even in his youth, the art of discriminative debate. Parmenides, therefore, tests Socrates initially because he voluntarily betakes himself to ideal types but spurns material forms, for since the essence of matter is deformity and is therefore opposed to the beauty of form, it is not surprising that the material form is the most defective of forms. Indeed, none of the forms that are subject to change or have any similar admixture in some way with material things, either in nature or in the soul or in some intellect, are perfect forms, but since the hierarchy of creation strives, step by step, towards perfection, and since the order of the universe takes its origin from the most perfect principle, we must finally reach the most perfect forms, that is, the ideal and intelligible types, which are totally devoid of all the limitations of material forms.

In these types there is pure beauty, just as there is downright naked ugliness in matter, but both matter and that beauty are very difficult for us to consider. For anyone who would consider matter is obliged to lay aside every form, and this runs counter, of course, to the usual operation of consciousness; and anyone who would contemplate Ideas is compelled to discard all the mists and wisps of material forms, an action quite contrary to the normal mode of human consciousness. In this way, Ideas are finally attained by the simple gaze of steady intelligence, a gaze utterly dissociated from all considerations of material things.

But it is the power of dialectic which trains the mind to reach Ideas and prepares it by means of living intellectual concepts, as it passes from type to type with a skilful meandering movement, if I may express it thus. That is why Plato calls this the roving faculty, for it seems to rove over contrary propositions, each in turn, with long labyrinthine movements. Socrates thinks that a similar kind of meandering should be applied to the intellectual types rather than to the perceptible types. There is no doubt that Parmenides, too, fully approves of this.

Chapter 36:
The rules of dialectic which pre-suppose being or non-being, and the number of ways in which non-being is described

PARMENIDES maintains that the most powerful form of reasoning is that which proceeds from hypothesis, and he examines carefully, with many steps, what follows if something is affirmed and what follows if it is denied, for this form of reasoning does not depend on any human contrivances, but relies on a rational succession of natural and divine things and has the hierarchy of the universe as its teacher of the truth.

Indeed, he directs that the hypothesis should be not only whether something is, but also whether it is not, and what follows in both cases should be noted. It is certainly to be observed, when we are seeking the specific causes and principles for any one thing or event – for the nature of principle is reason – that when something is supposed to be there is an effect, and when that supposition is removed the effect is removed.

For when this cause is supposed, that effect is also present simultaneously with it, but if the effect is not removed when the cause is removed, it takes its rise from yet another source. He therefore enjoins us to consider four things that follow from the two suppositions, the first supposition being that something, such as mind or soul, exists, and the second supposition being that mind or soul does not exist; for in both cases he wishes to examine carefully

i) what happens to that which is supposed in relation to itself

ii) what happens to it in relation to other things

iii) what happens to other things in relation to themselves

iv) what happens to other things in relation to the thing itself.

But when he supposes the mind or soul not to exist, how can he consider what happens to something that does not exist? The answer has to be given that it is not supposed at present that the mind and soul are absolutely nothing, for if that were the case there would be no question of what then happens to it; but the supposition is rather that this thing which is called mind and soul is not really the mind and the soul but is, or is imagined to be, something different.

Indeed, the followers of Plato generally understand non-being in two ways, or in a single way: firstly, as absolutely nothing, and secondly, as non-being. But *that* is indeed not *this*: no man becomes a horse; or because it does not exist for this reason it may exist for another reason: as a being created by some power, but not brought into existence by some deed. They call matter non-being, because it becomes nothing through a cyclical movement; and they call anything perceptible non-being, too, because on account of its fluidity and divisibility and capacity for intermingling it does not truly come into being.

They also call the inconstant conception of the soul non-being because it is not perfect being. They say that change in the intellect, even in the first intellect, is in some way non-being, since it is the reason why *this* is not *that*, and *that* is not *that yonder*; and they say that the One and the Good are non-being, since they are higher than being.

Thus they say that in many ways they suppose something to be inferior to non-being, while they do not so thoroughly eradicate that to which they deny being that, as they seek to know what follows when they imagine that One does not exist, or that multiplicity does not exist, or that intellect does not exist, they do not totally eradicate what they are laying down as a hypothesis. But, as I have said, they partially understand something, provided, however, that there is no possibility of concluding that One is either multiplicity or intellect.

Besides, what shall we say to Parmenides' hypothesis that One does not in any way exist? We shall reply, using all the assistance presently available to us, that it can be imagined that what is said to be One is in no way One, just as a crowd can be imagined that is quite devoid of unity. For the present I shall say what is necessary on this subject.

In relation to that which is called non-being we should add the advice given by Parmenides in the *Sophist*, where Melissus says that the great Parmenides has warned us to be careful never to apply anything of being to absolute non-being, that is, never to be rash enough to allow full opposition between being and non-being; indeed, at this point he does not want non-being to mean the One Itself that is higher than being, or to mean matter lacking the wholeness of being and having the lowest level of being, but, if I may express it like this, a deprivation in all respects. Anyone who pictures this has no further need of being shown what appertains to being.

But since number is not at the lowest level within being, it is not right, he says, to apply to complete deprivation either multiplicity or numerical unity. Nor is it right, either individually or with others, to declare, think or say that it is something, since something is said to be some being. Nor is it right to say that there is some one, for some one is this one being or that one being. But the first One, about which no mention is yet made there, is not one being, but simply One. For if it were one being, it would not be simply One, but some one which, through its association with being, undergoes modification.

However, we have written in greater detail on this subject in the *Sophist*.

Chapter 37:
The subsequent discussion is said to be difficult, because it is not only logical but also theological

FROM THE words of Socrates, Parmenides, and Zeno we gather that the subsequent discussion will be a huge and difficult task, a deep ocean to cross, not so much on account of the dialectical or logical form of the dialogue as the largely theological matter contained within it, without which it would have been improper to speak about it beforehand and so many times and in such splendid terms; nor, again, would it be proper for a veteran follower of Pythagoras to occupy himself with nothing but logic.

Does not Plato uphold everyone's true dignity? And to everyone who has dealings with him he makes due attribution. To Socrates he attributes instruction on morals and purification; to the priest, the mysteries of sacred love; to Timaeus, knowledge of science and mathematics; to Melissus, who was a follower of Parmenides, the teaching on being. Does he, therefore, attribute to Parmenides – his elder, his teacher, the pre-eminent proponent of intelligible being and of Ideas – a puerile kind of training? Of course not.

But let us hear Plato himself testifying to the divine excellence of Parmenides and of this book. In the *Sophist* Socrates addresses Melissus thus: 'Do you wish to speak to us in your own words or to ask questions in the manner favoured by Parmenides, whom I, as a young man – though he was well advanced in years – once heard holding forth in discussion and proffering the most exquisite of reasons.' Again, in the *Theaetetus*, when Socrates was asked to refute those who posited a single motionless being, he did not undertake to do so himself but gave this answer: 'Although I honour Melissus and others, who say that there is one self-consistent totality, for it may seem immodest of me to cross them, yet I honour them less than I do Parmenides alone, for Parmenides, to use Homer's words, strikes me as one who is sagacious and worthy of great honour. I once conversed with him when he was advanced in years and I was but a youth, and he struck me as having a wisdom that was profound and noble in all respects. This is why I fear that we do not have the slightest understanding of his sayings and expressions, and what he himself implied by his words is, I fear, even more of a closed book to us.' Finally, who does not understand that while he promises a discussion that is dialectical he is, at the same time, providing one that is theological, since both are the same in the writings of Plato, and the kinds and specifics of universal being are brought into the central argument one by one?

However, the statement that it would be ridiculous for a discussion of this kind to be presented to a crowd, especially by an old man, has two meanings. The first meaning concerns logical pretext, which the crowd thinks is trickery with words and sophistry, not realising that this system is the key to truth and wisdom. The second meaning concerns the theological matter which is being discussed and which is full of paradoxes, striking the crowd as ridiculous and the wise as meriting great respect, as Plato tells us in the *Phaedrus* and in his letters to Dionysius and the Syracusans. Nor is it fitting for a follower of Pythagoras or Plato, especially one who has followed this teaching for a long time, to divulge the divine mysteries to the profane.

What more should we say? Whatever has been discussed so far is long compared to what follows and compared to a theological preface, and with good reason; and what follows will indeed be divine: not some plain logic without any philosophical meaning, which some considered propounding prior to Proclus. Proclus speaks against them in his *Theology*, declaring that it will be unnecessary for him to pursue the fight, as they have long since been refuted by all the members of the Platonic family. But he himself, following Syrianus, thinks that there is a mystery lying hidden within each word and that the number of clauses equals the exact number of the deities.

I, however, following the middle way, think that, as is commonly said, there is as much hidden within theology as dialectical ingenuity gives access to; and for that reason there are within it opinions on divine matters, not totally continuous at all times but divulged from time to time. Indeed, if it had been Plato's intention to give instruction solely in logical argumentations, he would have accepted this comfortable teaching about the One and being, and about the different types of being – an easy teaching, yet one that would be a stumbling-block to his followers and not ready to be expounded to everyone.

On the other hand, if he had decided to connect all the divine mysteries together both here and in all other places, he would not have introduced a logical difficulty, a difficulty that is of no great worth in itself and is unbecoming to the deities. Nor at this time would he have chosen a young man for instruction, even though he was a young man who, being divine by nature, was asking questions about divine matters together with questions of logic, which were rightly handed down by Parmenides, who conveniently wove what would be a kind of divine discussion from his books dealing with divine matters, calling this discussion a serious laborious game because, behind a dialectical or logical exterior, he wished to conceal a divine theme taken from his books.

In brief, this book was unanimously described as theological by all the other followers of Plato, especially the most eminent ones, and Dionysius the Areopagite also seems to confirm this view, for whenever he refers to the One Itself he puts it above being, and he distinguishes the one being from the simple One Itself, saying that the One Itself is the beginning of Itself and the begetter of the one being. Indeed, he makes use of the reasonings, refutations, and words of Parmenides, frequently bearing supreme witness, in a divine work of the highest order, that the theme of Parmenides is divine. In the same way, by following the actual reasonings of the Platonists, he always puts the Good, which is the One, above essence. But more on this subject elsewhere.

Let us finally confirm, with some further evidence from Plato himself, that this book is not disputatious, but it is certainly philosophical: in the *Theaetetus* Plato puts Parmenides far above Melissus and Zeno; in the *Sophist* he says that Melissus had been a follower of Parmenides and was unversed in refutations and controversies. And to honour God, or at least to honour what is divine, no one should therefore suppose that Parmenides himself, who was older and much more divine, had been introduced by Plato as a logician who devoted himself to contentious refutations and to frivolous childish games.

Chapter 38:
On the hypotheses of Parmenides; and on the One and the Good, which, according to the words of Plato, is higher than being and higher than intellect

WHY PROCLUS and some others have drawn up nine hypotheses within this dialogue we have explained at the beginning of the commentary, where it should also be added that in their opinion the affirmations and refutations made by Parmenides concerning the One must, for both to be true, interpret the One Itself as having one meaning when it is being denied and a different meaning when it is being affirmed: for example, if the One, while being refuted, is explained as being neither the same nor different, this should be understood as referring to the One that is higher than being; but when the One is affirmed to be equally the same and different, it should be understood to refer to the One which has a connection with being.

Some others, however, tried to show that a distinction of this kind does not hold good in all circumstances, as when there is a consideration of what follows if the One is, and, again, what happens, and why, if the One is not, for they said that in this twofold enquiry it was necessary to take the One Itself with the same meaning in both situations, for otherwise the authority of the One could never be understood in the unfolding sequence of events, unless we know for certain that when the One is posited certain effects are also posited, and that when the same One is removed the effects are also removed. This enquiry should, however, meet with a response elsewhere.

But for the time being let us briefly review how the One Itself is higher than being and is the beginning of all being. It is shown in the *Philebus* that from the One, which is the beginning of creation, two are immediately produced: the principles of beings, or the two elements known as limit and limitlessness. Philolaus the Pythagorean also acknowledged this. From these two all beings are directly compounded, but before the compounding of other beings the first to be compounded and mixed from these two is the first being, which contains universal being within itself, so that just as any being whatever is made up from its own limit and from limitlessness, so the first being is a specific mixture of the first limit and limitlessness. From this there is the clear conclusion that the One Itself is above being, above the elements and principles of being.

For he speaks openly of both the limitlessness of beings and the limit of beings, and he shows that all beings are composed of these two. The first to be so composed he calls essence, whereas the author of the union of these mutual opposites he will aptly call the One. Moreover, in the same book he reflects on what is the highest good for our soul, and he shows first of all that there are three qualities of the highest Good which make it totally perfect, satisfying, and desirable. From this he deduces that intelligence alone, however penetrating it may be in itself, is not the Good itself for us, because by its very nature it does not fully comprehend those qualities of the Good, for intelligence is not sufficient for us to live in bliss, except through the presence of the Good itself.

However, since our intellect is the image of the first intellect, it seems to follow that, just as its own intelligence is not the Good itself for our intellect, so for the first intellect intelligence alone is not simply its highest Good; for if it were otherwise and the first Good were then defined through intelligence alone, the result would be that in all situations simple intelligence would suffice for all perceivers and would be the highest Good for everyone. For this reason, therefore, the conclusion is that the Good itself is higher than the first intellect, since for every perceiver happiness is defined, not through pure intelligence, but through the whole presence of the Good itself.

Listen also to the Platonic comparison in the sixth book of the *Republic*, where the same things are very clearly confirmed: Just as the sun produces, within the eyes and colours, generation, power and action reciprocal to the light, yet the sun itself is not the eye or colour or generation, but is far higher, so the Good itself bestows upon intellects and upon intelligibles their essence and power and action reciprocal to the very splendour of truth, yet the Good itself is not the intellect or the intelligible or the truth or essence, but is higher than all these in excellence and power. Again, he says in the same book that being itself appears at the same level as truth. Therefore, since he very plainly puts the Good itself before truth and intelligence, he likewise puts it before being.

Again, in the *Sophist* it is clear that in the first being there are all those things which are necessarily required for the perfection of being; they therefore possess life and intellect and the formative causes of all beings; possessing life, they possess movement and otherness, but possessing intellect, they possess stillness and sameness. There, these four, added to essence, are formally distinguished one from another, and essence is also distinguished from them, though mixed with all of them.

Being itself, therefore, is a totality, both multiple and single, and this totality is exactly the same as being itself. Again, this totality is related to the cause of essence, so that it is both all and one; and those things that harmonise with the whole harmonise likewise with being, that is, they are both multiple and single at the same time.

From this it is clear that being itself, insofar as it is subsequent, differs from the One Itself, especially since the whole of the first being, he says, is thoroughly mixed with non-being. Nowhere, however, did he mix the One Itself with the non-One. Indeed, he infers in the *Sophist* and demonstrates in *Parmenides* that the One Itself is absolutely distinct from the non-One and from all the kinds of being, since it is higher than being; and finally he shows in the *Sophist*, in exactly the same way, that the first universal being itself is subject to the One, both in its parts and as a whole. It is therefore not the One Itself, because the One Itself is not subject to the One, has no parts, and is not whole.

Again, a multiplicity of beings, composed either of opposites or of non-opposites, necessarily arises from a single being. But the single being itself arises from the simple One Itself, for when we call being hot or cold, stillness or movement, we are not asserting that any one of these is being itself, because if stillness were being itself, then movement would certainly not be being; and if movement were being itself, then stillness would directly lose its name of being. But this being is evident and it is imparted from the one primal being to stillness, to movement, and to the whole host of beings.

Therefore, being itself, which is the cause of the essence in all things and is shared by all, partakes of the One, not in the sense of *As being is to the first, so One is to the first*, but being itself exists and is not allotted according to its participation, but by its participation it is one. For this reason it is subject to the One and is the first being. These words are in the *Sophist*. Therefore, when the One Itself, the beginning of all, is thus shown to be higher than being, it has necessarily been shown to be above life and intellect and the intelligible, for these things are subsequent to being.

To put it briefly, as we have said elsewhere, the difference between the One and essence is clearly stated in *Parmenides*, where the One Itself, in its pre-eminence, is distinct from all the kinds of being and even from essence itself, as is seen especially in the aim of the first hypothesis; and so, as I was saying just now, the first One Itself soars considerably higher above the intellect. But in the intellect those individual kinds of being exist from which the One is independent.

Finally, we must not undervalue this sort of corollary: just as Plato consistently puts Parmenides and his discussions on the One above Melissus and his discussions, in the *Sophist*, on being, so he follows the truth by putting the One Itself before being, taking care, in both cases, to preserve what he always preserves in the natures and persons of the gods.

Persuaded by these words of Plato, his companions put the One and the Good before essence and intelligence; and, as Proclus tells us, so did some very fine followers of Plato, such as Plutarch, Ammonius, Plotinus, Amelius, Porphyry, Iamblichus, and Theodorus, together with their disciples. I think, however, that Plato appreciated that this was the point on which the earlier school agreed, beyond all dispute, with the later school; and the later school took its rise from Syrianus and Proclus, truly great men whose views were in full agreement on this same matter; subsequent exponents within this school who should be particularly mentioned are Hermias, Damascius, and Olympiodorus.

Chapter 39:
Next, how Plato proceeds to the First. Its name.
The Idea of the Good

THEN IN the *Republic*, and the *Philebus*, and, in fact, throughout his writings, Plato reduces perceptible multiplicities to intelligible unities, that is, to Ideas: for his intention is to relate each single multiplicity to a single Idea, and then to relate the intelligible unities to the simple One Itself, which excels the intelligible world by at least as much as the intelligible world excels the perceptible world.

That One he calls the pure Good itself, but among Ideas he does not place the pure Good itself but only the ideal Good, from which he distinguishes ideal Beauty, so that the ideal Good is not the cause of beautiful things but is the cause of good things. Nor does he attribute to things their first essence or supreme unity but some subsequent perfections which are known by the name of *Goodnesses*. But, as he says in his Letters, the Good itself is the maker of all good things and of all beautiful things; and, as he teaches in the *Republic*, it universally distributes the essences, the virtues, and all the perfections.

Yet it is not within essence, and it is not essence or the intelligible or any Idea, but it excels both essence and the intelligible in age, intrinsic worth and power, just as the sun excels generation and eyes and colours. But since it is totally unknown to the intellect and cannot therefore be designated by its own name, it is called the Idea of the Good because the ideal Good is very similar to it, and for a like reason it is known as the Brightest of Being.

However, it is very plainly declared to be above being and above the light of being, that is, above truth and intellect. These declarations are made in the *Republic*, where, while he shows that the Good itself, which unites all intellects with their intelligibles, is not the intellect, is not the intelligible, not the truth, not knowledge, not any cognition, not essence, he seems to be reproducing precisely the negation of all beings around the One, as proclaimed in *Parmenides*.

In short, the light of the Good within all intelligibles, within all intellects and within universal being is truly nothing but the quintessential unity and goodness divinely infused into the divine world.

Chapter 40:
Next, Plato's two paths to the First;
and two names of the First

PLATO RISES to the Supreme by two paths: by the path of analogies in the *Republic* and by the path of negations in *Parmenides*. Both the analogies and the negations affirm that God is set apart from all beings and from all intelligibles, and that He is also the beginning of creation.

Some negations, however, are better than affirmations; some are companions to affirmations; and some are worse than affirmations. The negations that are better are made when we show that the First is not being, since it is superior to being and the beginning of being. The negations that are companions to affirmations are when we show that non-being is mixed with being, as when it is said in the *Sophist* that non-being seems to be at least equal to being; for what is immobility is not movement; what is sameness is not change; what is heat is not cold; what is rational is not brutish; and what is gold is not iron. The third type of negations occurs when we give the name of non-being to ebbs and flows and to unformed matter, as if they were far below the wholeness of being.

But analogies really indicate a similarity and relationship, not of the First to the subsequent, but of the subsequent to the First, which clearly excels everything else much more than the other causes excel their respective effects. It does not excel some levels more and other levels less, for if that were the case it would have a stronger relationship with some and a weaker relationship with others. But if it were characterised by any relationship, it would not be simply the One and it would not be fully Absolute. It therefore excels all things equally.

All things are related to it, however, in individual ways, for some are nearer to it and some are further away. That, in turn, through what is single and indivisible, brings forth all things as if on a pivot. And these are related to, and turn towards, that in different ways, in accordance with the manifold nature of creation.

Just as our Plato rises up to the First by a two-fold path, so does he designate that First with two names in particular. In the *Republic*, where he ascends by means of analogies, he calls it the Good, for by the goodness that fills them analogies guide us to the First by starting with the likeness of things. In *Parmenides*, however, where he proceeds by means of negations, he calls it the One, for it is by negations that he defines God as the sole beginning of everything, totally simple and totally supreme.

Now the negations show the movement of all things from here, since multiplicity proceeds from the One that is ultimately devoid of all multiplicity; but analogies seem to show how all things turn towards the First. Indeed, since all turn towards the First through desire for the Good, things other than the First are sought by some and neglected by others, while the Good is necessarily chosen by all.

We do not, however, give it these two names, or any additional name, but when we turn to what follows from it and consider the development of all multiplicity from it, we call it the One. On the other hand, when we consider the turning we call it the Good. Yet even in the outward movement we appreciate the Good on account of its abundance, just as in the return movement we appreciate the One, since this is how all things are restored to unity. For this reason, when Plato, in the *Republic*, turns everything back to itself as to the Good, he declares it to be the unifier of the intelligible and of the intellect itself.

Chapter 41:
Some Platonic discussions follow which show that the One is the beginning of all things, and that the One Itself, the Good, is above being. The first discussion

UNIVERSAL BEING is either total unity or total multiplicity or both unity and multiplicity.

It is not total unity, for if it were we would be obliged to admit that opposites are fully identical and to declare that there are no dimensions containing many parts as well as a beginning, a middle, and an end. We would be obliged to assert that there are no numbers in creation, no differences of shapes and figures, no opposing qualities, no movements, no results, no actions, no feelings, no changes of motion, of time or situation, nothing to distinguish one cause from another, and no actual or potential effects.

Again, it cannot be said that universal being is total multiplicity, absolutely devoid of all unity, because if there were no unity within any particular thing or within all things, there would certainly be no multiplicity, for multiplicity necessarily consists of individuals, of which each and every one is individual and unified within itself. It therefore follows that if there is no unity, then there is no multiplicity either. Again, within a multiplicity in which there is no unity, what you think of will be either nothing or a totally limitless multiplicity, and the same reasoning can be applied endlessly to all the details of the parts. There will then be, first of all, that multiplicity which is assumed to be infinite, a mass of infinite clusters in an infinite number of directions, followed by more infinities. And either the whole of the first multiplicity will be greater than the other clusters, as if these were parts, in which case infinity will be greater than infinities; or it will not be greater, which brings us to the absurd admission that the whole is not greater than its parts. Indeed, neither the whole nor the parts will be anything without the unity and union that are necessary for the formation of the whole and the parts.

Finally, if multiplicity is incalculably infinite, what happens when the One is removed is the emergence of a multiplicity that is incalculably greater; and if the converse is assumed, a multiplicity that is incalculably smaller. On the one hand, therefore, an infinite host arises, while on the other hand it will remain finite, which is an absurd situation, universally devoid of all order.

Again, the removal of unity will mean that things will be both similar and dissimilar, as we have said elsewhere. They will be similar because they suffer the same deprivation. They will be dissimilar, too, because such deprivation means that as long as they lack the One there is no quality or condition in which they concur. Again, the removal of the One means that, for a similar reason, things will be both the same and other, for they suffer the same deprivation and, not having the One, are obliged to be different.

Thus, through the removal of the One, multiplicity can neither rest nor move. It cannot rest, for to rest is to stay in one and the same place; and it cannot move, for if what is imagined to be totally non-One ever changes it will surely change to its opposite, to the One, which is imagined to be nowhere. Therefore, since nothing can, through anything identical, suffer its opposites, surely those things which are contingent on the removal of the One in the way we have described are considered impossible.

For these reasons the universal, and any kind of being, is simultaneously one and many.

The next question is whether the unity and multiplicity within being are completely separate or whether they are, in fact, mixed together. If they were separate one from another, the same absurdities would follow which were adduced a little earlier about a multiplicity that was deprived of the One. They are therefore perfectly mingled together.

For this reason it is necessary for the principal cause to be above these two, partly to inspire this unity to be a unity, this multiplicity to be multiplicity, and partly to enable these two to be reconciled. For this multiplicity is not glued to some unity which enables it to be multiplicity, set against this unity as the efficient cause of unity. Again, this unity, though permeated by multiplicity and partaking of it, is not the prime cause of multiplicity, and it is not from themselves that this unity and multiplicity, which are mutually opposed, become reconciled, but from elsewhere, especially since neither is produced from the other. But it should not be thought that these two have combined by chance, for if that were the case they would be parted one day.

The next question is whether the originator is absolute unity or some kind of multiplicity. The originator cannot be multiplicity, since from him different things universally come together in unity. And if multiplicity were devoid of unity – an unlawful suggestion – or if multiplicity partook of unity or unity of multiplicity, this is not simply the One and the first principle, but something both limited and conjoined.

That the simple One, however, is the cause of every being and of the whole is clear from the fact that nothing is better for things than the unity of every single thing, and if this is absent then the mutual union of things is also lost: that union whereby every single thing comes into being, exists, and is maintained. Within things, however, that which is best must proceed from the first principle, while unity and the union of different things do not arise except from the One. On this reckoning, that which is One gives being to all, since being is lost through division. For that which loses the One loses being too; but that which loses multiplicity, or does not receive it, is not necessarily deprived immediately of its essence, for what is opposed to the One itself is the non-One, which in Greek is called οὐδέν. What is opposed to multiplicity or to the many is non-multiplicity or the non-many. Therefore, if the One and the many are not the same, then the non-many and the non-One, that is, μηδέν, will not be the same. Again, essence and the One are not the same, since it is through the very principle of essence that things are as they are, but it is through the principle of the One that each thing not only is, but is a particular one, partly distinct in itself from all others and partly entering into union with others.

Again, saying 'essence' is not making a statement, nor is saying 'one'. But saying that essence is the One is making a statement.

But now if essence and the One are the same, in the same way multiplicity and non-being will be the same, which is impossible. For multiplicity is within essence, and the One is not within essence. But since being and the One differ from each other in the hierarchy of the universe, are they ranked as equals, as two principles? Certainly not. For there cannot be a twofold origin of creation, since the One must be higher. But if essence be higher than the One, the One, like a participant, will be subordinate to essence.

Moreover, if being be prior to the One, in that very first moment in which there is being the One does not exist, since it is said to be naturally later. But that which does not yet exist cannot participate. Therefore, whatever the One is, essence will likewise be, but the converse does not hold, that whatever essence is, the One will immediately be. Thus any being will in no respect be the One, and so will be either nothing or an endlessly infinite multiplicity, which is impossible. Thus the One is above being.

Yet the One Itself is said to be beyond essence not on account of some deficiency but on account of some excess, since it is better than essence. But does it exist within essence as its apex? Certainly not. For then it would be a participator, belonging to something and within something, and it would not be the first principle of all. For it must be a non-participant, independent, and completely within itself and not within anything, with no obligation to depend on anything, and it must have no dual nature within it but be the totally absolute One.

Chapter 42:
The second discussion on the same subject

AGAIN, THAT in which all things somehow share is the beginning of all things; and on account of this participation all things turn towards it, having a relationship with it which is derived from it and which refers all things to it; so that that by which all things are made is also that by which they are perfected and maintained.

But what is this function which belongs to the first Self and is the common characteristic of the first Maker of all? It is not life or movement, for these are not within all things. Again, it is not stillness, because movement, being by its very nature the opposite of stillness, has no stillness within itself, and thus stillness is not common to everything. But nor is intellect, as such, common to everything. For it is not the case that all things understand or are conscious, since consciousness is the quality of intellect within things. Intelligence is the primal consciousness, the beginning of all awareness, and matter has no intelligence of any kind. All things seem to have essence within them, but even this is not completely true, since what is created for its own sake is not yet this very self which is said to be created, and as soon as it does become this very self it ceases to become anything further. Therefore, since something in process of being and that which is being itself are opposed to each other, it naturally follows that that which is becoming cannot, by its very nature, be thought to have essence. For this reason, whenever Plato discusses essence in the *Timaeus*, the *Sophist*, the *Republic* and elsewhere, he distinguishes it as something very different from generation, and he judges that things in flux become but are not. Hence it is that essence is not common to all things, for the characteristic quality of the first, that which is the most common factor of the most common principle of all things, is, for whatever reason, within all things.

Reflect, therefore, that all things, to some extent, have mutual opposites: same and other; stillness and movement; becoming and, as I might say, having become; and others of this kind.

The One indwells all things both individually and collectively; and within the very multitude which seems opposed to the One, the One Itself makes the multitude, for what is a multitude but one repeated over and over again? And how may a whole be composed of many if there be no union? And how may a part belong to a whole or to a number unless it itself is something, by which I mean some one? The One, therefore, indwells all things, and if it were taken away each and every thing would be lost.

For this reason, when the ancients wished to speak directly of that which is in all respects nothing, they said οὐδέν, that is, not even one, as if more is negated by saying 'not one' than by saying 'not being', as if the function of the One forsook all things later than essence does, and as if vanishing into total nothingness were the same as losing the One outright. This One, therefore, which is absolutely common to all, derives its existence from the simple One which is the most common of all.

Chapter 43:
The third discussion on the same subject.
Also on the simplicity of the first and the last

IN THE hierarchy of the universe there is the first and there is the last, and each of these is of necessity one and simple, devoid of multiplicity. If this were not the case, neither of them would be simply the first or the last, for within the simple first there must not be something later, and within the simple last there must not be something earlier.

If you could divide the first or the last into many, in both cases you would find something higher and something lower, for these cannot be divided. If they could be continually divided, their measure would not be the first or the last in the universe. Therefore, just as with a long line a point is reached in both directions which has no length at all but is totally indivisible in so far as regards size, so in the universe we move to the first and the last, each absolutely one and indivisible in existence and nature.

Concerning the first, there must be no doubt that if the last could be divided into many, then it would not be this absolute last, but rather that into which things will ultimately be resolved. Since the action of the first, however, extends further than the actions of those that are subsequent, it surely follows that within the last there will be no functioning of anything else, only the pure and absolutely simple nature of the first itself; so that nothing can be considered simpler than the last other than the simplicity and unity of the first, especially since it is unable to devise anything new within itself. But that which is closest to the first, although simple in nature, multiplies itself through its own power of fertility.

Moreover, every division, every differentiation, every multiplication takes place either through variation of forms or through division of forms, as far as regards measure and number. All these have form, but in matter nothing of itself has form; and so within matter there is no power to multiply. Therefore matter is in the greatest degree one, and since it has within itself nothing of the many it has the power to assume the many, just as the first, being none of the many, has the power to create the many. Certainly matter is in the highest degree one in its ability to receive form, just as the first being is in the highest degree one in its power to impart form. But neither of these is the simple One Itself.

Who therefore, considering that the One is predicated equally of the greatest being and of the least, would say that the One and being are absolutely identical? And the extent to which formative multiplicity is negated in respect of matter is the extent to which being is negated and the One affirmed. And because matter can assume an infinity of forms but, being undefined itself, has the same relationship with all, this may be why Plato, in the *Philebus*, accords it a place in the category of the unlimited; yet he will not for that reason consider it to fall short of one, but rather to be one in the fullest degree, since it naturally possesses nothing of the unlimited.

For in that dialogue he frequently gives the name of One to the unlimited itself, because, of its own nature, it has no multiplicity, but rather contains the host of all those which, at every step, play their part beneath it. In the *Philebus*, too, when he uses the term 'unlimited' he does not intend us to understand merely matter that is subject to bodies; especially since he says that all beings are composed from the unlimited. And yet not all things are composed from this matter. Therefore the universal possibility of receiving form, and the unrestricted potential of undergoing any kind of differentiation, are said to be the unlimited.

For this reason, when matter is taken back to the level of the unlimited, Plato does not call it multiplicity, either in the *Philebus* or elsewhere, but in the *Timaeus* he calls it the one receptacle able to receive all differentiation. And he shows that matter is further from being than form is, since material form is related to a real being as an image is. But matter is not related, except perhaps as a shadow or as an opposite, since matter is as formless as true essence is impressed with form.

However, as he shows in this way that matter is almost devoid of being, he is also stating that it has no small share of the One, for he says that of matter it can be truly declared to be 'this and that'. And, on account of the different elements of which it is composed, it never changes its nature.

Then, just as the followers of Plato arise, through negations, to the One that is simply itself, so, through negations, they also descend to utterly simple matter, which has, as we have said, the least possible being, if any being at all, but is unified in the highest degree.

Of course, just as by negating mass, shape, surface and length we reach a point which to the highest degree is one with respect to dimension and has the least possible measurement because it is not measurement but some sort of measurement, that is, a limit, so by negating beings through the negation of forms we descend into matter, which is simply one. But the least possible being is not really being in fact, but something of being, the possibility, if I may put it like this, of being moulded into being by being itself.

In exactly the same way we proceed from the body to its mirror image, which is certainly not the body but is something of the body; and from this we proceed to its shadow, which is the least bodily thing there is. By a similar progression we move from Ideas, which are true beings, to the bodily forms, which are images of these beings; and from these we proceed to matter, the shadow of the universal being.

Formlessness in matter, which admits any differentiation but prevents essence from having a set form, necessarily forms a single being. Now in order for matter to be one, something definite is assigned by form, through which the One approaches this appearance or that appearance, but in order to be one it also has something indefinite from the One, which is simply itself, since it depends solely on this One as being totally beyond all limit. But in the *Philebus* we discuss this subject, and others, in greater depth and detail.

Moreover, according to the author of the *Timaeus*, material form does not meet with essence in any degree, but only in name, since it is derived from it and is related to it as an image is. It therefore falls far from the ideal image, just as the mirror image of a man falls far from human nature; and yet it does not make a similar departure from the One. For although nothing from the nature of being or of man is in the image, it is not for that reason that this image is something less than the One, that is, in representing one individual man or one individual Idea as different from others.

When beauty is preserved, so is the Good, but it does not equally preserve essence. In the same way, mutually opposite movements, although they fall away from essence on account of their tendency to flow, do not each have less than the One through their own distinctiveness, which marks them out as distinct from others. Each also has its own good, by which it is directed to its end and which is conducive to the Good.

Again, neither matter nor form is as far from the Good as it is from being. For form has both beauty and goodness and, as the image of the Good, it invites us to the Good. But perhaps matter is to be judged good as often as it desires appearances and gladly brings them forth as parts of the Good; and perhaps matter is as good as it is necessary for the universal work of the Good itself. However, it is through the very lack of forms, the lack by which it seeks the Good and is also necessary to the Good, that, as I have said, it is very far from being; and through the same lack it is urged towards the Good and approaches the Good.

Through what we have said the Platonic teaching is confirmed, that the One and the Good are to be deemed higher than being. In brief, the One, which is shared with multiplicity, and is a particular One, that is, one multiplicity, has been mixed with an appropriate multiplicity. Above this One, therefore, rises the One which is beyond participation, absolute, pure. This is the beginning of all multiplicity, and through the One which has entered into multiplicity it orders the multiplicity and holds it together and calls it back to itself.

Finally, just as above forms which are everywhere mixed with their opposites or with forms that are alien to them there exist the Ideas, which are pure in themselves, and just as above any being which is in some way mixed with non-being there is a being which is pure in its first cause, in the same way above the One which is conjoined to multiplicity there exists the One which is absolutely devoid of multiplicity and in which nothing is not One. On this One depends every One, as well as the non-One. Indeed, since everything of that kind exists from the first it is the One, but since it exists beyond the first and below the first, it unfolds within itself both multiplicity and the origin of differentiation.

Chapter 44:
The fourth discussion on the same subject; and on the contemplation of the Good

BEING ABOUT to perceive the single best principle of the universe, we are obliged, first of all, to lay aside whatever is most at variance with it, that is, evil and multiplicity, and to use all our powers to be called back to our unparalleled and best quality, back to the simple and peaceful contemplation of sublime intelligence.

And so, according to the measure of the divine light shining within the first intellect and within Ideas, we look up to that in exactly the same way as we look up on a clear night to the stars in the firmament, employing all our powers to contemplate that intellect through our own intelligence and to contemplate Ideas through the ideal forms innate within our own intelligence.

If we progress by long perseverance in such contemplation, the new and incredibly wonderful light of the Good itself at last flashes upon us from on high, just as the radiance of the sun illumines astronomers who have been observing the stars until daybreak, the radiance which miraculously removes the stars at once from their eyes, just as the light of the Good itself, if it is to be perceived, obliges us to put in second place its intelligence as forms, as well as the intellect itself and Ideas and all intelligible things.

Just as we look up at the sun with half-closed eyes, so we look up at, or rather worship, the light of the Good with half-closed intelligence. For it is not permissible or right ever to direct the gaze of the intelligence upon that which is above the intelligible. Surmising this, therefore, or rather looking towards it by some flashing light, we quickly come back to the intellect and to intelligible things, just as, with half-closed eyes, we come back from the sun to the firmament and to the stars.

Moving next to rational discussions once more and to conversations and finally back to this world, what is the most important thing we can conceive or say about that world? Of course, because it is very similar to the state of the mind which has come thus far, a state of this kind is in the highest degree one and simple and excellent. And so, on account of this state we describe God as totally one and good; yet when we say one and good we are not eulogising two but one and the same.

For since the Good cares for everything and is therefore sought after, it is no wonder that it unifies the essence of whatever seeks it, just as evil, or some destructive force, disperses essence. Hence the goodness of everything is union, and union is its goodness.

For these reasons we consider the One Itself and the Good to be absolutely identical; and all the more so since the nature of the Good is, as it were, to diffuse itself through all things as they evolve, and on the other hand to recall all things to itself, the One, through the desire implanted within each. And this is how it makes the universe fully united.

But when we say One, we do not mean one being, but simply the

One. For since it is not essence that preserves unity, but rather unity that preserves essence, which means that essence is different from the One and lower than it, we must not say that the first single being is One, for that would be mixing it with multiplicity.

Again, when we speak of the Good, we are endeavouring to indicate not some good being but the simple Good itself. For since being does not perfect the Good, and the Good does not desire essence, the reverse being true, the nature of the Good is different from the nature of essence and of being and is higher than it. For this reason, if anyone joins being to the Good itself, linking the worse to the better, he will produce not only something good in place of the Good itself but also something less than excellent in place of that which is excellent.

Now the common agreement of all on the definition of the Good, by the grace of which all things exist and which all things seek, seems to show that the Good does not exist by the grace of any other and does not seek any other; that the Good, therefore, is not some being or some good within a being, for every essence seeks the Good, that is, seeks to exist according to its nature and to conduct itself well and perfectly.

It may perhaps seem that, for the sake of its own substance, the Good has also been sought within essence, but if it conducts itself perfectly according to its nature it is not simply the Good, or the Good of all, but merely the good of something and the good within something, and thus some particular good, which for this precise reason has been sought, with a view to approaching the Good itself by means of it. Therefore beyond the good which is being, or within being, or of being, there is the Good which is higher than being. For just as any being seeks its own individual good as something other than it, and seeks the Good itself within its individual good, so the universal being consequently chooses the Good itself as something other than itself and higher than itself.

Finally, if it can in any way be right to describe the Good itself, look around at all the perfections in the creation, which are to be sought for their own sakes. Their well-spring is therefore the Good itself, which resides as the centre in all things that are sought, in part producing perfections to be sought after within desirable things, and in part, with these perfections as baits, enticing all that seek to come to itself.

Chapter 45:
The fifth discussion on the same subject; and on the naming of the First

WHEN WE name the First, we usually do so with some very common epithets of perfection, such as essence, life, mind, truth, and virtue. But these may be taken as concrete or as abstract: if as concrete, for example a living being and so on, they do not match the simplicity of the First; if as abstract, they seem more appropriate on account of their simplicity – essence and life, rather than being or living. But again, if they are considered as abstract like forms and formative causes within concrete things, they will not be applicable to the First; if they are considered as external, then essence will not convey life precisely, nor life convey mind, but, through desire, mind will strive towards life, and life towards essence. For this reason neither essence nor life is appropriate for the First.

But perhaps intelligence is more fitting; yet not even this is right, because it is not given to all to understand. And intelligence itself strives towards the truth and, through truth, towards the Good. But the Good is nowhere changed.

In brief, of those that we have already enumerated the early ones are inappropriate for the First because they do not include the later ones but merely strive towards them. Then again, the later ones are also inapplicable to the First because they are not the earlier ones and they have no part in them, and also because they produce more limited effects, and it is not fitting to call the First by the name of being or living, since being is an activity taking place by means of its essence within a concrete being, while living is an activity taking place by means of life within a living being.

Now if anyone wishes to designate the First with these names, we should be happy to accept a name that is causal, if I may put it like that, rather than a name expressive of form, such as would not be strange to the followers of Plato and such as might have been often used by Dionysius.

But since the First has these qualities – that it alone comprises the perfections of all things, that it seeks nothing beyond itself, and that it imparts its own substance to all – while the Good and the One possess that single quality, this is rightly the special name of the First. But essence, of itself, does not include life (as we have said), life does not include intelligence, and intelligence does not include the truth in its simplicity. And yet essence, when made perfect through the Good, has life; life, perfected through the Good, likewise has mind; and mind, perfected through the Good, now possesses truth, joy, and fulfilment.

The First itself is not this truth or this or that power, so that it will not be defined as a particular good or as failing to comprise all things good; unless perhaps it be composed of all things, which is a wicked thing to suggest, for the First Good itself is simply and solely every good.

Chapter 46:
The sixth discussion on the same subject; and what is chosen is not simply being, but well-being and the Good

ESSENCE, LIFE, consciousness, desire, and action are distinguished from each other through methods of opposition. Essence is akin to stillness, and life to movement; again, life is akin to direct movement, and consciousness to reflected movement. Essence and life maintain the specific quality of their own forms, while consciousness is conformable to all.

Again, consciousness perceives things as they are within itself, while desire, on the contrary, perceives them as they are within themselves; and finally, desire remains within the desirer, but action moves outside.

The more these two differ from each other, the more they differ from essence, so that they are not even like gradations of essence but are like some additional forms – its perfections, and good things that are dependent on the higher Good. For either these do not exist of themselves, since they exist in another, or essence naturally perfects the imperfect, but is itself perfected by the Good, which is higher than essence.

Moreover, just as sense is related to the sensory good, in exactly the same way the intellect is related to the intelligible Good. Thus, just as the desire for the Good follows the sense of the Good, because the

Good differs from both sense and desire, in the same way the desire for the Good always follows the intelligence of the Good. Here, in fact, desire is always the mean between consciousness and the Good.

But it is evident that the desire for the Good is not the Good itself, and so it is also evident that consciousness, however precise, is not the Good itself. And it is even more evident that essence, which is below consciousness, cannot be the Good itself.

But now, since no essence, by virtue of being simply essence, rests within itself, but produces action and, through action, moves towards something by reason of the Good, what, I ask, does it seek? Certainly not being; for it has being before it has desire, and it cannot desire unless it first exists; nor does it desire to be more than it is or to be other than it is, for if that were the case it would be seeking, in the face of nature, to change its own type.

I pass over the fact that neither essence nor being can receive any more or any less. Therefore neither strives for anything beyond what it already is, unless it be to be well or better, that is, to conduct itself better; but this is nothing other than to desire the Good as the seasoning of essence. Neither being nor existence has anything desirable in itself. If it were otherwise, the present being would be desired, and what everyone has would be everlastingly sought, and what appeared the greater being would be loved more greatly.

Something, therefore, is desirable not because it exists but because it is good. The Good and the desirable are interchangeable terms, but being and the desirable are certainly not interchangeable. And it frequently happens that something absent, or yet to be, having less being, is more desirable to us than is the present, as if it were better. Therefore being and the Good are not the same, but the Good is loftier; because if the Good be compared to a being, even being has a cause for its end and its movement.

Possessions, of course, provide more reason for being than do deprivations. But, by reason of the Good, we often choose deprivations as well as possessions, and sometimes more so. The nature of being, therefore, is not the same as the nature of the Good.

Do we not choose not to do good as often as we choose to do good? To feel annoyed as often as cheerful? To know when we have been offended as much as to acknowledge something pleasing? Being totally deprived of all hope of good things and at the same time being oppressed by evils, do not some people choose not even to live, just as others choose to live profitably or at least in the hope of good things?

In this way those who choose not to live destroy themselves in their rejection of life and essence without the Good, although it is on account of the Good that they have loved both of these.

Chapter 47:
The seventh discussion on the same subject; and how the cause of being differs from the cause of the Good

ESSENCE ITSELF, as essence, does not increase or decrease. But the Good, as something other, both increases and decreases. In addition, it often seeks, as an end, what is more essential within things; and what is less essential in these things, such as action and movement, it seeks as something better or as something through which it may at some time conduct itself in a better way, as if essence and the Good were not the same.

Moreover, created beings seek something external and its enjoyment as good, not because it is good, or even because it may be good, but mainly because it is appropriate and profitable to what is good.

Again, the opposite of being [*ens*] is non-being [*non ens*], but the opposite of good is evil; yet evil and non-being are not exactly the same. For evil is said to be not only the total removal of being [*essendum*], if I may put it like that, but also a certain eclipsing of the Good and a certain disposition in opposition to you and something particularly hostile to you. The more being [*ens*] these things seem to have within them, the more evil they are for you. But in truth the opposite of the Good is the not-good, just as non-being [*non ens*] is the opposite of being [*ens*].

But the not-Good and non-being are not exactly the same, for the not-Good is not only the removal of being [*essendum*] from anything but also an eclipsing of the Good. On the other hand, as we have said, the more being appears, the more evil arises.

In the same way, the final formal perfection of essence is the intellectual form. The perfection of this form, if I may express it like this, is the presence of intelligence. But this has most being when it is most

77

assured. Yet assurance, as such, is not the aim of intelligence; but when it perceives its own good with assurance this good is not what is called being in the highest degree but is the highest degree of consistency and delight, as if the cause of being and the cause of the Good were different.

Is pleasure not sought before all else, as if it had the highest proportion of the Good? Pleasure, however, does not consist in feeling some vast and powerful being, but in appreciating something that is concordant and good for you. But if you also considered that something with more essence or being is more sought after, I certainly do not think that you would consider essence to be greater in mass or in number, of longer duration, or more involved with qualitative gradations; for essence, as such, is simply detached from size, number, time, and quality; and these things which I have just mentioned are sometimes rejected in favour of their opposites. Again, you do not call essence more substantial, if I may put it like that, for larger and smaller are not attributes of substance.

The alternative is that you will judge being to be greater and more desirable because being is better. What is better, however, is considered to be better by virtue of goodness itself. But the goodness in essence is a quality of essence and a condition of being. Above this goodness, therefore, exists the absolute Good itself.

In addition, just as matter is indifferent to forms opposed to each other, and class is indifferent to mutually opposed variations, so essence is indifferent to the living and the non-living, to the sentient and the insentient. It is therefore drawn out to these things by means of something other than itself.

Indeed, life is related to essence as its perfection and goodness, and in the same way sense is related to life, and intellect to sense. Life is not a greater being than essence, through which it itself is, but it is better than essence; sense is not more alive than life, through which it itself lives, but it is better than life; and so it is with intellect and sense. Yet at every step that which is better arises by means of the Good and not by means of essence, which never moves of itself towards what is better, but moves therefore by means of the Good, which is higher than being.

If you say, however, that the Good itself is totally identical to being at its height, my answer is, firstly, that just as within any being [ens] there is a cause of being [essendum] but a different cause of well-being [bene essendum], so there is a cause of being [ens] at its height, and a different cause of the Good itself; secondly, that what you were calling being [*ens*] at its height will not be simple being but will have some addition through which it does not simply exist but exists to the full, that is, as perfectly as possible and as well as possible, by means of some perfection and goodness imparted directly by the simple Good itself. But when we say the simple Good itself we mean all Good, without limit and without admixture.

Again, is perfection a two-fold goodness, formal and final? If anyone proves, therefore, that formal goodness is a kind of increment in essence, he will not be able to say the same about final goodness, which is most powerful and excellent. This is why the Good is considered to exist apart from essence. And it often happens that what is apparently incidental in something or around something is preferable and better because it is more essential. Indeed, this cannot occur without the seasoning of the Good, whether it be formal or final, especially because what is apparently incidental is preferable because it operates externally around the Good itself. If this were not so, it would never be desirable, for the end of substance cannot be incidental. Its aim, therefore, is the Good itself, in the presence of which the substance turns by means of that incidental.

Moreover, essence and life and intellect differ among themselves formally, for they have different definitions; and non-being, non-living, and non-perceiving are not identical, and some are compatible with more things than are others. Nor do they differ in being larger or smaller, as if essence, like heat, had a first level and a second and a third. For essence is substantial, while heat and light perhaps differ in the way that dryness does.

Indeed, if we do not otherwise distinguish being by way of quality into its first level and its second and third levels, we shall imperceptibly come to the point of supposing just a single essence or substance, like a single heat that is sometimes gentler and sometimes fiercer; and we shall remove the levels of substantial forms together with the distinctions of things pertaining to providence.

But perhaps someone will say that essence is not susceptible to a greater or smaller degree of quality, but that in any compound there can be many ways of being [*essendum*], so that our soul first has its own natural being [*esse*] and secondly assumes the nature [*esse*] of tranquillity, thirdly of wisdom, and fourthly of happiness, and that there are as many levels of goodness as there are ways of being [*essendum*]. We, for our part, shall be happy to accept this, but we shall add that every level of goodness is formally distinguished from the mode of being [*essendum*] which it accompanies; for in all places being [*esse*] seeks the Good, rather than the converse. Being [*esse*] is perfected through the Good, but the converse is not true, and we would reject any being [*esse*] that was totally devoid of all good, but we can never reject the Good.

But to sum up, since the soul seeks wisdom beyond its natural being [*esse*], it does not seem to seek it as if it were some higher level of being [*ens*] or of essence; for either essence does not have levels of this kind or perhaps that first being [*esse*] is more essential, on which it is based as a substance, while the second being [*esse*] and the third are, as it were, adventitious. It does not, I say, seek a subsequent level as something consisting more of essence, but as something better, participating more of the Good and leading to the Good itself.

For this reason the first level of being [*ens*] is universally directed towards the second as to its end. But being [*ens*], as being, is not necessarily an end, but as something good it is therefore directed towards the Good, for the first does not seek the second, and the second the third, unless it profits from being encouraged to go towards the Good.

Finally, if we follow the teaching of Plato, we shall conclude that everything depends on the first principle and is directly related to it; and that the more it depends on it, therefore, as on its creator, a being [*ens*] exists and can be spoken of; and furthermore, that the more it is related to it as to its end, the more it is good and is described as good.

This is for two reasons: for as it relates to that through a specific characteristic, it brings with it the natural good; but as it is turned towards it through some desire, it acquires an adventitious good which is sometimes better than the natural good.

Therefore, just as it is one thing to depend on the First or be produced by it or proceed from it, and another thing to be related to it by going back or by turning back, so, within any object, being is one thing, and the Good is another; and in the same way, outside any object, being itself is one thing, while the Good itself is another. But the Good is always and everywhere related to being as its end.

The Good is therefore higher than being; and everywhere it is higher according to the extent to which the cause of the end is higher than the cause of the maker. But, as we have said, things are granted essence by God Himself as the Maker, and they obtain the Good itself from God Himself as from their end; and so the Good, as we were saying, should be considered higher than being itself.

I believe that Aristotle himself will not deny this, provided that he remembers that he has received from the ancients the following description of the Good: The Good is what all beings seek. For since some things are full of desire, but that which is desirable is something different and more excellent, the Good is certainly striven for by all beings and, as must be admitted by Aristotle, it is higher than the whole ensemble of beings. This is why God, he says, governs and moves all things purely in His capacity as the desirable and the lovable, that is, as the Good and as the End.

Aristotle is right, together with his teacher, to give the title of the Good to the cause of causes, with the additional name of the End, since the final cause precedes all others. But whenever Aristotle makes being equal to the One and the Good he is perhaps judging it to be equal to that One and that Good which can be perceived by the intellect and comprehended by the being. His Plato, however, proclaims this in loftier tones, while Aristotle, as if it were something totally ineffable and unknown, does not honour it with words but pays it silent homage.

Chapter 48:
The first principle of the universe is the simple One Itself, the first in every rank, and most truly One. On the sun, on nature, on intellect

JUST AS division is the worst condition for all things, dragging everything to ruin, so union is the best condition: union of the parts with each other and with the whole, and of the whole with its cause, which is its origin and nature.

But union is ultimately produced from the supreme unity, which is thus recognised as the first principle of the universe, the principle which bestows the finest gift and perfects everything by uniting it and converting it, just as it made everything by bringing it forth. Hence it comes about that, in every kind and order of thing, that indeed is the first principle which is the most uniform of all within it and which is the simplest of all. For the moment I pass over the fact that unity is the first principle of number, the point of dimensions, and the moment of time.

In some way that which is very small in nature becomes the first principle of the natural body, the uniform seed-power itself and the origin of the omniform body.

But let us take up greater subjects. We see light flowing forth from innumerable stars, from fire, from countless eyes, and from precious stones and such like. These things are vastly different one from another, both in type and in kind. But the light emanating from them is everywhere very similar and, as I might say, most truly one.

Therefore the one principle does not require differences, for differences would make it vastly different. What then? A single sun is the first principle of all the light in the world. Although many things under the sun seem to be principles of light, it is by means of a single solar nature, power, and property that they shed a light which is so uniform. Moreover, if we seek the most powerful principle of light within the sun, shall we say that the very mass of the sun is the principle of light? Certainly not, if we follow right reason, for indeed many parts of that sphere give forth many lights. There will therefore be many principles; but we are seeking a single first principle, for the light which of all worldly lights is most truly one and simple, incorporeal and supreme, requires a principle that is one and single, incorporeal and supreme.

Does the very soul of the sun therefore generate light? Indeed it does, yet not by means of its living multiplicity, for if that were the case it would shed different lights. It therefore creates visible light by means of intellectual light: not through intellectual variation, but rather through the unity of the intellect, the unity which excels that intellectual soul as a sign of that simple unity which is the first principle of the universe. That intellect, through its own unity, is most fully united with this principle. Through the same unity God is, and is proclaimed. This divine unity of the sun, therefore, is the first principle of the uniform light of the world, just as simple unity and goodness are the creator of intelligible light.

In the same way, if we seek the first principle of universal creation we shall eventually come to the One, when all creations in one single rank strive towards the single form of the universe. This first principle is none other than the generative life of the world.

But since within this there are the countless seeds of all created things (yet there must needs be a single first principle), it is through its primal unity, by which it itself is divine and is fully united to God supreme, that it is the first principle of all the creativity in the world.

To those who further enquire what the first principle of all consciousness is, perfect awareness, or the first intellect, immediately appears as first and foremost. Yet it is not on account of its numerous types and concepts that it is the first principle of cognition, for this ultimately has to be one, but it is on account of its own unity, by which God exists, that it bestows the power of cognition both on itself and on all others.

Chapter 49:
The first principle of creation is unity and goodness, above intellect, life, and essence

PERHAPS SOMEONE will think that the first intellect is the simple First. Anyone who thinks thus, however, should note that, when he speaks of the first intellect, he means exactly what he is saying, not simple being but a first which is bound by particular conditions and a fixed intellectual system.

In the same way, what is called the intelligible itself cannot be the simple First, especially since it has a relationship with some intellect, a relationship that is incompatible with the first principle.

But you who wish the intellect to be God, first and supreme, please say how it will have such a title. It will not be merely as intellect, for if that were the case everything would possess some intelligence or consciousness, since everything must bear the mark of the first, supremely powerful Creator of all. For intelligence is the primal consciousness, if it is through intelligence itself that all things are truly and chiefly expressed, and especially if intelligence is nature itself at that point, for just as life naturally begets living creatures, so natural intelligence naturally creates beings that are intellectual or conscious.

Moreover, that first intellect, being intelligent, betakes itself to the intelligibles presently existent and to what are called beings; and it has no function of its own except to observe clearly those things which are. For this reason, therefore, it cannot be the first principle of creation, whose property is to make all things, preserve all things, and perfect all things. Just as there is a gulf between making and observing, so there is a gulf at least as wide between the intellect and the first principle of creation.

Finally, intellects are composed primarily of intelligent souls: either daemons or angels, but not gods, unless they also have the function of universal providence.

The ground of intellect, therefore, and the ground of principle cannot be considered the same. But should that first intellect, insofar as it is life, be called the first principle? By no means; for if that were the case everything would be alive. But perhaps insofar as it is essence? Not then, either; for that whereby intellect exists, or even life, is more perfect than that whereby essence exists. And so it is on neither of these counts that God exists.

Again, no essence rests within itself, but through its actions every essence strives towards the Good; nor does anything seek merely to be, but to be well and to be with the Good.

From this it is clear that above simple essence itself there is something more, which is the Good itself, especially since being and essence, unlike unity, can admit of multiplicity. Thus unity is simpler and prior. But more on this elsewhere.

Furthermore, not all things have their own being and their own essence, such as those things which are fully constituted by outside agencies and those things which simply pass away, as well as deficiencies and unformed matter. All things, however, should exhibit an unmistakable sign bestowed by the first principle: the best gift, I say, provided that the first principle makes all things from its own nature and expresses all things with power.

By what reasoning, therefore, is the first intellect considered to be this principle and to be God? Because it renders absolutely everything similar in some way to itself, through the unity and goodness granted to all. For everything is, in some measure, single and good. The intellect, therefore, is single and good by virtue of unity and goodness, and yet these fundamentals are not within the intellect, not even within the first intellect, for in the intellect unity and goodness are not simply themselves but, rather, certain things, such as the intellectual, in conformity with their own intellectual nature and capability. For the principle of unity and goodness is, in fact, always different from and higher than the principle of intelligence, since intelligence does not pervade everything, as they do, and intelligence is not content with itself but strives for union with the Good itself and partakes of some multiplicity and compounding, which the primal unity necessarily shuns.

Now when we think of the simple unity and goodness above the intellect, we are not considering two, but one alone; for to unite and to do good are universally the same, and neither unity nor goodness admits of anything higher, since nothing can be thought of that is simpler than unity or better than goodness.

The simplest and best is indubitably the First. But the First is utterly single; to the First truly belongs that incomparable simplicity which we call unity itself, as well as that universality which permeates everything and which we call goodness itself. Through unity it is absolutely simple. It is therefore by virtue of unity and goodness that the First is all-powerful, since goodness held in unity is universally more powerful. It is also by virtue of unity and goodness that the First permeates everything with its power, and here is the Good in its fullness. Indeed, simple unity is simple goodness.

Finally, since all things, including ebbs and flows, as well as formless matter, participate to some extent in unity and goodness, and since all and sundry yearn for union and the Good, let us consider that which is simply one and good to be the first principle of everything.

If only that admirable young man had carefully pondered the foregoing debates and discussions before confronting his teacher so boldly and propagating so recklessly a judgement opposed to that of all the followers of Plato, namely, that the divine Parmenides was simply a logician and that Plato, together with Aristotle, equated the One and the Good with being.

Chapter 50:
The unity above essence; the unities within essences; the gods; the general aim of Parmenides in his hypotheses

JUST AS simple unity itself is above universal being, so in the hierarchy of creation the unity of every being is to some extent higher than its essence. In relation to this unity and to what accompanies it, essence stands as does the circumference of a circle to the centre. Indeed, unity, in the manner of a bond, holds essence as its servant by uniting it to itself; and by keeping essence away from what belongs to others, unity perfects essence and strengthens it as if it were its pivotal point and something superior to it. It is not unity itself, but the union of being, that is equated with being, for unity is more extensive than being; it also shows that any deficiency is one, that any characteristic is one, and that the actual matter of form is no less one than are form and compound, although matter falls further from being [*ens*] than from being [*esse*] and essence.

Only the One and the Good, therefore, which is imparted to all things, demonstrates, as we have said, that the simple One and Good is the principle of all things, since it is the property of the First to imprint its own character strongly on each and every thing. But where the being is not true, as in things that are totally transient, the unity is not divine; where essence is true, however, as in everlasting substances such as rational and even individual souls and the heavens, the unity is now divine. Yet since these are not closest to God, being types of compounds and being in movement, their unity is not God; but where essence is absolutely true, as in minds that have no attachments or as in celestial souls, their unity is God; alternatively, there are as many extra unities as there are essences, and they are called gods.

Unity, therefore, is the proper name of God, the unity that is completely above essence, God single and first; while the pre-eminent unities within sublime essences are the numerous favourable gods. And on account of such unities, which have a greater power to express the primal unity, those essences have assumed all the names of the gods and have apportioned universal providence, which is a property of divine goodness.

These unities are everlastingly united to the first unity, just as rays are united to light, and as lines are united to the centre. They are joined to each other, for since union takes place by virtue of the unity in all else, much more closely are the unities united to each other, but at the same time they are distinct from each other, for the power of unity is to unite to itself, rather than to others, the natures that are related to it. For this reason, notwithstanding the general union, it unfailingly maintains its own unity and its special character that is distinct from all the others.

This is why Parmenides, though treating in manifold ways of the One on account of the wonderful union of all unities in relation to the first One and in relation to each other, touches at times, as very many followers of Plato did, on that first One which is beyond the limits of universal being; and at those times he does not concede to that One any of the properties of beings.

At other times he speaks of the One which has essence as its companion, and on those occasions he affirms the function of being and of beings, and he affirms all of them when he speaks of the first essence. Again, he emphasises some of them before others when he treats of some essences, and invariably when he treats of divine matters.

Proclus therefore thinks, as we have indicated previously, that the significance of the One Itself, which is found everywhere, actually varies in the different hypotheses, but at the same time the One Itself, which precedes hypotheses, can to some extent be seen to be invariable by virtue of that mutual union of the divine unities.

But the things that are subsequent are universally subject to much greater variation, in order that the clear distinction among the same unities may be revealed. For in the subsequent the whole is sometimes posited, while sometimes a part is posited, and at other times a very small part. Indeed, there are also times when the consequence is positive, and times when it is negative.

He adds in some places that the One is sought above being, as we have said; while in other places he says that the One and the many unities within being spread extensively throughout the levels of beings. In yet other places he declares that the One is not truly bound within being, from which, however, there may be an immediate and convenient return.

The aim of the whole dialogue in all respects is to consider what happens when something is posited and when it is not posited: what happens to it in relation to itself and in relation to others, and what does not happen. In the first hypothesis, therefore, the inquiry is: Given the One, what fails to happen to the One in relation to itself and to other things? In the second hypothesis: What does happen? In the third: The things that happen and those that do not. In the remaining two the questions are: What happens to other things in relation to themselves and to that which is being hypothesised? And, similarly, what fails to happen to them in relation to themselves and in relation to that? In the four remaining hypotheses – for there are nine all told – changes occur in a similar sequence when the One is posited.

His thinking throughout is that the similarity of the hypotheses indicates the marvellous union of the divine unities which are fundamentally inherent in the First One. The dissimilarity, however, indicates differences among the divine unities, inasmuch as they depart in one way or another from the One.

It is necessary, he says, to notice that from the first five hypotheses true conclusions can be drawn when the One is posited; while the later four show what absurdities follow when the One is withdrawn.

For the proposition put to Parmenides is to show how, given the existence of the One, all the levels of beings come forth from it; and how, on the assumption that the One does not exist, all these levels are removed; and this is what he affirms throughout the treatise, partly by asserting the true and partly by eliminating the false.

He discusses providence in a similar way, with the following reasoning: If providence exists everything will be rightly arranged, but if it does not exist all will be in disarray. Providence therefore does exist, since everything is in order.

Finally, his intention is to arrange the principles of creation with five hypotheses, and in the following four his aim is not so much to posit new substances as to show the numerous impossibilities that follow if the One be removed; for when the One is in place all things are in place, and when the One is removed all things are removed.

This One, therefore, is not a name invented by some logician, but it is the very principle of the universe. This is the mark of the sole principle of all things.

Chapter 51:
Plutarch's analysis of the hypotheses of Parmenides

THAT THIS dialogue was held to be divine among the ancients is attested by Plutarch, who, after many methods of exposition, introduced the method which we shall shortly describe, a method consisting partly of the views of the ancients and partly of his own view, and one which Proclus commends for its structure, which we alluded to in the preface. But let us now proceed to the understanding given by Plutarch, following it as closely as possible and not departing from it, except perhaps fractionally when we consider the final hypotheses.

The first hypothesis treats of the first God; the second, of the first intellect and the purely intellectual structure. The third hypothesis treats of the soul and, likewise, of its structure; the fourth, of material type; the fifth, of formless matter. These are the five principles of creation. The first three principles are discrete, while the following two inwardly complete the system.

In the manner of the Pythagoreans, Parmenides calls the One, on account of its simplicity, any discrete substance. Things other than the One he calls matter and corporeal form on account of their movement and differentiation, which are far removed from the divine. The particular reason for doing so is that these two – matter and incorporeal form – are the subsidiary causes, rather than the main causes, not so much of themselves as of other things, as we read in the *Timaeus* and the *Phaedo*.

The three hypotheses, therefore, which investigate how the One stands in relation to itself and to others, are justifiably considered to treat of the principal causes. But the next two, which examine how other things are related to each other and to the One, are seen to introduce type and matter. In these five hypotheses, therefore, these principles, together with what is within them and around them, are confirmed by the positing of the One: the One, I say, which is above being, within being, and beneath being.

In the other four hypotheses he shows how many absurdities follow if the One that is within beings does not exist; so that we may understand that much greater absurdities follow if someone denies the simple One itself.

The sixth hypothesis shows, therefore, that if the One that is intelligible has no existence in beings, so that it partly exists and partly does not exist, there would be in the hierarchy of creation only that which is perceptible by the senses. For when the intelligible – which is the One – is not present with true being, what remains is merely that which is perceptible by the senses, which is said in some way to be; and there will be no other apprehension beyond that of the senses. In the sixth hypothesis it is clearly shown to be absurd that in the range of cognition there are only the senses, and in the range of the cognisable there is only that which is perceptible by the senses.

The seventh hypothesis demonstrates that if that One be not present within beings, so that it does not exist in any way at all, there would be absolutely no cognition and nothing cognisable, which would be a ridiculous thing to say. This is what the seventh hypothesis shows. Again, if that One exists in part and in part does not exist, as the sixth hypothesis was suggesting a little previously, then all other things will be akin to dreams and shadows.

The eighth hypothesis refutes this as an absurdity. But if the One does not exist at all, then all other things will be less than shadows or dreams: they will be nothing.

The concluding ninth hypothesis proves that this is a monstrous suggestion.

This is why the first hypothesis is to all the other hypotheses as the principle of the universe is to all else. The four hypotheses that immediately follow the first deal with those principles that follow the One itself; and the next four prove that, if the One be taken away, all that has been laid forth in the previous four will totally vanish.

For whereas the second hypothesis demonstrates that, if there exists the One which is conjoined with being, the complete ordering of the soul also exists, the seventh hypothesis makes it clear that, if that One does not exist, then all power of cognition perishes, together with reason and imagination and sense. And whereas the fourth shows that, if that one being exists in some way additionally to the simple One itself, then material types also exist which clearly partake somehow of the one being, the eighth hypothesis shows that, if that one being does not exist, there will be but shadows and dreams, which are here called things perceptible by the senses, having no formal distinctiveness and no substance. Again, whereas the fifth hypothesis teaches that, if that one being exists, there will also exist matter which partakes of the one being not because the one being is being but because it is one, it does not explain the fact that if that one being does not exist, then there will not be even a shadow of anything.

This is what Plutarch says.

Chapter 52:
The meaning of the negations and of the
affirmations within the hypotheses.
Which ones are dealt with and in which order

SINCE THE first hypothesis focuses attention upon the simple One Itself, which is higher than being, it negates all the conditions of beings with respect to the One, which is detached from all things, being their final principle, a principle which is especially – even predominantly – efficient.

In the entire hierarchy of final and efficient causes, the most powerful is the one which is furthest from its respective conditions of effects; so that heaven, or an Idea, is a greater cause of man than is some other man, and the sun is a greater cause of vital heat than is fire.

But since the second hypothesis deals with the simple one, that is, the one being in which, beyond the simple pre-eminent principle of unity, there is also the principle of essence which departs from simplicity, it affirms all the formal characteristics of beings when it discusses this one being. For this is not so much the final cause of beings as their efficient cause, and not so much their efficient cause as their model and, in some way, their form, which is equally uniform and omniform. For this reason those negations relating to the First are not unmitigated negations, for they indicate that this One is the cause of all and is pre-eminent, not to a certain extent, but more than words can express, so that none of their forms is within it, nor any model differentiated into many things, nor any relationship or type of similarity to these things. But we speak of these matters time and again with Dionysius the Areopagite in our commentaries on his writings.

However, the affirmations relating to what follows the first do not add to it their own structure or nature, but they add their models, types, and effective powers, which are there distinct, one from another, both absolutely and according to their forms.

If we then follow Proclus, we shall say that every pre-eminent principle, especially the One, of any multiplicity reproduces a multiplicity which is like itself, that is, exalted unities which are similar to each other, rather than a multiplicity that is far removed and particular unions of individual things within the multiplicity. Therefore, just as the first intellect initially creates pure, separate intellects and then the intellectual powers within souls, so the simple One Itself first creates the superior divine unities, which are also known as gods; then it creates the unities which are implanted within things, and then those which are related and specific to those things that are united.

The One Itself, however, differs from those unities, for it is absolutely free of all characteristics, while those unities are derived from it through the influence of diverse attributes, which is why the gods have diverse names and functions. He advises us, moreover, to observe something which, to tell the truth, I consider very difficult to observe: how, in the second hypothesis, divine hierarchies of this kind are transmitted, followed by their designated attributes, which are as numerous as the conclusions which jostle one another for position.

Now the third hypothesis is considered to deal not simply with any particular soul, but with the entire divine soul. That the soul is there treated of, Parmenides himself bears witness when he states that the One partakes of time there, while the first time is in the soul. But *was* and *will be* are not applicable to the higher minds, though being, ever present and eternal, is applicable. In the second hypothesis I have discussed these minds and the question of whether the soul is actually a goddess. In the third hypothesis I have discussed the soul, not as a goddess but as divine.

Now, to go over the same points briefly once more: the first hypothesis, if we are allowed to believe the ancients, deals with the way in which the first God creates and orders the respective hierarchies of gods; the second hypothesis treats of the divine hierarchies, how they have come forth from the One, and of each essence that is conjoined by God to every unity; the third hypothesis deals with those souls which do not possess substantial divinity but do have a manifest likeness to the gods; the fourth hypothesis treats of material forms, how they proceed from the gods, and which ones depend on which respective order of gods; the fifth hypothesis deals with primal matter, how it is not composed of formal unities but depends on the unity that is above essence, for the action of the first One extends right through to final materialisation, which in all manner of ways sets limits to the unlimited nature of the One through particular participation in unity.

The first hypothesis and the fifth hypothesis proceed by way of negations, but the first, which negates everything in relation to the first step in creation, demonstrates by its negations the incomparable power and supremacy of the cause which is independent of everything; while the fifth hypothesis, which negates everything in relation to the final step in creation, points to deprivation and deficiency.

The second hypothesis and the fourth hypothesis employ only affirmations, but the second hypothesis includes models, while the fourth includes images.

The third hypothesis, being in the middle position, corresponds to the soul, which is at the mid-point of creation, and on account of this correspondence it is made up of both affirmations and negations, and through some sort of association it has the negations conjoined with the affirmations.

Chapter 53:
The aim, the truth, and the arrangement
of the first hypothesis

THE *SOPHIST* demonstrates that since all things partake of the One, the One itself must truly be. Since all other things more truly are the more they partake of the One, and since whatever partakes is not, on account of the multiplicity which characterises it, truly the One (and yet these things really exist), that true One itself, which has no trace of multiplicity, must truly exist with itself in its own nature. And the more it precedes all else, the more truly One it is. For wherever something is true by nature it is prior to, and earlier than, that which is false.

The final conclusion is that there would be no beings if there were not in fact that One itself. The One Itself, however, is totally indivisible.

This teaching, which is imparted to us in the *Sophist* by Melissus, one of Parmenides' hearers, is in all points identical to Parmenides' first hypothesis, which proves that the One Itself has no plurality and no parts. From this conclusion all the conclusions that follow are interwoven in an inevitable sequence.

From this it is clear that neither in the *Sophist* nor in *Parmenides* is there a discussion of a one which has been logically created by some mere name, or of a fictitious being, but there is a discussion of the One that is, as I may say, the One that exists or abides. Indeed, when he negates essence in relation to the One, he will necessarily affirm that the One itself is above essence and is God supreme. For in relation to the One, which he values so highly, he does not negate essence because he thinks it is nothing, for he shows that if it does not perhaps exist nothing remains; or because he judges nothing to be below essence, for below essence he has temporal things, fluctuation, and matter, from which he detaches the One Itself in a masterly way. Therefore the basis of this hypothesis is the One Itself, not a name invented by someone in a discussion, but the principle of the universe.

This is what Dionysius the Areopagite, the zealous follower of Parmenides, proved in particular. For every time he refers to the One Itself, which he does frequently, he places it above essence, and with this name he always designates the principle of the universe.

Some of Plato's followers have thought that the first hypothesis, by using this name of the One Itself, is referring not only to the first God but to the others as well, since all the gods are universally exalted unities and are called such, but the principle of unity that relates to the First is certainly not the same as the principle of unity in relation to those that follow, for the gods that follow are indeed to some extent unities which are above essence. However, they abide in essences which are the most perfect of all essences, while the first God has no associated essence.

For this reason the first hypothesis concerning the One, which it presents, negates essence, as we have said, together with being. Such a negation cannot be made in relation to the other unities, and from this it is clear that the question here concerns the sole and simple One in its own right, and the others not in their own right but insofar as they derive from the First and are subject to the First.

Moreover, it is clearly necessary for every nature that resides in another, as though it were imperfect at its own level, to rise to a nature of the same level, or of a similar level, or at least of the same name, a nature that is already perfect and self-existent, as, for example, to rise from a material type to an immaterial type; from life totally centred on the body to life which is none other than the soul, distinct or distinguishable from the body; from the intellect which is within the soul to the intellect which is pure and substantial.

But shall we, in the manner of Proclus, rise from the intelligible which is within the intellect to the intelligible which is outside the intellect? Indeed, wherever the intelligible resides within any intellect – not the intelligible complete in all respects, but some intelligible, and not, in fact, identical with the substance of mind – there we shall search for a more exalted intelligible.

But after we have reached the first intellect, where the intelligible is so complete and so deep within the intellect as to be the very essence of this intellect, we shall yearn for no intelligible beyond this.

However, since the unity here is not simple unity itself, but a unity which is essential, intellectual, and intelligible, and which has formal number as its companion, we shall proceed from here to the simple One Itself, from which, as from a watchtower, we shall contemplate the divine unities, the gods, flowing forth in their hierarchy.

Here it seems that a very apt example will help us. Since a line is the first continuum and is divisible, it therefore partakes of the indivisible, the point. Although the point has a state superior to that of the line and is indivisible, it is within the line and is the beginning of the line. Again, many lines within a circle touch the centre of the circle by means of their respective points, and in the same way the intelligible and intellectual essence, being the first manifold, is constituted of surpassing unity. Although this unity is not essence and is not subject to essential differentiation, yet it abides within essence, or rather it is conspicuous as the apex by means of which every intellectual essence is a god, enjoying the divine unity to the full; and just as everything is placed in its type according to its form, and we are what we are according to our soul, so the gods, according to their respective measures of unity, are considered to be that which is most powerful, namely, God.

In short, the aim of the first hypothesis will be to free the simple One Itself from all the characteristics and conditions of the intellectual unities everywhere, which are the gods, and, by freeing it, to indicate how all things proceed from it.

But our aim in pursuing these mysteries has been to reach the simple intelligences of beings through the logical discourses of our reason; and through these intelligences to arouse the One Itself, which dwells within us and is within us and is supremely divine, so that we may cognise this simple One; for when, through consideration and understanding, we have correctly negated from the first principle all the conditions pertaining to beings, we shall run the risk, after all the conceivable negations of things and functions, of being deceived by our imagination into thinking that we have come to nothing or to exile, to something empty or indeterminate, formless and confused, unless we counter our negations through the arousal of the divine energy of our unity by some loving emotion. This will instantly transport us, by means of our own unity, to the unity above us, so that we shall enjoy the divine unity when we have set aside the movement of reason and the multiplicity of intelligence, as we strive through unity alone towards the One Itself, and through love towards the Good itself.

Chapter 54:
When the characteristics of beings are negated with respect to the One, this indicates that the One surpasses and creates all these

AFFIRMATIONS concerning almighty God are very misleading and dangerous, for in our everyday affirmations we usually think of a particular type and characteristic to name and define something. But to do this in relation to the First is unlawful.

Negations, on the other hand, always leave the thing undefined and free in its range. Negations also render the soul more conformable to God, since they separate it from human conditions and limitations and entrust it, now almost devoid of limits, to God, who is utterly devoid of limits.

And, of course, we understand what we often say in agreement with Dionysius, that negations with respect to God indicate no deficiency, but sheer abundance. For when we say that God is not mind, not life, and not essence, we wish it to be understood that He is higher than all these and is their source.

But to negate hands in respect of a craftsman is to indicate a deficiency, he lacks the instruments necessary to him. Yet to negate hands in respect of nature is to declare the excellence of nature, which needs no hands to act. Indeed, just as that First is the cause of all, so the ingenious negations concerning it are the causes of the affirmations that follow. For this reason, whatever the first hypothesis negates concerning the One the following hypothesis affirms.

In this way it is made clear that all things are made by the One, for the very reason that the One is not one of the all but is above all. For just as the soul or nature, not being the body, produces and governs the body, and just as the intellect, not being the soul, creates the soul, so the One itself, not being subject to multiplicity or number or shape, creates multiplicity and number and shape. For none of those things which it creates can be the One itself; and no other cause, albeit excellent and universal, is the same as its effects or allied to its effects.

Therefore, when we negate form or shape in respect of God, we are not suggesting some deficiency, such as when we are considering matter that has no shape or form, but we are contemplating a God who is not circumscribed in any way but who circumscribes matter with forms and shapes. Since in negating all things with respect to God and with respect to matter through some dissimilar similarity we wish the same things to be negated in relation to each, we are in the habit of saying that because neither the soul nor nature has eyes or feet, they generate eyes and feet within the body in the same way that they generate the body.

Similarly, the One Itself is said to be neither whole nor part, neither same nor other, neither stationary nor moving, neither simply one of the opposites nor both, so that it moves all these equally. Nor is it similar to anything, lest it be obliged to conjoin with it in some higher cause of similarity, but rather that it may be able to bring about all similarity. Nor is it opposed to anything, lest it be subject to some cause of opposition, but rather that all oppositions should depend on it.

Chapter 55:
On the one being. On the simple One Itself. On the aim of Parmenides both here and in his verses. The aim and conclusion of his negations

PERHAPS IT would now be useful to repeat briefly what we have said many times before: the principle of unity is different from the principle of being. For the principle of unity spurns all multiplicity, while being does not reject multiplicity.

Secondly, the principle of unity is no less compatible with passive, formless power than with all else. But this is much less true of the principle of being.

Finally, by virtue of its inherent simplicity, unity precedes being [ens]. And the man who denies the One is denying more than the man who denies being [esse]. This is why the wise bestowers of names did not call total deprivation by the name of οὐδόν, which in Greek means 'non-being', but they called it οὐδέν, which means 'not one', that is, absolutely nothing. They do not attribute to the One 'is' or being or essence. But they do attribute 'exists' and existence, thereby indicating the simple effective act and presence of the One Itself, although they do not intend such attribution to suggest a composite, but merely simple witnessing.

Similarly, in the *Sophist* Melissus, the follower of Parmenides, considers one being before many beings. For in any hierarchy many similars may be reduced to a higher one. Indeed, the one being is related to a single unity, of which the one being, coming subsequently, necessarily partakes. On the other hand, it should not be imagined that unity likewise partakes of being; for if that were so, unity would no longer be simple but a multiple and a compound.

Then he demonstrates that this one being is a whole which is also multiple, in which there is both a principle of being and a principle of unity; and he thinks that this universal being should be considered to be the well-spring of all beings and to be subsequent to the One.

Parmenides, as Melissus witnesses, composed a book in a poetic style concerning this one being as the second principle. For we declare the First to be beyond words. Many things which in the first hypothesis are negated with respect to the One itself are affirmed, in the second hypothesis, with respect to the one being.

Therefore, when Parmenides says that he will begin from the One, he is indicating a difference between himself and Zeno at the beginning of the discussion. For Zeno started from multiplicity, while Parmenides starts from the One. And since all things are here negated with respect to the One, when Parmenides says here that he will begin the discussion from that One of his, we must not understand him to start from the one being but from the simple One Itself, of which this one being is composed; and for this reason he rises instantly from *this* to *that*, negating in *that* and affirming in *this* all the things which he had also affirmed in his verses, namely, that the intelligible universe is spherical, and so on.

Indeed, since there is firstly simple unity itself, that is, supreme simplicity and power, what the One creates first is what it creates most fully, and since the creator has no particular relationship with anything but is equally related to all things and is equally above all things, either the creator does nothing – which is a wicked thing to say – or the creator creates everything at the same time within that One, which is what we were saying just now.

And so we say with Plotinus, and equally with Parmenides, that the first One is above all, while the second one is all, as the creation of an absolutely perfect Creator is the most perfect of all. But how the Creator and the creation are one is a subject we deal with in the *Christian Theology*. Plato, on whom we are now commenting, seems to have considered them as two. But let us proceed with what remains.

The negations are made with respect to the First, not so much on account of the weakness of our intelligence, which is not strong enough to deal with the matter in any other way, for even the first intellect does not consider the First in any other way, as because the First cannot and must not be reached in any other way; nor does the intellect attain it except by putting its own individual multiplicity in second place and by simply offering unity to unity.

Now in the first hypothesis the conclusion of the negations and their arrangement is this: the One Itself is not multiplicity, and it has neither whole nor part. Again, it has no beginning, no middle, no end, no limit, no shape. It is not within another and not within itself. It neither stays nor moves. It is neither the same nor other. It is neither similar nor dissimilar to itself or to others. It is neither equal nor unequal to itself or to others. It is neither greater nor less than itself or others. Again, it is neither older nor younger. It does not partake of generation or of time or of what is said to be being. It cannot be named, spoken of, thought about, or known.

Chapter 56:
On the universal being and its properties; and why these are negated with respect to the First. Which multiplicity is negated, and why it is negated

IN THE commentaries on Plotinus, whom I follow more gladly than I do Proclus, both here and in many other matters, we have often shown that the intellect, the intelligible, the first being, the first essence, and the first life are in fact a single substance, although within that substance they do differ in principle.

In that substance the five kinds of created things and the Ideas are distinct one from another by virtue of their formative principle, for since the first essence possesses all the perfections of essence, it has life and intellect: I mean the first life and the first intellect. If the intellect is perfect, possessing perfect intelligence, then it also possesses the deepest level of the intelligible. If anyone would separate the intelligible from the intellect by means of essence, we should then be compelled to admit that the first intelligible, being perfect, would be intelligible to itself and would therefore have intelligence within itself.

On both counts, then, we come back to the same point, being obliged in both cases to link the intellect with the intelligible within the same essence, in which all intelligibles and beings are included intelligibly and intellectually. We call this the intelligible world, the universal intelligible sphere.

In his verses Parmenides sings of the one being and describes it. In the *Sophist* it is said to be the first being but not that which is truly the One, because it is not indivisible, and therefore it is not the first One, because the true One is totally indivisible and partakes of no multiplicity, for if it did it would also partake of the One; and so it would not be that first true One, to which reason compels us to proceed from the one that is untrue, just as it compels us to transcend untrue forms, untrue life and untrue cognition and to move towards true forms or Ideas, true life and true cognition.

If the intelligible world is the first formative being, the beginning and the model of all beings, generating and forming all things by its own form and nature, then all the properties which are compatible with it are also compatible with all beings, inasmuch as they are beings; and conversely, all the properties which belong to beings, inasmuch as they are beings in form and are perfect within their respective types, also match the former properties, although such properties exist more fully within the intelligible world.

Iamblichus and Syrianus and Proclus, on the other hand, do not put the natural differences of kinds and of Ideas within the first being, because, since it is nearest to the One itself and, for that reason, very closely united with it, it cannot admit opposites. A strong additional reason which they give is that in the first being there is nothing that is not being, and therefore we do not find those opposites which say that the same is not other, stillness is not movement, the rational is not the brute, fire is not water, man is not horse.

Another reason is that simple being is predicated of absolutely everything, but none of the opposites and no Idea is affirmed with respect to absolutely everything; and this is what we are told in the *Sophist*. Therefore they put difference of this kind in the intellectual essence, which is subsequent to simple essence, and this is where Plato also puts the origin of numbers.

But we, following the more ancient authorities, say that those differences are to be located in the first being, yet not at the first level, which is simply being, but at the next level, which unfolds by means of life and intelligence. For in this way the objections that we have mentioned are avoided, and within the first being are located the immediately subsequent properties of all things.

Indeed, five kinds unfold more fully within the living essence of an Idea, or rather within the living intellect, for they are scarcely discernible within essence. Present within that, however, are the properties that are universally necessary for all beings.

All these properties Parmenides enumerates, one by one, in the first hypothesis, as we have mentioned in the previous chapter, negating them in the One, but soon affirming them in the one being, so that, after he has negated, with respect to the first One, all the properties of the universal being, he may thereby demonstrate that the One itself is above universal being. This he also clearly confirms near the end of the first hypothesis, negating, with respect to the One, what is called *esse* and *ens*, for if this were not the case all those things which accompany and follow the *esse* and the *ens* would be compatible with the First.

But such things, on account of their differentiation, cannot be compatible with that simplicity which is the simplest of all; for how can the multiplicity and the assemblage of Ideas which differ among themselves, how can the opposition of properties such as sameness and otherness, stillness and movement, the similar and the dissimilar, the equal and the unequal, and other such oppositions, which in the first being are the absolute principles of lower properties that differ among themselves, how can these be harmonious with the First?

In this context Syrianus and Proclus, the authorities on all conclusions, consider that some gods exist in isolation, so that multiplicity is a god, a part is a different god, and the whole is yet another god. In the same way, they say, the plane figure and the solid shape, youth and old age, similarity and dissimilarity, and so on, are all deities which are judged to be lower than the First on account of all their negative consequences, while their positive consequences are also arranged in their own order. But this seems to be a poetical device rather than a philosophical one.

However, let it be sufficient for us to take these as the properties of the universal being; in their own way they are within the first being and within subsequent beings. We need to remember that Parmenides, in his negations, begins with the more universal properties and moves in a regular series to less universal properties, for when the first have been negated then the others are later negated; and, in the same way, if anyone denies that this is an animal he has denied that it is a man, although the converse affirmation does not produce the opposite conclusion. Indeed, if you affirm *man* you have affirmed *animal*, but the converse is not true.

But since it is always right to start from the known, that we may, through the known, easily discern the unknown, Parmenides, in his negative conclusions, firstly negates multiplicity with respect to the One, which is clearly different from it; later, after a great many points, it is by means of multiplicity, which is not unknown, that he negates essence, or being, which seemed to him almost identical, and yet it is not identical; and if it be added to the One it introduces composition or property. Finally, he denies that the One Itself is merely a one, lest perchance there be two, something and one together, or lest there be one and the limited in some kind or order.

This is why Plato, in his letters, forbids us to inquire, in relation to the First of all, what it is or what its nature is, for any such terms undermine and restrict its universal pre-eminence; and he forbids us to ask questions concerning the nature or substance of the One, the nature of life, the nature of essence, and the nature of the Good.

In his affirmative conclusions, however, he affirmed this from the first with respect to the one being, that is, he affirmed the One and the being with respect to the intelligible world; and soon afterwards he affirmed, in addition to its essence and unity, that which is very strongly connected to it, namely, multiplicity, by which I mean the multiplicity of the ideal types and kinds.

By means of these wholly familiar points, which are very obvious, he will affirm things which become ever less familiar, and for this reason the first hypothesis does not ask what follows if universal being is the One, for, if that were the case, once the nature of being and of the universe has been given, that is, once the nature of all things has been given, the inference would quickly have to be made that the One contains multiplicity, parts, limits, and so on, and finally essence. But, in fact, all these are denied, because the hypothesis is not whether all things are the One, but whether the One Itself *is*; and the converse to this is put as a hypothetical question after the fifth hypothesis: if the One does not exist, what follows?

But when he negates multiplicity with respect to the One as fully as he can, this is not the multiplicity of perceptible things, or the multiplicity of the living power of thought. For it was not seemly to take pains to refute those things which no one would assert with regard to the First, but he negates with regard to the First that multiplicity which he will assert with regard to the second, that is, the intellectual multiplicity which befits the first intellect and is filled with the intelligence of Ideas and of kinds.

This multiplicity also befits the subsequent intellects, which are pure and divine, yet it in no way corresponds to the first principle of all, because all multiplicity is subsequent to unity and because within what is truly the First there must be nothing that is not the First; and also because unity and utter simplicity thrive within boundless goodness; and finally because in that which finds perfect joy and fulfilment within itself there can be nothing but itself. But concerning the wondrous simplicity of the First and the formative multiplicity of the second we have often spoken at length with Plotinus.

Perhaps someone will ask whether multiplicity is opposed to the One. Our reply is that opposites are to do with the same subject, as with number that is even or odd; length that is equal or unequal; quality that is similar or dissimilar; substance that is the same or different; motion that is swift or slow; essence that is one or many – whereas multiplicity is not sundered from union, and as one it is not sundered from multiplicity, for this one is the one of multiplicity, but it itself is not multiplicity in spite of being lodged within multiplicity, and because it is one it cannot be many; yet because it is the one of multiplicity the one can undoubtedly be termed the many.

However, the simple One Itself, which is above essence and beyond essential number, is so absolute that multiplicity is considered not to be opposite to it but merely different, for just as the first heat, the first light, the first essence and the first Good have nothing cold, nothing dark, nothing that is non-being, nothing that is not good, so the first One admits nothing but the One and casts out all multiplicity, which differs from it, for if multiplicity be within it (to speak in the manner of Plato), it will not be the One Itself but will be united, yet not united by itself; just as something that is formed by something other than itself, so it will be united by the simple higher One.

Now the fact that the Platonic reasonings which remove multiplicity from the First do not detract from the Christian Trinity, in which, through the intrinsic simplicity and unity of its nature, a single relationship makes a distinction but not a compound, is clearly set forth by Nicholas, the Greek theologian and bishop of Metho; but we touch upon this in some notes on him.

Finally, let us conclude, with the followers of Plato, by saying that when Plato negates multiplicity with respect to the One, he merely means that nothing higher can be thought of; that the One is utterly simple and unmanifest; and that from it the whole multiplicity of the form of things proceeds as numbers proceed from unity. What Plato here calls the One that is above being, in the *Republic* he calls the Good that is above essence, but, as we learn from the *Phaedo* and from *Parmenides*, the One and the Good have the same property of perfecting all things, containing all things, and pervading all things.

Moreover, nothing is better than the Good itself, and so nothing is higher; again, nothing is simpler than the One, and so nothing is above the One. If this were not the case, then what is imagined to be higher is either nothing or it is a multiplicity which, being infinite, is totally devoid of union. But since there cannot be two principles, the One and the Good are the same in all respects; yet, as we have said elsewhere, we call it the One on account of its uniqueness and surpassing simplicity, and we call it the Good on account of its abundance and all-pervasiveness.

Chapter 57:
Through the negation of multiplicity, parts and totality are negated with respect to the One: number is prior to essence, and all multiplicity partakes of unity. The first essence, life, and mind are identical

WHENEVER PARMENIDES denies something with respect to the One, remember, as I have suggested in other places, that he means not only that God, being above that thing, is not that thing, but also that that thing has been created by God, although God has in no way been touched by this effect or changes His bearing in any way.

Therefore, since multiplicity is negated first, it is being made clear that God is in no way multiple; that what is first created by God is multiplicity; and that all multiplicity is gathered together within the One, like a deity derived from unity, in which all numbers are held.

Again, when it is next denied that God is any totality or has parts, it is being made clear that, apart from That which is in no way compounded, every compound, and the first above all, is created by That. Of course, it is on account of the simple One Itself that any one of the parts is some kind of a unity and that all the parts are united into a single form of the whole.

It is within the intelligible world itself that the first compound is made from the limitless and the limited, as from matter and form, and also from essence, life, and intelligence; and again, in some way, from the first kinds of beings and from Ideas.

Moreover, as we have said elsewhere, in dealing with negative conclusions we should rightly begin from more general propositions such as: *If it is not a living being, then it is not a man.* In dealing with affirmative conclusions, we have: *If it is a man, then it is a living being.* Therefore, since Parmenides, through the very negation of multiplicity, consequently negates both totality and parts, he declares multiplicity to be more general than parts and their totality. For he says that if the One is some kind of totality, and therefore has parts, it will necessarily be multiple.

Of course, when he is making affirmations he begins from more particular points, such as: *If it is a man, then it is also a living being*; and similarly, *If it is a totality, and therefore necessarily possesses parts, it is multiple or a multiplicity*. For this consequence is more general than its antecedent; and when this is negated, namely, that the One is not many, what had been the antecedent is immediately negated, while it is inferred that if it is not multiple, then it is not the whole and does not have parts. But what is multiple or a multiplicity is prior and more general, and hence it is clear that any totality is made of many parts; that there are many parts everywhere; that these are related to the whole and the whole is related to them.

However, not all manifolds, if separated, are parts of something or comprise a whole. In addition, multiplicity *per se* does not determine any definite end for itself; indeed, by its very nature it seems to go on multiplying without end. But parts, combining through their own nature into the single form of the whole, are limited by some limited appearance of the whole.

Lastly, even if the many never combine and are simply the many, parts, on the other hand, become and combine into a whole when they have come together according to a definite principle. In the hierarchy of creation, therefore, multiplicity is anterior to both whole and parts.

But how the One is anterior to being, just as in the intelligible world multiplicity, or number, is anterior to the host of beings and all the compounds of totalities, whether they are created at that point or subsequently, we have explained at sufficient length, with Plotinus, in the books on Ideas, on the kinds of being and on numbers; for unless there were certain natural principles present and anterior within the first formative being, which is the source of countless beings, the multiplicity of beings would be distributed, as it were, in the manner of the waters, or at least the whole plethora of beings would spread hither and thither by chance, without order, without definite measure or limit, and without cease.

Accordingly, if we are seeking the first cause of multiplicity, we shall find that its source and the source of union are the same. For the fact that every single thing and all things together are somehow one is incontrovertibly due to the simple One Itself, which we often call unity itself. Again, the fact that there are many is due to the same. For through multiplicity itself there are many, just as there is one through unity; but multiplicity itself – not, I say, this or that multiplicity, or the multiplicity of these things or those things, but simple multiplicity as such – is nothing other than certain secondary unities generated from simple unity itself and dispersed universally.

For this reason the followers of Plato will not accept the dictum of the followers of Aristotle that unity and multiplicity somehow follow after being itself as some of its conditions; but rather do they precede it, inasmuch as they flow from the simple One Itself towards being and beings, and more can be predicated of one than of being, since any deficiencies, such as conditions, are described as one, for just as sight is one and sound is one, so blindness is one and silence is one; true opinion is a particular one, and falsity is a particular one; and more is predicated of multiplicity than of being.

Indeed, since not only things themselves but also their deficiencies are called many, and since not only things present but also things to come and things past are declared to be many, and since true opinions are called many, as are false opinions, therefore unity and the multiplicity of unities, which is the simple first multiplicity, are seen to precede the order of beings. These beings, therefore, are not only effectively from one but are also formatively from the first being. But the many are solely from the simple One Itself, from which the host of unities is infused into beings.

If anyone equates the cause of the multiplicity of beings with simple multiplicity itself, he will not differ from the followers of Plato, but if you seek the cause of simple multiplicity elsewhere than in the One, you will greatly err.

For where do you wish multiplicity itself to start from? If it be from another multiplicity, you will fall unwittingly into infinite regress. If it be from no cause, then multiplicity is the first cause of creation and there will be no union and no order within creation.

Finally, if any multiplicity necessarily partakes of unity, then it certainly depends on unity itself as on a higher cause. But if it does not partake of unity, none of the parts will be a particular one, and no particle of a part will be one, but each will be an indefinite part for ever; again, parts will have no union with parts and no relationship with the whole, and there will be no definite form of the whole, but an infinite form an infinite number of times, not united by its own parts, since it lacks the One, but, so to speak, torn asunder in all places. Therefore the One Itself is the beginning, the preserver, and the end of all multiplicity, all combination, and all order.

The theologians Gregory of Nazianzus and Nicholas have it that the divine Trinity is devoid of such conditions, for that multiplicity partakes of unity and is later than unity, which is a kind of number of certain parts composing something. But in their view the divine Trinity is not number or multiplicity, not accidental or essential, but is above essence; nor does it comprise anything except the whole; it does not exist outside unity itself, but is the characteristic naturally necessary to the unity of the divine nature. This Trinity therefore pertains to unity. It participates in unity yet is not united by its participation, but it has the deepest experience of natural unity, not dividing, but preserving, the natural unity.

Certain followers of Plato strive solely to assert the absolutely simple nature of God Almighty, but they never contemplated the personal attributes which are above our understanding; and on the simplicity of the divine nature there is no dissension between the followers of Christ and the followers of Plato.

Moreover, Proclus and Syrianus introduced a trinity of three substances outside the first: the first essence, the first life, the first intellect. Indeed, according to them that essence is the principle of being for created things, that life is their principle for living, and that intellect is their principle for understanding. They put essence before life, since the function of being extends further than the function of living; and for a similar reason they put life before intellect. If, as we have said of both of them, we follow Dionysius and Plotinus, we shall not accept an ordering of this sort, for since the function of the higher cause must be more perfect than that of the subsequent, it will be nobler to be than to live, nobler to live than to understand. This is not true according to its fruit, and therefore this is not the true ordering of principles.

Moreover, it is vain to imagine more principles to produce these effects, since one principle is sufficient and proper. Indeed, since the first essence has all the perfections natural to it, while life is an innermost movement or the act of the first essence, and intelligence is a reflection of life back into essence, then within the very nature of the first essence there is simultaneously life and the first intelligence.

We shall reply that being extends further than living and, again, that living extends further than understanding, not because those three principles are distinct one from another in substance or because in the universal hierarchy essence is superior to life, and life superior to intellect, but because, as Plotinus maintains, within the intelligible world, while it itself is being created from the First in accordance with some principle of such creativity, that essence of the first being is somehow prior, but it soon lives and it soon understands, for it _is_ before it moves, and it moves before it is reflected back to itself through movement.

But, in brief, if that intelligible substance were perfect at its first level, it would not be turned, by any desire, towards the beginning and the Good itself. However, it is necessary for all beings to be turned towards That. It is therefore born without being totally absolute, but so that it might be further perfected by That from which it is produced. Therefore, what is first given there to the offspring, inasmuch as it is related to the need to receive life, is, in the subsequent effects arising therefrom, earlier and more general than life; and in the same way, since life strives there towards intelligence as if towards the more perfect, the function of living is granted to many forthwith before the function of understanding.

But the gift of the One Itself and of the Good, being the gift of the almighty Maker of all, pervades all things and is the choicest of all gifts. For this reason the One Itself, the Good itself, wondrously surpasses all the levels and orders of the universe. That this is above intelligence, above life, and above essence is not only maintained by the followers of Plato but is frequently confirmed by Dionysius the Areopagite.

But we have already digressed too much. Let us return to the theme in hand.

Chapter 58:
An opinion affirming the abstracts of abstracts with respect to God. Again, negations and relative affirmations about God are safer

SOME OF the earlier followers of Plato used some absolute affirmations with respect to God, thinking that, since God is the absolute cause of all, and especially of those things which are prior and most extensive, He holds directly within Himself their powers and roots, by means of which certain absolute affirmations may be made concerning God, but nothing in any way concrete, such as that God is being, that God is living, or that God is intelligent; and no abstract affirmations bordering upon these, such as that God is essence or life or intellect; but rather abstractions of abstracts, if they can be pronounced, or if they can be heard without laughter: essentiality, vitality, intellectuality, and other similarly perfect specimens after their kind. These, they say, are for some reason totally united in God and, though completely hidden from us, are known to God alone. Perhaps they thought that abstracts which border on concretes have some of the qualities of concretes.

But distant abstracts, or abstractions of abstracts, are, in their view, totally devoid of all the passions of concretes, so that affirmations concerning God convey nothing petty, nothing changeable, nothing of multiplicity or of division or of any combination, but they show the supreme power of perfecting the best; so when they say 'essentiality' they do not mean some form or type distinct from life or vitality. Similarly, when they name 'vitality' they do not imagine a type different from essence or intelligence. Again, when they say 'intellectuality' they do not mean a type distinct from essence and life. For these three, as well as wisdom and truth and virtue and similar qualities derived from these, are such that each one of them is distinct from all the rest and is not itself what they are. Each one of them, therefore, is a definite and circumscribed good, not the simple All-Good.

And so, through what we have called the abstracts of abstracts they mean to indicate neither the good within this or that nature nor the assemblage of different goods, but that which is absolutely, uniquely and pre-eminently the All-Good, which – when the limits of all natures have been totally removed, and when all multiplicity has been taken away – brings forth the good things of all natures through its unparalleled power for effecting essences, lives, minds, wisdoms, truths, virtues. These, I say, were perhaps what the earlier followers of Plato contemplated.

But the later followers of Plato, after the negations, which in company with Plato they choose before everything else, admit affirmations which are not indeed absolute but merely relative: not absolute, I say, because they fear the possibility of defining anything close to God and they fear to attribute to God anything related to our own nature, which Plato most providentially forbids in his epistle to Dionysius, where he declares that this error about God is the source of all errors.

However, they propound relative affirmations which neither indicate the essence or nature of God nor express His name or any concept of Him, for Parmenides says that such things are beyond our powers, but they declare how things are related to God: thus, when we speak of the beginning, the middle, and the end, we understand that things are created, preserved, and brought to completion by God; when we speak of the Good, it is as the most perfect end of all, sought out by all.

But if ever we seem to affirm the One, we are either attributing our own properties to it, as if these qualities are thereby united, or we may be denying that it itself is multiple or in any way compounded.

Chapter 59:
If the One has no parts, it follows that it has no beginning, no end, no middle

NOW JUST AS, through the negation of more general multiplicity and then of that which is more particular, he has denied that the One has parts, so henceforth, through the negation of parts, he denies that it has beginning or middle or end, as if that is also more general than the other.

But first he draws a positive conclusion from the particular to the general in this way: If it has a beginning, a middle, and an end, it follows that it has parts. Then, changing tack, he draws the negative conclusion that it has no parts, and so it does not have those things. That it is more general to have parts than to have those things is clear from the fact that you can conceive of parts as something more common and available before you distinguish them and arrange them in such a way that you are aware that this one occupies the beginning, that one the end, and a third one the middle place between the two.

Moreover, the parts are to a certain extent in twos. Yet the initial distinction of beginning, end, and middle is not into two but into three; and with the majority of numbers a distinction of this kind is not easy. In short, what is there to stop us considering a countless, never-ending multiplicity of parts? Yet we are not allowed to contrive extremes or middle within this multiplicity.

But when Parmenides says that if these three exist they will be within the One and will be parts of one line, he presents us with a difficulty. For in this analogy two points make the beginning and the end, between which a middle point is also indicated, and yet the points are not parts of the line. For magnitude does not consist of indivisibles. And the parts of a line are not infinite. But nothing prevents us from considering innumerable points.

To this we shall reply that within a line there may be things of differing quality, so that something may be a part of it, while something else is its end; but in the One most of all they are made conformable to themselves. If something has been allotted as the beginning or the middle or the end, it will also be part of the One. But who has forbidden Parmenides to name as parts of something whatever belongs to it, whatever helps to complete it, whatever has dealings within its hierarchy? In this way, therefore, he will be able to call points 'parts of a line'.

Finally, even if points are not understood as parts of a line, because merely a line is being considered, yet, because the line is supposed to be limited, the points at its ends are to some extent thought of as parts of the limited line. But take these things as you will, there remains another doubt, as he declares in the *Laws*. Here he denies that God holds the beginning and the middle and the end of all things.

We shall briefly reply that he is there speaking of another god, namely the intellect, as the founder of this world, in which are discerned the models of all the beginnings and middles and ends within the creation. Here, however, he is speaking of the simple primal One, in which there are no absolute distinctions of Ideas, but by its utterly simple abundance the intelligible universe brings forth, to speak in the style of Plato, through itself the perceptible universe too.

Alternatively, if he is also perhaps speaking of the First in the *Laws*, he does not mean that it has a beginning, a middle, and an end as parts of itself within itself, but that through its own pivotal nature it holds within itself the beginnings and the ends and the middles of all things; and that all things are related to it as to their own beginning and end and middle; for all things come forth from it, all things seek it, all things are preserved unshaken while they fix their centres in the centre of That.

Chapter 60:
In what way the One Itself is called the limitless and the limit of all

IN THE preceding arguments he has demonstrated that, since the One has no parts, it consequently has no limits. He now demonstrates that, since it is without limits, it is unlimited or infinite; but nothing of great import seems, at first sight, to follow from this, for perhaps by a similar process of reasoning anyone may prove that because mathematical unity, which is the beginning of numbers, and the point, which is like the beginning of dimensions, have no parts and therefore have no limits, they too are infinite. The mountains are in travail, and a ridiculous mouse will be born.

We reply that this unity and point can be called infinite in some respect within its own kind, because unity has no numerical parts and the point has no dimensional parts or limits; and nothing prevents either from replicating itself endlessly through the limitless numbers arising from the former or through all the dimensions produced from the latter. And so they both seem to be limitless, but within the universal order of creation they are both finite and in some way they have their respective parts and limits.

For neither of them exists simply and absolutely, but each of them is something specific within its own kind, and each is constituted by its respective differentiation within its own type, and consequently each has its own properties and is subject to events and is limited by its nature or by a higher cause and depends on a specific end and has its force measured for a particular purpose. Therefore, possessing parts and limits of this kind, they are indeed finite, and in the same way all other things, apart from the First, are composite and finite.

But the simple One Itself has nothing of this kind; for it admits of no multiplicity and no condition.

As we have shown in the commentaries on *Philebus*, all things other than the First are composed of the limitless and a limit, that is, they are composed of some passive power, unformed as such, or the deformed power of other things that inclines further and will come, ready to assume form, from another source, and also of the form or the act which limits this kind of power and inclination. This limitless and this limit are the mutually opposed elements of created things, reconcilable from above by the simple One Itself.

This One is not any such limitlessness, for in that case it would be limited from above; nor does it, as if in opposition to itself, put any limit upon subsequent unlimited things; nor is it any such limit, for if it were it would be confined within things and would not be able to create, in contrast to itself, things unlimited. It is therefore above these and above all pairs of opposites, so that it is free to govern and perfect all things. And so it is limitless, because it has no internal limits and is subject to no external limits through which it could be defined by any cause, end, subject, perception, or condition.

Its levels of power and action are without number and without measure. It is not some limit, or a limit of something, or a limit within something, but rather the originator of all limits whatsoever.

Syrianus and Proclus consider that these two elements – the limited and the unlimited – exist before all the levels of beings, withdrawn within themselves below the First and distinct one from the other, since they must exist in their simplicity within themselves, each pure element separate from its opposite, before there are compounds and even before the opposites are mixed together.

But I, in company with Plotinus, do not think that these two are separate from any compound, especially the first compound, by anything other than the principle of being formed. For within the first being, there is its first limitlessness, that is, its capacity as such for receiving form; and there is no limit, that is, no first universal form; as yet it has no such limit and no trace of such a limit. Furthermore, a limit of this kind, as such, has no form. It is limitlessness that is able to receive form. Nor does it have properties of the limit, but properties opposed to these.

Socrates, however, in order to show that these two are not two separate substances, has already said, not that God made or begot these two, but that He revealed them. Yet, he says, the first compound being was begotten and made from these by God Himself, as if to say that this is real, while those are not at all real.

From these discrete elements, when they are fused together, are composed all remaining things, that is, Ideas, minds, souls, all things in heaven and all under heaven. It seems futile to imagine that this limitlessness, that is, this incomplete capacity for receiving form, which is still unformed and has still not attained a desirable end, can exist of itself and independently within itself, just as it would be foolish to imagine, if someone separated unformed matter from form, that that limit which is the intrinsic end of this limitlessness were likewise separated, as if someone had somehow separated a material form from matter.

In fact, you can never separate matter from form, but if you can conceive of form apart from matter, you have gone beyond the form that was just now in front of you and you have transcended kind, so that you no longer have this sort of form, but the ideal form. In the same way, if you transcend the limitlessness and the limit which are within a being, you will directly find a different sort of limitlessness which is not subject to form but is the author of all forms, and you will find a different sort of limit, not a limit conjoined to limitlessness, but a limit which, from on high, allots limitlessness and the higher limits to limitlessness and individual limits to each particular thing.

Thus the unlimited and the limit, which are mutually opposed within things, are, when beyond things, simply the One Itself.

Chapter 61:
How shape is negated with respect to the One, as well as straight lines and circular lines

That which has a limit is more general than that which has a shape, for whatever is endowed with shape is enclosed within limits, but anything that is not bounded by limits, such as a line, still has a shape. He therefore denied that the One, being more general, has limits before it has shape. And from this general negation he rightly adduced a particular negation.

Furthermore, he negated shape as something general before he drew forth from the mid-point particulars such as the straight line and the circular line. And conversely, while he denied that the One partakes of the straight shape or the circular shape, he drew forth from the mid-point not only these two extremes of shapes but also the middle shapes which partake of the extremes: the cone, the cylinder, the triangle, and the square.

However, it would be ridiculous to negate mathematical shapes with respect to the One as if one were undertaking a great task. What is certain is that the One exists above every unbroken kind, indeed above every general being; and so, with respect to the One, he negates shapes that are more exalted than mathematical shapes, while very clearly negating these too.

In this regard, mark what we have mentioned elsewhere: Parmenides is always engaged in making negations by means of opposites – one being and the multiplicity that is opposed to this one; the parts and the whole; the beginning and the end; the straight and the circular; something positioned within itself or positioned within something other; rest and motion; and similar opposites; so that in all cases he is indicating that the One Itself is not both of the opposites, for if it were it would be manifold and not the simple One; nor is it either of the two opposites, for if it were it could not create the other one and it would suffer opposition through not being simply absolute.

He is often happy, in company with our Proclus, to consider a little whether Plato's negation of shape with respect to the One had the same significance as when, in the *Phaedrus*, he denies it with respect to the supercelestial realm, that is, with respect to intelligible nature. For there he speaks of perceptible nature beneath heaven, or of living nature in the heights of heaven, of intellectual nature throughout the celestial realm, and of intelligible nature throughout the supercelestial realm.

How right he is to call nature unshaped. But when he there affirms many things of her, such as essence and intelligence and others, which here he denies with respect to the One, then, of course, he is saying that unshaped nature means something different from the unshaped One; but I reply, more with Plotinus than with Proclus, that the essence of the first mind, which is immediately intelligible to itself, does not yet have a shape, that is, a precise distinctiveness of Ideas which the power of the same intellectual mind conceives within itself, immediately turning itself back into its own substance.

The One itself has no shape means that within itself it has and will have no distinction made by the Ideas which differentiate the absolute qualities from each other; for if that were the case it would not be the simple One and it would now be bounded and confined within some Idea.

Again, *It does not have a straight shape within itself* shows that it undergoes no inner transition from this to that; that it depends upon nothing; and that it does not change direction.

Lastly, *It is not circular* points out that it does not, through a manifold intelligence, employ that reflection which the intellect employs to reflect upon itself and upon its cause. But Plotinus often speaks of this, and when Parmenides speaks of it directly in his poetical composition on the one being, or the intelligible world, he compares it to a sphere and he describes it by using the actual definition of a sphere; and he confirms this here in his second hypothesis, when he is going to talk about the same thing, namely, the one being; but in the first hypothesis he negates the circular and the straight with respect to the simple One Itself, as if these two were properties of the intelligible nature and the intellectual nature.

In any case, no one doubts that the circular examination of oneself or of one's cause is a property of intelligence, and that straightness, too, is a special property of intelligence, for straightness indicates a movement, not any kind of movement, but one that never inclines or veers, one, indeed, that is unwaveringly intent; and it is by such a movement that the intellect proceeds from the supreme Father. Again, life inwardly proceeds from its own essence, and intelligence from life; while power proceeds from nature, operation from power, and work eternal from operation.

Indeed, movement is the beginning of differentiation, for by means of movement the levels of creation are differentiated by their generating cause and by the extent to which they move towards the first levels of the universe, or towards the intermediate levels, or towards the lowest levels.

And so, in a straight movement of this kind, the intermediate precedes the two extremes. For if you go downwards the last is in front of you, and if you go upwards the highest is in front of you. But the turning movement which is denoted by the circle completes a union, for through it every single thing is united to itself inasmuch as it gathers individual things to its innermost centre; and all things are in turn gathered together; for all things, through some common longing for the good, move towards the Good itself and are in harmony with each other; and just as true uprightness is within the intellectual nature by means of an unvarying movement such as we have described, so the true circuit is within the same nature, not only because this nature turns chiefly towards itself and its cause, but also because all the things, apart from its centre, that are within it are, as if on the circumference, equally distant from the centre and turn equally towards it and, by means of it, turn equally towards the common centre and the common Good. But in all else no such equality is preserved.

Finally, within the simple One Itself we cannot trace any movement by which the One proceeds from a cause or by which something proceeds from something else; nor can we trace a turning movement through which it is turned towards its cause or towards another good, or through which its outermost elements turn towards the innermost, for if that were so it would not be the first of all and it would not be the simple One; but that the One Itself is the beginning of the universe is evident from the fact that nothing can be found anywhere that is better than unity and union; but if by any chance there were a cause higher than this, it would provide something better for things than union.

Chapter 62:
The One Itself is nowhere, because it is neither within itself nor within something else.
How discrete things are said to exist of themselves or to be produced from themselves

IN HIS poetical composition Parmenides affirmed that the one being abided within itself and around itself, whereas now he denies that the simple One Itself abides within itself or within anything else, granting it, in fact, no location for being. For it is not within a cause, since it is the cause of causes, and it is not within any of the things that follow, since it has no leaning towards them and no such semblance; for certainly no one can believe that that which is the First is within place or object or kind, or is like a part within the whole, or the whole within parts; and furthermore, that which is utterly simple is not within itself, in which there is not one and another, with one cleaving to another, or the parts residing within the whole, or the whole striving to enfold itself.

However, the one being, the first intellect, is everywhere. Firstly, it is within its cause, which is the Good itself, the begetter of intelligence. Secondly, it is within itself, where there is intelligence within life, and life within essence. Ideas consist in the very differentiation of intelligence. Thirdly, it is within whatever follows, carefully regulating every individual thing, wherever it may be, and distributing in all places forms which are to some extent similar to their model; but because it is nowhere really confined even in this function, it is equally present to all individual things everywhere.

Indeed, it is a property of the intellect itself that while it is within something else – its father – it nevertheless abides within itself, that is, it is turned back to itself through some perfect form of attention, and it is not encompassed or influenced by anything that follows; but that property of the intelligence to be within another and at the same time to dwell intellectually with itself does not belong to the simple One Itself, for it is fitting that the One Itself is nowhere.

This is demonstrated by ample analysis: for if it is somewhere, either it is within itself or it exists within something other; but since it is neither within itself nor within something other, it is therefore said to be nowhere. In the same way, when he demonstrates that the One is not in something other, because there would be many points all around where it would be touched by the other and where it in turn would touch, he seems to be denying merely that it is, as it were, in some place or container which would certainly be something light and in some measure common to all that is indivisible and incorporeal.

Yet it must be considered that Parmenides is here denying that the One is within something other, as if this were a property of the One; but it is not by any means within something other, since there are multifarious ways in which something can be within something else.

We shall therefore say, in company with Syrianus, that it is here denied that the One Itself is within something other, in the sense that is used in the second hypothesis, where it is affirmed that the one being is within something other, since the one being – that is, that first intelligible, or even the intellectual essence – is within something other, as though within its cause, that is, it is within the One Itself, the Good, which encompasses it as if by a sphere, being its beginning and its end, preserving the centre, and extending beyond the one being in all directions, both because it is more noble and because its scope of operation is wider and vaster. But the one touches the other at many points, as Parmenides says, that is, by means of many of its parts, powers, Ideas and acts it cleaves to That, and through number it strives to imitate its unique abundance as far as it can.

Now it is a property of this intelligible essence to be especially within the One, since it is as close as possible to the One and it cleaves to it uninterruptedly and unwaveringly. Another of its properties is, in fact, to be within itself and to enfold itself within itself by means of the reflection into itself of virtue, intelligence, and will, the most precise of all reflections.

In the same way, the most significant property of the One Itself is not to be within another in any way, and particularly as if it were within its cause; and it is not within itself through the agency of any self-understanding known to any intellect. If it were otherwise, there would be within it two disparate parts, or powers, or principles: at least there would be one principle to understand and a second principle to be understood. Such divergence, indeed such opposition, is totally alien to the very principle of the One. For nothing can tolerate simultaneously as opposites the same whole and a second whole.

Therefore, once one admits those things which I was talking of just now, it assuredly follows that a second other, and another belonging to it, contains itself through one principle and is contained through another principle; for because it moves of itself, although it does not do so by means of two parts, yet seeks through two different powers to be also within itself, not only is it said to be that intelligent substance on account of a measure of self-awareness, but by some principle it also brings itself forth to some extent; for just as some things are moved by something other, and some bodies, such as souls, are moved by themselves, so some things, such as bodies and all things corporeal, are brought forth only by something other.

Some things are not only from another but as soon as they come forth from it they exist as separate independent substances. To the extent, therefore, that they bring themselves forth and maintain themselves by their own power, to the same extent are they brought forth and maintained by themselves. Indeed, within all substances that are endowed with intelligence there are two powers: generative and transformative. By means of the generative and fertile power they develop within themselves a further form and life and action whereby they seem to generate and, as it were, to regenerate themselves. Moreover, they develop something similar into something other, when they seem to manifest themselves outwardly also. By means of the transformative power they turn back to themselves and to their cause, when they seem to transform themselves and to fashion themselves.

These intellectual substances, therefore, according to the followers of Plato, are said to be or to be brought forth from themselves and within themselves. Such a condition clearly does not strive for the One, in the presence of which, beside practical existence itself, there is no further power different from existence, as is the case within all other things, an existence which can be said to exist therefrom, or through which a further form or action is developed inwardly. Again, that in which no deviation or difference can be conceived has no need of any transformation.

Chapter 63:
How the One is said to neither move nor rest; and how movement and rest are in everything except the First

IN ONE of his poetical compositions Parmenides affirms both stillness and movement with respect to the one being, and he will make the same affirmation in the second hypothesis. In the first hypothesis, however, he denies both movement and stillness with respect to the simple One Itself. Indeed, in his first poem he says that the first being is single and motionless. Then he attributes to it an intelligence that is linked to the highest intelligible.

That intelligence cannot be motionless he adds in the poems that follow, where he seems to concede movement in addition to stillness, since intelligence resides in life, while life is a vigorous movement of essence, that is, an act emanating from essence, the beginning of all life and movement. Intelligence, however, is a living limit upon such movement and a reflectiveness which observes its own nature.

Therefore, inasmuch as intelligence resides in life and thus observes so many things, there seems to be a movement. But inasmuch as it acts as a limit, restraining the expansion of life and re-attaching it to its centre, stillness, too, is revealed.

In our *Theology* we have shown that in everything after the First there is a differentiation of these four: essence, being, power, and action. Here, therefore, essence seems to be drawn towards its own being, while power goes forth directly from it and moves instantly into action. The whole process can be seen as a movement in which stillness is considered in relation to being inasmuch as, while the things that are subsequent move forward, the initial things stand firm and finally come to rest in their own end.

But in relation to the One Itself, as we have said, it is wrong to attribute any power or action (other than simple existence) by means of which we can imagine a forward movement or conceive of a stillness which is opposed to such a movement. In fact, power, action, and movement have a cause that is distinct from the One, and so they should not be applied to the One, as if the One produced all things through them. It certainly does not create through movement; nor, as it happens, are all things subject to movement. Again, either it produces movement through movement, or we are obliged to locate movement in the One. Yet these three which have just been mentioned strive universally towards the Good, as if they were not the Good itself.

And so the Good Itself, the One Itself, creates and perfects all things, not through something else, but by its own unity and goodness. For if whatever is closer to the One and the Good is universally greater and produces things both greater and more numerous, it follows that all things are made purely by unity and goodness.

For the time being I make but passing mention of why Proclus eliminates action from the One: just as whatever is from being has being, so whatever is from the One necessarily has the One. Therefore matter which proceeds from the One is the One, yet it has no action within it, but it would have if it proceeded from the One by means of some action inherent in the One.

Furthermore, although Parmenides here seems to negate with respect to the One only those corporeal movements described as change and conveyance, it must be remembered that the task would be light and trivial if he removed only those movements from the One. But, in fact, with this description he has removed all movements, both incorporeal and corporeal; for he says that the former are the only movements and that the One is not moved by any movement. Indeed, a movement of change within the soul occurs when the soul, as if now changed, undergoes the emotion, the life, the form, and the action of things that are higher or of things that are lower. There is a direct, inward, rational movement from the higher to the lower, an outward change of place, and a quickening of the body.

There is also a circular movement within the soul when it observes itself or repeats the same things. But within pure minds change means being transformed by the intellectual power into something intelligible. There is a circular local movement related to themselves and to their cause, but perhaps they pursue a straight movement insofar as they contemplate one form by means of another.

The simple One Itself is therefore detached from all such movements. But when you hear the word 'change', understand not merely a change from one quality to another, but all change in addition to that of place: generation, corruption, increase, decrease, transference of qualities, and similar changes.

Finally, it is reasoned that whatever moves or changes or is conveyed, the One Itself neither changes nor is conveyed, and thus in no way moves. Firstly, he shows that the One does not change, and then he will show that it is not conveyed. For if it changes, either it is completely transformed or it changes in part. If it is completely transformed, either it changes into multiplicity that is devoid of the One, which cannot be, or it changes into nothing, in which case there will be within things nothing greater than the non-existent One. But if it changes in one of its parts, there will be two different things within it, one of which remains, while the other departs and something foreign is accepted; and so it is not the One, but a sort of multiplicity, and it changes according to its movement.

But we have admitted that the soul changes as it adjusts itself, now to one set of circumstances, now to another, in keeping with its emotional basis and its way of acting and living. We have agreed also that the intellect changes as it applies itself to the intelligible and is moulded by it and is further fashioned either by discerning an object or by applying itself to more intelligibles. In this way, therefore, both the soul and the intellect, while remaining what they are, become multiple, a situation abhorrent to contemplate with respect to the One.

He then shows that the One is not moved spatially in this way. Whatever moves spatially, as it were, either moves around the same point in a circle or goes from place to place in a straight line or, by a combination of straight and circular, moves obliquely. But the One cannot change in any way, either into a circle or into a straight line. In the same way, it cannot undergo any combined movement arising from these movements which are foreign to it, and thus it is not changed by any movement.

Chapter 64:
The One moves neither in a circle nor in a straight line

HE SHOWS that the One does not move in a circle because a centre is necessarily given to a circle and it has its extremes around its centre, and the centre remains within it when all else changes; and thus it has both parts and a whole.

Such things, however, cannot apply to the One on account of its absolute simplicity. Therefore it does not move in a circle. From the One he removes circular motion, both the corporeal circle and the incorporeal circle. Of course, its actual centre remains within the soul and the intellect, as does unity itself, together with their respective powers or substances, while the other parts and powers and actions ebb and flow and work in many different ways, which indeed seems to produce a circle that is totally alien to the simplicity of the One.

Furthermore, he demonstrates in the following way that the One does not move in a straight line. Anything that moves in a straight line goes from this place to that; either it is completely here and there at the same time, therefore, or it is completely neither here nor there, or part of it is here and another part is there.

If the first be granted, then it does not move but remains in both places simultaneously. If the second be granted, neither this place nor that seems to belong to it in any respect. If the third be granted, then it is divisible. Since the One is indivisible, it cannot therefore engage in such movement.

It has been shown earlier that the One does not exist within something, since such a condition is beneath the dignity of the One. But since being made within something, that is, recently touching something, or being conveyed by something, or being changed in some way is worse than being within something, so much less is it deemed applicable to the One.

Indeed, it can be said that something exists fully within a place and outside a place simultaneously, such as the mind and the intellectual soul. It is all the more absurd to say that the One, fully within all and at the same time fully outside all, comes into being through movement. Here I remind you once more to consider that, while he is removing from the One corporeal movements and parts, those that are incorporeal have been removed at the same time.

Since the soul, though divine, moves through multiple forms and intelligences by means of the supreme intelligible, turning in time and motion about the eternal, and passing, as it were, in a direct movement, now through this form and action of its own and now through that, attains that, yet it is not divided by time in the same way. In this straight progression, therefore, the soul is neither wholly within that intelligible nor wholly separate, but it is partly there while it is reaching that through its action and it is partly not there yet on account of other actions which are to be revealed later.

Even in the divine mind we can detect a movement which is, as it were, straight, and by means of which multifarious Ideas move out from their centre. Indeed, where part of the mind or of intelligence seems to exist within this Idea, and part within that Idea, although the whole essence is simultaneously within all things, such conditions, assigned not only to bodies but also to souls and minds, cannot be applied to the One.

In a word, all things in which power and action are distinguished in some way from essence seem to move to some extent, because power proceeds from essence, while action proceeds from power, but, as we have said earlier, in relation to the One Itself, on account of its supreme simplicity, these two cannot be imagined as distinct for any reason from essence, especially since, if you do so imagine, we shall ask whether the One Itself has produced its own power and action that come forth by virtue of another power and action, or rather by virtue of existence itself.

If you will perhaps grant the first, you will at once open the door to an infinite regression for all things. If you grant the second, you will place the One Itself with existence alone, keeping it far from subsequent power and action. But what you have imagined to be close to the Self in the form of power and action will not be the Self or anything that belongs to it, but a particular condition subordinate to the

Self. Indeed, the power of what you have imagined will be the very essence of the first being, but life and intelligence are the effective characteristics of the first essence.

Of course, the sure sign of the first principle is that around the Self there are, instead of power and action, substance and substantial action, to be made known directly after the Self. But to preclude the possibility of division and movement within the First, perhaps Aristotle, too, thought that it should be clearly called the final cause rather than the efficient cause.

Chapter 65:
How stillness is negated with respect to the One

WHEN HE is going to show once more that that One does not stay still, he puts forward anew a proposition that has been proved previously, asserting that the One does not dwell within anything. Therefore, if it does not dwell within anything, it follows that it cannot remain permanently within it, and therefore it cannot stay still; for staying still is usually defined as remaining permanently in the same place.

Perhaps everyone will grant that the One cannot be called moving or still, in case it be thus understood to be composite, for it is still and steady in stillness and mobile and moving in motion. But no one will think of preventing us from calling it stillness itself or movement itself. We, however, reject this view for a reason that has already been demonstrated: that the One transcends all opposites and all things which are in any way mutually opposed, so that opposites may be both created and also reconciled in the One, for they are joined by the power of the One, a power opposed to divided opposites.

For if it were both of the opposites, it would be a compound produced by the supreme reconciler of differences; but if it were one of the opposites it could not create the other opposite and all that pertains to it. Indeed, no one could possibly say that the worse of two opposites is the One itself, the beginning of all. But perhaps the better cannot be this either, for it will be considered to be in a class with its opposite, and its opposite will have no part in it; for an opposite, by its very nature, has no part in its opposite. Whatever, therefore, has no part in the One and the Good can in no way be the One or the Good.

In brief, stillness itself, however perfect, and movement itself, however effective, belong to a particular type and a limited perfection; for they are sundered from each other, and the perfection found in one is not found in the other. And so neither of them is absolutely perfect, and neither of them is the First. For the First, standing apart from every limited perfection as the simple principle of the Good, fully contains within itself the perfections of all things, just as it contains the single universal perfection that represents them all.

Chapter 66:
The five kinds of being; the three levels of negations; the ten predicates negated; a few words on the same and the different

THE FIVE kinds of being are dealt with in the *Sophist*, and we have dealt with them at some length in the *Philebus* and the *Timaeus* as well as in Plotinus. And so, for the present, we shall review them briefly, firstly remembering what we recalled earlier.

While Parmenides negates, with respect to the One, all kinds and characteristics of being, he is negating all being with respect to the One, in relation to which, after openly negating all the characteristics of being, he will finally negate essence; but while he is negating, with respect to the One, whatever pertains to being, as if such things are unworthy, he is placing the One above universal being.

I shall state once more that, just as the whole multitude of such things or of such beings is reduced to this single being, so all such beings particularly and all such things are eventually reduced to the one simple first being. This one being depends on the simple One Itself. For this reason, therefore, this one being simply is, and it selects its essence from the One. It exists by proceeding in this way, and from the One it obtains change and movement.

Again, by existing in this way it turns from the One and towards itself; and when it turns towards the One it obtains sameness and stillness. Indeed, through essence it is second, because the One exists first. Through difference it is distinct from the One, distinct within itself, and distinct from other things. Through movement, too, it moves forth from the One, it moves within itself, and it strives to move towards other things. Through sameness it is similar to the One, and it also harmonises with itself and with all other things. Finally, through stillness it does not move away from the One or from itself; it keeps a firm hold on its own characteristics and does not allow itself to be adulterated by things outside itself.

For the moment I make but passing mention of the way essence, being dependent on the One, is not the One and yet is the One. Because it is not the One its lot is boundlessness; but because it is also the One it acquires a limit. Its boundlessness is related particularly to life, its limit particularly to intellect. Again, through its boundlessness especially it possesses movement and difference, while through its limit especially it possesses stillness and sameness. We really deal more fully with these matters in the *Philebus* and the *Sophist*.

After the five kinds of things, which are within the First on account of their intrinsic worth and within all that follows on account of their individual nature, multifarious Ideas suddenly appear within the First, and many forms manifest in what follows.

But before we examine how Parmenides, after negating stillness and movement with respect to the One, negates sameness and difference, it will perhaps be worthwhile reviewing the threefold nature of negations, as carefully noted by Proclus.

Some things, of course, are negated with respect to the One according to the degree of internal harmony that it has in relation to itself, and this, according to Parmenides, is the first level of negation. Others are negated according to the degree of harmony that it has with itself and also with other things: this is the second level. Lastly, yet others are negated according to the degree to which it considers other things only: this is the third level.

For he denies that multiplicity and the whole and form are within anything, and he negates movement and stillness with respect to the One insofar as the One is directly concerned. But from the One, in relation to itself and also to other things, he removes the same and the different, the similar and the dissimilar, the equal and the unequal, the older and the younger. For it is the same neither to itself nor to other things, and this is also true of the other items that follow in this list.

Finally, from the One in its relation to other things he removes the conceivable, the knowable, and the nameable; for in this state it is quite unknown to all things.

Therefore, since movement and stillness belong particularly to the first level, while the same and the different belong more to the second, he has, of course, negated movement and stillness before negating the same and the different; especially because he has made it clear that the first being, on account of its movement, is different from the First and different again within itself; but on account of its resting within the One he has revealed its sameness. This is why the latter are prior to the former.

Observe, meanwhile, how he negates predicates with regard to the One, for while he is negating the same and the different he is removing substance from the One; while he is negating the similar and the dissimilar he is removing quality; and while he is negating the equal and the unequal he is removing quantity. Whenever he removes the older and the younger he has taken away occurrence and action, together with movement; and he took away place when he denied that the One was within anything; and he also removed custom and relationship everywhere when he showed that it possessed nothing since it harmonised with nothing.

But in addition to the ten predicates he also removes the transcendent being with which at least those five kinds universally harmonise, though clearly this is only if the One be negated. Many think that the ten predicates are inferior to the intelligibles, especially the first intelligibles, and that that substance which is defined as comprising mutual opposites is not within them; and much less will there be type and kind, since they are of less substance than the substance defined earlier; least of all will there be accidentals, since they are more tenuous than types and kinds.

It is therefore in no way strange that the predicates are negated with respect to the First if they are generally negated with respect to all divine things. Nor is it greatly to be wondered at that the ideal types are negated with respect to the First, for they are lower than the intellectual and intelligible unity. Firstly, therefore, the first and most extensive kinds of being, which are prior to Ideas and belong to the vital essence, are negated with respect to the First.

I mention briefly what Proclus adds: that the individual orders of the gods are in this way negated with respect to the First, which excels all.

Finally, Parmenides, in his poetical composition, expressly affirms the same and the different with respect to the one first being, and he will make the same affirmation in the second hypothesis. In this first hypothesis, however, he negates them with respect to the One, declaring at the same time that above the one being there exists the simple One.

Chapter 67:
The One is neither different from itself nor the same as the different, but is completely free of all conditions

HE DRAWS four conclusions concerning the same and the different, but since a start needs to be made from the ones that are more obvious, he denies with respect to the One that it is different from itself or the same as others – these being the more obvious negations – before he denies that it is the same as itself or different from others, these two being more difficult to prove.

Moreover, since difference is more alien to the One than is sameness, he first reasons that the One is not different from itself, an argument that is quite easy to accept, before he reasons that the One is not the same as others.

The first proof is as follows: If the One were different from itself, it would be different and divergent from the One Itself and would therefore not be the One Itself.

This is the shape of the second proof: If the One were the same as the different, it would be the different and would therefore no longer be the One Itself but the different, something other than the One and in addition to the One.

But understand here that the One Itself has no identity or communion with other things, for if it is true that the higher the cause the more distant it is from the characteristic conditions of its effects, surely the highest Cause of causes stands completely aloof from all the characteristics of all beings. Thus it accords with nothing in type, kind, or order.

If this were not the case, not only would it be something which exists but it would also be a partaker of type, kind, and order; and it would no longer be the simple One. Surely something that partakes is not only that of which it partakes but is something other as well; for otherwise it would not partake of it but would simply exist as itself. Thus the One Itself partakes of nothing, lest it cease to be simply the One.

Indeed, things that are lower than it do not partake of it, being quite unworthy of its sublimity, while nothing higher can partake, for what is higher than the One? In fact, the higher we rise through the levels of creation, moving step by step to a higher cause and then to one even higher, the closer we come to the One and to the increasingly simple. And so the simple One Itself is above all.

Again, it should not be imagined that the real One Itself is double: this and that. If that were the case, how would the One differ from either of the others? It would be necessary, however, for them to be distinguished if there were two. Thus *this* would be distinguished from *that* through some characteristic which *this* possessed in addition to the One Itself, while *that*, likewise, possessed its own particular characteristic; each would therefore be a mixture, something both multiple and single, and so neither would be simply the One.

Since, therefore, the One Itself is sole, single, and alone, if it were imagined to be the same as something different it would, of course, become the same as something which is not really the One; if the One Itself were imagined to be the same as this and to harmonise with it to some extent, it would be subject to the general ordering and it would become, with this, a partaker of the general nature. It would no longer be simple and absolute.

If, however, it became the same as this, if, that is, it arose directly as this itself, then that which he previously asserted to be the simple One would be wholly this which he later declared not to be the true and simple One.

Indeed, since all other things are classified by type, kind, and order, they can be related to sameness in such a way that they each have the power to be that sameness to a certain extent, yet, though of the same type, they are neither inwardly the same, as Socrates and Plato say, nor absolutely the same; and this is how it is for all other things. But if the One Itself, which stands aloof from all fellowship, were also imagined to be the same as anything else, yet cannot be imagined to be the same through any external condition or fellowship, it would now necessarily be inwardly identical to this nature through its own uniqueness.

Chapter 68:
The One is not different
from other things

ANYONE might think that it is an easy matter for the One to be different from other things and identical to itself, for the general view seems to have been accepted that the characteristic of the One is to be outwardly distinct from others but inwardly indistinguishable from itself.

Parmenides, however, after weighing these matters rather carefully, deems that neither the different nor the same should be predicated of the One, whether you take the different as something different in form or as something partaking of difference, and likewise whether you take the same as sameness or as something partaking of sameness. But since sameness seems to relate more closely to the One than does difference, he proves, starting with the easier proposition, that the One is not different from other things, before showing that the One is not the same as itself, though both these views are beyond the common range of conception.

Remember first of all that what is different from other things is different either because of a difference of which it partakes or because of itself, inasmuch as it is difference; and remember in the second place that the principle of the One is different from the principle of difference. For the One is absolute, while difference refers to something other. Moreover, it is a characteristic of the One to unite, but of difference to divide. For this reason difference is not only different from something other but is actually alien to it.

If, therefore, the One were said to be different from other things, although it is not different through the fact of its being One, perhaps it would be deemed to be different through partaking of some difference, and therefore, admitting a difference alien to itself, it would no longer be the simple One. Nor again could the One rightly be said to be different from other things, as difference itself. For difference is different from itself, but the One is not different from itself, for the One cannot by any means be made different, since the principle of the One is different from, and alien to, the principle of difference. But when we say that the principle of the One Itself is alien to difference and quite aloof from the kinds of being and from universal being, we are in danger of admitting that the One is different from all these.

But remember that difference is rightly described as a divisive factor implanted within beings and directly opposed to the sameness brought about through unification. God forbid, therefore, that through a factor allotted to beings and allied to opposition we should grant that the One Itself, the source of all beings, be separate from being. For when we say 'separate', we are considering the ineffably supreme in its incomparable simplicity.

For there is one way – that of place – whereby body is separate from body. There is another way – that of separable substance – whereby soul is separate from body. There is a third way – that of essence itself, or at least of the formal difference in principle – whereby intellect is separate from soul, intellects are different one from another, and Ideas are different one from another. And there is also a way – that of the utterly simple pre-eminence that pertains to the One and is unmatched by anything else – whereby the One Itself is separate.

Difference, therefore, may be admitted with respect to beings; but with respect to that which exists above being, or with respect to nothing, it should not even be mentioned. For who could rightly say that nothing is different from being, as if it were something additional to being? In the same way, no one could rightly say that the One Itself, which is higher than being, is separate from being on account of difference, which is a condition of being.

Chapter 69:
The One is not the same as itself

THE PRINCIPLE of the One is different from the principle of sameness; for the One is absolute, while sameness is relative. For there is always something that is the same as something else, and for this reason the One, being absolute, has no sameness, which is relative.

Moreover, if you have one wax tablet here and four wax tablets there, and you wish this one tablet to be made the same in number as those four, you will divide it into four. Thus, by means of division and number, this will become the same as those. If you further wish the original four tablets to differ in number from these tablets, you will make them become a single tablet. And so in this way difference occurs through unification, just as sameness was produced a moment ago through division.

The conclusion from this, which I have proposed, is that the principle of unity and the principle of sameness differ one from the other. If this is so, the One Itself cannot be the same as itself, for if it were it would partake of sameness (which would allow it to be the same as itself) and by admitting an alien nature it would cease to be the simple One; or it would perhaps be sameness itself in order to be the same as itself by its very nature.

However, it cannot be sameness, since there is understood to be one principle for *this* and a different principle for *that*. Further confirmation is given by the fact that sameness has a connection with difference and number; for sameness consists in at least three items, because of necessity it requires that *this* is the same as *that* and is the same in a particular state. But the One Itself cannot be subject to any such connection.

Proclus objects that Parmenides held that one multiplicity was made equal to, or equivalent to, rather than the same as, another multiplicity. Parmenides replies that in this way reference is made to essential number rather than to accidental number. Therefore, when number reaches outwardly the things which are numbered, equality or inequality may rightly be spoken of, but when number is essential and innermost, sameness may be spoken of, since sameness is a kind of communion in nature.

Finally, each single order of subsequent things brings something new with it, something inferior, in addition to what was in the previous order. The region beneath the moon brings change in substance to the motion of the heavenly bodies, a motion which of itself does not change the substance. The heavens add a localised orbit to the living non-localised movement of the celestial soul. The soul adds temporal discursiveness to the unmoving intelligence. The intellect brings the yearning for intelligence to the being which of itself has not yet striven to obtain intelligence. Lastly, this intelligence, in addition to the other kinds and opposites which were not in the First, undergoes difference with sameness, restores its unity by means of sameness, and by difference manifests its pre-eminence with full power.

Chapter 70:
The One is neither similar nor dissimilar
to itself or to anything

AFTER HE has negated, with respect to the One, which is higher than all, the sameness and difference which belong to that intelligible essence, he proceeds to negate the following pair: similarity and dissimilarity.

Now similarity follows sameness, and dissimilarity follows difference, and they are less significant. After these he will negate equality and inequality: the first is put after similarity, and the second after dissimilarity. The first two relate to the formative powers of the intelligible essence, and the second two seem related to the actions, measures and modes of those powers.

But now, in the intelligible world, where the powers are diversified and multiple modes can somehow be found, similarity and dissimilarity, equality and inequality, being universal, need to be distributed to all that follow, according to the individual capacity of each. These soon manifest in their own intelligence as Ideas: ideal similarity, and so on. But in the One Itself they cannot be distinguished in form as kinds, even the most widespread kinds, or as Ideas.

Now Parmenides will formulate four propositions on this matter: the One is not similar to itself; the One is not similar to another; the One is not dissimilar to itself; the One is not dissimilar to any other.

That the One is not similar to itself or to others he proves in the following way. Whatever is similar to something necessarily partakes of some sameness, but the One cannot partake of sameness, and therefore it is not similar to anything, either itself or another. Indeed, the One Itself is the cause of sameness, while sameness is the source of similarity and, in fact, of equality itself. For those things are said to be equal which are in a certain manner the same in quantity; while those things are said to be similar which concur in the same quality, that is, which have attained the same type of quality. But the One, as has been proved above, does not participate in sameness. Since sameness is by nature different from the One, it is therefore manifold; for this reason, if the One admits of sameness it will become multiple and will cease to be the simple One.

He shows subsequently that the One is not dissimilar to itself or to other things, and he reasons briefly as follows. Just as similarity depends on sameness, so dissimilarity depends on difference. For those things are called dissimilar which exist in different kinds of quality. Therefore, since the One Itself cannot admit of any difference (as we have said above) in case it ceases, by upholding the alien and the multiple, to be the One, it certainly cannot be dissimilar.

However, if anyone says that other things are dissimilar to the One or similar to the One, he will not be speaking at all correctly, since the One cannot, along with other things, be related to the Idea or genus of similarity or dissimilarity. But he will have the correct view only if he deems that other things are dissimilar to the One since they have nothing in common with it, or that they are also similar to the One since they each have a common one received from the One.

Those, I say, who partake of a principle which bestows unity are carried hither and thither by a common desire. On the other hand, however, that One must not be called similar to other things, because it cannot partake of similarity or sameness.

The fact is that images are described as similar to their original, but the reverse is not true. Now just as the ideal original is related to its own sequence of forms which stretches out from it through many levels, in exactly the same way the One Itself, the Good Itself, seems to be related to all the levels of beings, inasmuch as they partake of the One and the Good.

Indeed, on account of this comparison Plato, in the *Republic*, called the one principle of the universe the Idea of the Good, not because it is a type or Idea, for it is much higher and much more extensive, but because, as we have said, any Idea, in its development, imitates to some extent the universal development of all things from the Good itself.

Chapter 71:
The One is neither equal nor unequal to itself or to others

IN THE intelligible world beyond limit and limitlessness, which we have expounded elsewhere, they posit sameness on account of the essence of all forms, which is one and always the same; but they also posit difference there, on account of the multifarious Ideas; as well as similarity, because they are similar and always maintain the same appearance; and dissimilarity, because they differ among themselves in principle and they therefore make things dissimilar.

They also posit equality there, because the way of virtue and action is always equal and because, by the equality of proportion, they equalise all individual things one with another. Finally, they posit inequality there, because the parts, the powers, and the Ideas are not absolutely equal; for there are formative levels, and they do not make things that are equal. There the levels of kinds and Ideas are said to be commensurate with each other, but are not considered to be similarly commensurate in relation to the essential intelligible unity.

Yet we cannot posit such variety within the one author of the one intelligible world, where, if there is neither limit nor limitlessness, it follows that there cannot be those things subsequent to limit, such as the same, the similar, and the equal, or those things related to limitlessness, such as the other, the dissimilar, and the unequal.

Parmenides, therefore, after negating, with respect to the One, the same and the similar, the other and the dissimilar, as if they were sources, goes on to negate the equal with the unequal which depends upon it; and he intends the four propositions, as stated above, to be understood: the One is not equal to itself; the One is not equal to others; the One is not unequal to itself; the One is not unequal to others. But in all his words, as we have remarked elsewhere, when he speaks of sensory phenomena he is also negating, with respect to the One, all vital, intellectual, and intelligible phenomena.

When, therefore, you hear the equal and the unequal spoken of as if they were at the physical level, understand that incorporeal equality and inequality are being negated. In relation to this he says that those things are equal which measure the same, as when a foot measure equals this foot and that foot; but he says that things are unequal when some have the same measure and others have different measures. Indeed, a two-foot length of wood is unequal to a one-foot length, but is commensurable with it because they have a common measure; for a foot measure which measures less than this wood, when applied once, measures more than it when applied twice. But the length is not considered commensurable in the same way to the width; for the width is not a definite measure which, when repeated a certain number of times, is judged by one thing to equal another. But it is simply that this is said to have a greater measure and this a smaller measure.

The reasoning, therefore, is as follows: What is equal to something has the same measure as it, and for this reason it also partakes of sameness; and so, since the One cannot partake of sameness it does not have the same measure and it is certainly not equal to itself or to others.

The power of sameness is very widespread, for we speak of the same type, the same kind, the same order, the same time, the same quality, the same quantity, the same place, the same measure, and, in brief, the same 'everything'.

But things are compared as being equal in type, for who would say that a line is equal to a surface, that a surface is equal to a solid, that change is equal to augmentation or to localised movement? But we say instead that a line is equal or unequal to another line, and we speak of all the other things in the same way.

Therefore, since sameness and difference have been negated, with respect to the One, as being very extensive, it follows that equality and inequality, being less extensive than they are and being dependent upon them, are also negated. If, however, the One Itself cannot be compared to the manifold things emanating from it, how can it be equal to them, or even unequal by virtue of its contrasting inequality? But it has no need of equality, whose principle is different from it, and by virtue of which it may be equal to itself, for the One Itself is better and nobler than equality.

Nor do we name it the One as if it were some quantity or belonged to unbroken quantity or to number, or as if it were some unity having beginning or number or some likeness with them, conditions which would at least enable it to be called equal or unequal; but in the name of the One Itself we proclaim unique simplicity, which is totally indivisible, supremely pre-eminent and unparalleled, the cause of unity in everything, and, in brief, the author of unification. For whatever exists is either a unity or consists of unities.

However, all things receive this gift only from the simple One Itself, but they have received all other qualifications, which are more detailed and come later, from other causes, too.

Chapter 72:
Confirmation of the above

THE PRINCIPLE of equality is different from the principle of the One, for the One is absolute, while equality is relative, since equal is related to equal. Moreover, the nature of the One strictly excludes multiplicity, but the nature of equality includes at least three: for this is equal to this or to that.

Again, by bringing forth the unity in some places the One renders unequal what was previously equal, while in other places, with the addition of unity, it renders equal what was previously unequal. Thus it appears that the One Itself is above equality and inequality and begets both equally.

In this discussion we have passed over the point that, if the principle of equality differs from the One, the principle of inequality certainly differs from the One. Since, therefore, the nature of equality is something other than the Good itself, the One would adopt an alien nature and would not be the simple One if it were in any way equal to itself or to another; for whatever you added to the One would immediately remove simplicity and you would be taking away the simple One Itself and you would render the One something multiple. If, however, you said that the One was unequal to itself or to others, it would likewise cease to be the One, for it would become unequal through inequality, which is something other than it.

Indeed, something that is unequal has more measures if it is larger and fewer measures if it is smaller, but in both cases, so to speak, it is measured by a canon which is appropriate to it and which touches with its parts the parts and details of what is being measured. For this reason, if the One could be measured it would already have a number of parts and would thus no longer be the simple One.

Nor should we imagine that the One is the measure of itself, by means of which it is equal to itself, for if that were the case the One would have two principles, indeed, two opposing principles: the principle of that which is measuring and the principle of that which is measured; and also, in fact, the very principle of measure, which is also different from the principle of the One; and it would no longer be the simple One.

But who would say that the first cause is equal to created things?

For the first cause, on account of its unparalleled simplicity, pre-eminence and power, admits of no connection with created things. If this were otherwise, it would not, on account of such a connection, be fully absolute.

Again, who would say that the first cause is unequal through an inequality which is in turn opposed to equality and which centres on the same subject? If that were so, it would by no means avoid all dealings with created things; in fact, it would experience the better of the two opposites but be consigned to the first one. How, therefore, could it be the measure of created things? This is what we learn from the *Philebus*, *Theaetetus* and the *Laws*.

It would certainly not be a measure applied to the things that are measured; if that were the case, it would not be absolute. Nor, again, would it be the internal measure of things in the way that unity is the internal measure of numbers; if that were the case, a part of the multifarious nature of creation would be less perfect than the whole, and some one would have been united with all other things, any one of which, through its assumed difference, would be a particular one. If this is an impossible situation, then the One Itself could not be a particular ideal type within the intelligible world, for then it would be deprived of the particular perfections of all the other types.

Nor could it be that whole world, for, as is demonstrated in the *Sophist*, if it were a particular whole it would be multiple and a partaker of the One rather than the One Itself.

Let it therefore be the measure of things inasmuch as it allots to the individual things and to the levels of creation produced from itself their respective ways of being and of well-being; while individual things, for their part, turn and approach it according to the extent to which they have moved away from it.

But it should not be thought that Parmenides is making such great efforts simply in order to negate with respect to the One something patently alien to it: the equality of quantity. For he further negates equality with things, for the sake of simplicity, virtue and excellence, and he negates inequality likewise. For comparisons of this kind tend to be made rightly between *this* and *that* when they concur in one particular which can be perceived in both parties equally, or more so in one and less in the other. But within the One and things there is simultaneously nothing which would allow such a comparison to be made, for if this were not so the One would be multiple and susceptible to combination.

And those men are not to be granted audience who attribute to the One Itself those characteristics that are proper to things, calling it at the highest level 'most stable' or 'fastest' or 'most equal'. For the foundations on which these superlatives are built – stillness, movement, and equality – are not applicable to the One, since how can superlatives match it? It is therefore far higher than all superlatives.

Chapter 73:
In relation to itself and to other things, the One cannot be younger or older or of the same age

IT IS right to consider that there are three ways in which something can partake of time and of movement. For either it changes through action and substance in the flow of time, as does the body; or it changes through action alone, as does the soul; or it changes through some process and original nature, as does the intellect.

Parmenides proclaims that the One Itself is free of all these conditions of time and movement, and he asserts that the One is the beginning and end of everything which is circumscribed by movement and time. For from the beginning we have said that it should be noted in all the negations that whatever is negated with respect to the One should be clearly understood to have proceeded from the One, as from that which is beyond all comparison.

But Parmenides first examines the properties of all those things to which time is in some way relevant. There are three such properties: being of the same age, being younger, being older, in relation to other things or in relation to themselves.

Now he proves that the One Itself stands aloof from these properties, for he also separates from all participation in time and movement those things which can be imagined within the supreme intellect. But it would not have been worth while proving that the One is free from movement and time at the physical and even animate levels, for all intellects are free of these.

Within any intellectual substance, in accordance with their origin and order, essence is before life, life is before intellect, intellect before power, and power before operation. Therefore intellect, by virtue of those things that are prior to it, is older than itself, and by virtue of those subsequent to it it is younger than itself and also of the same age as itself.

For those things which properly pertain to essence have been conjoined to each other through their comparable origin, and the same is true of those things which pertain to life, and true of all those that follow. The intellect, moveover, is younger than the intelligible but older than the soul. But most intellects are of an age, and the same is true of the multitude of souls.

In a similar way, Ideas which are more universal are older than those which are more particular; the most particular are of an age, and each one is the same age as the members of its own class. Furthermore, within the divine and blessed souls which enjoy the intelligible world there are certain revolutions moving through types that become ever more inward.

In this way there arise the younger age, the older one, and that which is the same, for those that prompt more universal revolutions are older than the souls which seek to put one of the more universal revolutions on a par with many revolutions that are particular. They are of the same age if they produce the same revolutions; they are older if they move through forms that are more universal; and they are younger if they move through forms that are less universal. But they are the same age as themselves whenever they resume all comparable forms, or the numbers of such movements and times, whether they pertain to divine souls or to intellects and intelligible things.

Indeed, in the second hypothesis they will be affirmed with respect to the one being to which are inclined all substances that are in any way divine and intellectual. But in the first hypothesis they are negated with respect to the simple One Itself. Now the reasoning is as follows: Whatever is of the same age assumes equality and similarity of time; whatever is younger or older is subject to inequality and dissimilarity in time; but it has been demonstrated earlier that the One Itself is beyond all equality and similarity and their opposites and is not, therefore, of the same age as itself or other things; nor is it younger or older.

This reasoning, too, like the others, proceeds by means of the more universal, for the more universal is simply equal or similar or simply unequal and dissimilar, rather than being so in relation to time. However, he links similarity with equality in order to make comparisons of age, not between a man and a dog, but between a man and a man, between a dog and a dog, that is, between beings of the same type.

Chapter 74:
The One Itself is above eternity and time and movement. It cannot, on any basis, be said to be within time

THAT THE One Itself is above eternity was demonstrated when it was reasoned that it was above stillness and abided in nothing. But eternity is stillness within the same and is a measure inherent in things which are eternal and constant. Therefore it was asserted all the more strongly at that point that the One Itself is above the eternal and the constant; and that it is also above time, although this is more properly declared when the One Itself is shown to be above movement and change, the necessary concomitants of time.

The One Itself, therefore, is not time, in which movement and change necessarily take place; for if the One Itself were time or movement it would create only things that change; whereas a superior cause would produce things that are better than those subject to change. But who would say that the principle of the universe is movement, which is by nature imperfect and inconsistent? For to move is to proceed towards something by going forwards, since movement, which by its very nature does not embrace stillness or limit (these being its opposites), wanders and strays about of itself; it is still not absolute, though it is unlimited, having a kind of limitlessness that is derived from outside itself.

In short, if the One Itself is not movement or time, much less can it be subject to movement and time. In the same way he demonstrates that the One is not within time. This is his proof: That which is within time is older than itself; but since *older* implies *younger*, while it is older than itself it is also younger than itself. But these conclusions cannot apply to the One Itself, as has been shown earlier, and so it is not within time.

The setting forth of this considerably more difficult reasoning admits of three explanations, that is, in that part where he proposes that it is made younger at the time that it is made older.

The first explanation is that it does not pertain to age as such, but rather to a relationship of one age to another. For that which becomes older in time counts as older in relation to its previous self, which is younger; and the converse is also true.

The second explanation is this: Someone born ten years ago is older than nine, and in relation to his ten years he was younger when he was nine, but at the same time when he was nine he was older than when he was eight; and this is true of any year or month or hour or moment, for in any of these he is simultaneously related to himself as older and younger, according to whether one is looking forwards or backwards.

The third explanation is that of Syrianus. It is related to the periods of the divine souls, where a movement which is almost straight seeks an end that is other than the beginning within its own time, which is likewise consequent upon the movement.

Indeed, the beginning is one thing, and the end is another; and so the man who precedes something cannot become simultaneously older and younger than himself except by virtue of the relationship which we have just described. But in a continuous circular movement, which is appropriate for souls which are, properly speaking, divine, and then, on the principle of transference, is appropriate for celestial minds, too, every moment is equally the beginning and the end.

Therefore that which moves at any moment becomes simultaneously older than itself and younger than itself: older, inasmuch as that moment which it has reached through its movement stands as the end and limit in relation to the preceding movement; and younger, inasmuch as that same moment stands as the beginning in relation to the subsequent movement of a continuing series. Therefore, divine souls are, at any moment, older than themselves and simultaneously younger than themselves.

It is also permissible to conjecture a somewhat similar state of affairs for the period of life within the circular movement and course of the lofty intellect, provided that what moves through the stream of time within the soul and the body by means of a beginning and a progression is immediately fulfilled by it within minds.

It is wrong, however, to fabricate any such thing within the simple One Itself.

Chapter 75:
A rule for relatives, with some confirmation of what has gone before

IN THE meantime he transmits a rule for those things which, under different names, are opposed to each other as relatives, in the way that younger is related to older, father to son, and servant to master.

Of course, whenever there is a mutual relationship between such people, the condition by which one of the two is accepted requires the other to be accepted too, provided that this opposition is one of true relationship. Thus the reason why the servant now serves is to be related to the reason why the master now rules. Again, the servant who formerly served is to be related to the master who ruled over him at that time. And again, the man who is one day going to serve will be related to the man who is going to rule at that time.

When someone becomes the servant of someone else, the latter at once becomes his master: as long as he is the servant of someone, that person is his master; and the converse is also true. Yet it is not right to relate a future servant to a past master, and someone who will soon be a servant is not to be related to a man who is currently a master.

We think that similar statements can be made with regard to junior and senior.

Chapter 76:
Since the One is above time, it transcends the conditions of time and of things temporal

AFTER HE has denied that the One Itself is within time – both real time and figurative time – he denies as a consequence that the One has the necessary conditions of temporal things, however these conditions are assumed: whether really or figuratively.

Time, which is dependent on eternity, possesses mostly its own nature, but also something of eternity. Therefore, inasmuch as it has acquired some image of eternity we normally speak within time and the temporal realm of 'is', 'was', 'has been', 'will be', and 'will have been'. For these simple words are, and they relate to some present: one that is now present, or one that has existed, or one that will exist.

On the other hand, inasmuch as time falls away from eternity, we normally speak within time and the temporal realm of 'becomes', 'was becoming', 'has become', 'had become', 'will become' and 'will have become'. For these words convey above all the sense of a simple existing flow and creative process.

None of these can affect the One Itself, which transcends time. This is clear for all the words which have just been given, except for the word 'is', which indicates the living present and about which some will perhaps entertain a doubt, thinking that it unites this present with itself. However, since this present is nothing but the fleeting moment between past and future, and it relates to time exactly as does the mid-point to a line, it cannot accord with the One Itself, which transcends even eternity.

It is in this sense that the prophetic utterance 'He who is, who was, and who is to come is the Almighty' should be expounded; and we have given a full exposition in our commentaries on Dionysius. For through these words almighty God is proclaimed as the Creator of all the things which are, which have been, and which will be. These words, therefore, which seem to be temporal names, do not declare the temporal form within God, but affirm His causal power and His authority over all the aspects of time and over all things temporal.

Chapter 77:
The One Itself does not partake of essence; it is neither essence itself nor being itself, but is far higher

THEN PARMENIDES asks whether there are ways of partaking of essence other than those which have been mentioned. The reply given to him is that there are no other ways, and he approves of this reply.

Therefore, since you know of a certainty that Parmenides placed the eternal above the temporal and stationed true essence within the eternal, while it was within the temporal that he allocated false essence, which he considers to be produced and not to be, take care not to imagine that in his question and his approval of the reply he is introducing only the participations of essence that are within the three divisions of time: the past, the present, the future. For beyond these participations, which are held to be false in the writings of those who follow Plato and Pythagoras, are the eternal participations, the true essences. That question, therefore, should be seen as the epilogue to the whole of the first hypothesis.

Indeed, since he has expounded step by step all the kinds and properties of being, in which there are the various ways of partaking in essence, and since with his negation of kinds he has already negated all such ways with respect to the One, he rightly denies, in this summary of a universal question, that the One itself partakes of essence.

However, if anyone persists in maintaining that this investigation relates to the divisions of time that have just been mentioned, he should remember that, just as movement and change are declared to be within even the primal being, so time, too, in its own way, is located within a starting-point, as we have said, on account of its movement from this to that, earlier and later, and its sequential development; and these things are negated with respect to the One. But let us now move on to what remains.

As we have said earlier, we should always begin with the obvious. And so he was right to first deny multiplicity to the One, and to do so beyond all controversy. But finally, and by many means, he also negated essence, it being closely related to the One and most difficult to distinguish from it.

In the second hypothesis, on the other hand, he will affirm that essence in particular has the most obvious relationship with the One Itself. Parmenides here above all seems to take being [*ens*] as concrete, essence as abstract, and being [*esse*] as the innermost activity of being [*ens*] through the agency of essence. For just as living [*vivens*] has living [*vivere*] through the agency of life, so being [*ens*] has formative being [*esse*] through the agency of essence.

Therefore, since he has denied that the One partakes of essence in any way, he consequently negates all being [*ens* and *esse*] with respect to the One; the whole of being [*ens*], I say: not just the temporal, but the eternal as well. For he says that essence is in no way a partaker and that being [*esse*] is in no way a partaker.

There may be some who will grant that the One does not partake of essence, and on this basis they will negate being [*ens* and *esse*] with respect to the One; but they may doubt whether the One Itself, simple essence itself, actually exists: not whether there is something called being, but what essence itself is. This is why Parmenides expressly demonstrated that the One in no way is. This is so true that the One is not One, that is, is not one with essence, and has no cause or nature other than its own; for just as life accompanied by intellect is not simply life but a kind of life, so being, when accompanied by life, is not simply being but is a kind of being, that is, it is accompanied by something different which enables it to be alive. In the same way, when the One is accompanied by essence it is not simply the One, but a kind of One accompanied by this difference by which it has been taken up.

We have often said that the principle of essence and the principle of the One itself are different, for essence as such does not directly preclude multiplicity and does not introduce separation. But the One, simply as the One, transcends all multiplicity and is detached from everything; and for this reason, if you were to apply the One to essence, you would take nothing away from essence, whereby it would be less than essence and less than perfect, but you would perfect it.

On the other hand, if you were to apply essence to the One, as we have said, you would completely remove the absolutely simple pre-eminence that is characteristic of the One Itself. This essence does not benefit the One, being inferior to it; but the fact is that the One perfects essence, being its cause and end.

The One, indeed, cannot partake of essence, for if that were the case it would no longer be the simple One. But all essence, even the first essence, necessarily partakes of the One. For just as the first essence is wholly essence and is wholly one, so above the one which has been made a partaker of essence there is the indivisible One, which is above essence.

This is what Speusippus, Plato's nephew, expressed in clear words, as is witnessed by Proclus, who adds that Speusippus confirmed this from the view of the ancients when he said that they deemed the One to be better than being and that the principle of being was absolutely unconditioned in relation to all that follows, just as the Good itself is absolutely aloof from the condition of something that is good. However, Speusippus there names the first being as the proper beginning of beings, the unending divinity dependent on the higher One.

What more? Why do we seek the evidence of Speusippus, since in the second hypothesis the One is most clearly distinguished from being and is proved to be so when essence is applied to the One and is said to be multiple and to unexpectedly partake of combination, which obliges us to posit the simple One Itself above the one being?

Finally, we must not call the simple One Itself being [*ens*], which is relatively concrete; and we must not call it essence, which is related to being [*esse*] as if it were some power, such as an activity; and we must not call it being [*esse*], which is within essence, as the activity of essence; and we must not call it some being [*esse*], on the grounds that being is not within essence; for it is not lawful to separate shining from light, knowing from wisdom, living from life, being from essence. However, if you have separated the being [*esse*], you will be left with the One Itself rather than the being [*esse*].

Moreover, since being [*ens*] is one thing, and the One, being simpler and more universal, is another, we have inquired elsewhere whether these two, in the final analysis, are to be considered equal or whether one is higher than the other. If they are equal, it follows that there are two principles of creation, and this conclusion we have refuted in the *Theology*.

The next question is whether they are united or quite separate. If they are united and intermingled, there will be something higher which is the cause of them both and the cause of the intermingling, as is demonstrated in the *Philebus*. If they are separate, this separateness will be totally within a condition of unity. And so, either there will be nothing or there will be an infinite multiplicity where the whole will not be the One and where no part or particle anywhere will be a particular one.

On the other hand, if one of the two is higher than the other it is not lawful to put being before the One; for if that were the case it would not partake of the One, and so it would be either nothing or an infinite number, and the One, being subject to being, would partake of being and would no longer be the simple One.

This is why we must be no longer tossed between Scylla and Charybdis, but we must put the One before being, the One which, insofar as it imparts unity and union, gives to each what is its own and maintains it. And so, anything anywhere that falls away from unity and union also slips down from essence.

Finally, we have shown elsewhere that above the form that resides in matter, above the life that is mingled with the body, above the intellect that is infused into the soul, there is something which is self-existing, stimulating life within itself, and illuminating the intellect within itself. And next to any order of multiplicity there is the head of the order itself, self-existent, the simple transcendent One. Again, the head of a higher order always transcends its own order to a greater degree than the head of a subsequent order transcends its own order.

Therefore, since we find the One taking part in all beings, we proclaim that above the universal being there is the transcendent One, in its incomparable simplicity and limitlessness, prior to each essence and prior to universal essence.

Chapter 78:
How essence, or being, is negated with respect to the One; and why the One cannot be known or named

WHEN PARMENIDES takes essence and being, which are lower, away from the One Itself, he in no way removes the One Itself. For, with the aim of proclaiming the One Itself, Parmenides produced poetical compositions, and his disciple Zeno held many discourses and later, with this as his chief aim, gathered together in a long series a vast number of conclusions, so that he could distinguish the One from everything beneath it and declare that the One Itself is the principle of all beings and that if this were to be removed absolutely nothing would exist.

Thus there is one way by which being is negated with respect to nothing, which is inferior to it, and another way by which it is negated with respect to the One, which is superior to it. This is what our Areopagite carefully notes.

Thus a man who denies that the One is should not, however, at the same time deny that it exists; yet, as far as he can, he should understand existence in place of essence, lest he be in danger, after the denial of being, of slipping into nothing; for it is significant, as we have said elsewhere, that whenever the ancient Greeks wish to remove everything, they do not, of course, refer to being, for they know that if being were removed the One might remain, but they say μηδέν, *not one*, as if to say *not even one*.

Therefore, after Parmenides has denied being with respect to the One, for the One is incomparably superior, he justifiably denies all connection with being. And so he first says that nothing of beings belongs to the One or is of the One, and he quickly adds that the One has neither name nor speech. Again, there is no cognition of the One, for sense has connection with the sensible, belief with the believable, knowledge with the knowable. Therefore, since sense, belief, and knowledge are properties of certain beings and have connection with objects, it is no wonder that the sensible, the believable, and the knowable are counted in the hierarchy of creation.

For whatever kind of being they belong to, the One Itself therefore, while rejecting, on account of its absolutely simple pre-eminence, all contact with being, also refuses to be cognised, even more to be named, for name depends on cognition, and also refuses to be spoken of, for speech is made up of names. Indeed, if knowing means cognising something through its cause, then the One, having no cause, cannot be cognised by knowledge and, moreover, it cannot be perceived by intelligence, the guide of knowledge. For intelligence is multiform, and through form it observes the forms of beings and therefore cannot attain the One.

If it is not perceived by knowledge and intelligence, much less will it be perceived by the lower faculties of imagination, belief, and the senses. This is what Plato maintains in his Epistle to the Syracusans, where he says that the Self can in no way be taught or declared, but that at length the light of the One suddenly flashes on those minds that are fully turned towards the One Itself through unity and silence, that is, through the absence of the usual activity.

When you hear in these words that the One transcends sense, belief, knowledge, and intelligence, understand that these four pertain not only to human beings but to daemons and to divine beings as well; for the ancients located the senses within daemons, too, and within the world-gods. Hence Homer says that supreme Jove cannot be detected even by the senses of the sun. In the same way, we should consider that the First cannot be cognised by belief, by knowledge, or by intelligence, however exalted, but may ultimately be perceived only by the unity of love that is divinely illuminated.

But the question is: If the principle of creation cannot be named, how can we use the name *One*? The reply is that with the name of the One the actual nature of the First is not being affirmed, but on the one hand it is being partly negated with regard to multiplicity and composition and communication, and on the other hand all things are declared to be produced, perfected, and preserved by that gift of unity and union.

The words of our Proclus are very satisfying: By the name of the One it is not the One within itself that is being expressed but that which is deep within us from the One, the one hidden concept of the One; for within all beings there is an innate yearning for the first principle as the end of all. And so, before the yearning there is a hidden sense (if I may so call it) of That. Indeed, through this natural sense, which is completely hidden from the other senses, the heavy and the light choose places along a straight line that naturally suit them and reject those that do not suit them. The roots of trees choose moisture and shun aridity; the leaves cleverly shun the shade and welcome heat and light equally.

And so, by this marvellous sense and yearning, all things are turned towards the First, even though they do not cognise the First; and the soul likewise, even prior to a clear notion and choice made by her own counsel, seeks the One Itself by her natural sense and inclination through a single impression made by it upon her. Being frequently guided by this yearning, she finally uses the name *One*, not daring to say *First* so much as to express her bright yearning for the First and to put forth her own single conception, as it were, of that First.

Furthermore, we declare that of all names the *One* deserves the highest respect, since indeed it is within all and it creates, perfects and preserves all things, which of their own accord grow weak through division and perish.

But now, just as all things are turned to the One, so they are equally turned to the Good, and they flee division and evil equally. For the fullness of the One and the fullness of the Good are the same; and their power is the same.

But there cannot be two natures, the nature of the One and the nature of the Good, for then there would be two principles of creation. The Good is not before the One, for then the Good would perhaps lack union, and the One would become composite thereby. Again, the One is not before the Good, for then it would be something better than the Good itself and beings would seek something higher and greater than the Good.

The final question is: Can the One be cognised in any way at all? The reply is: Parmenides does not think that it can be cognised in no way at all, but it cannot be cognised by sense, belief, or knowledge. For Plato, too, says in his Epistles that an Idea is not cognised by sense or belief or even by knowledge, since indeed knowledge, with its divisions, definitions, and demonstrations, is always so multifarious and changeable that it has nothing in common with the simplicity and steadfastness of an Idea; but he thinks that after such discussions an Idea can be perceived by the simple, steady observation of a sharper intelligence.

Parmenides, however, thinks that the One Itself is not directly attainable even by intelligence, the guide of knowledge, since intelligence takes many forms and it is through forms that it is conveyed to beings. But after the clarity and the flash of intelligence, another light now shines from above – the light by which our own unity is miraculously united with the One Itself.

Just as he says in his Epistles that an Idea is unknown, not through a defect in the state of matter but through an excess of light, so here Plato calls the One Itself uncognisable, not because it is something subtle or empty, for then it would be unworthy of lengthy consideration, but because it is far higher than universal being and all the powers that are cognisant of beings.

Finally, in his Epistle to the distinguished Hermias and his companions, Plato gives evidence that the supreme God can in some way be perceived, for he says that if, through the right practice of philosophy, we seek God, the Guide and Father of all, we shall eventually cognise Him clearly, as it is given to the blessed to cognise Him.

Chapter 79:
On the unshakeable nature of the first hypothesis. The One is higher than being

TOWARDS THE end of the first hypothesis Parmenides asks the young Aristotle, 'Is it therefore possible that these things are disposed in this way around the One Itself?' Aristotle replies, 'Not as it seems to me.' But take care lest, through a question such as this and the reply, you suppose that all the conclusions previously reached step by step concerning the One are weakened so as to appear less feasible and so that the One, which is considered higher than being, is seen as nothing but a name because absurdities are thought to follow from it.

All consequences are necessarily adduced from their antecedents. The simple One Itself, being devoid of multiplicity because it is the basis of all consequences, is absolutely necessary if there is to be, within any level of creation, an upward movement towards the First, which is One, completely free of all that is external and inharmonious, and therefore above any particular one. Because there is in all places an individual one that is also to some extent multiple, there must be the simple One Itself, which is free from any extraneous multiplicity.

This is also demonstrated in the *Sophist*, where it is said that being suffers the One and is a partaker of the One, being lower than the One; and again, that that which is the whole, that is, is composed of the many, cannot truly be the One and the First.

And here, in the next hypothesis, it is shown that the one which has a connection with being is already undergoing multiplicity. Hence we are compelled to search for the true One Itself above essence.

There is the further consideration that, as Socrates discusses in the *Republic*, the art of discernment is theology itself and, as we might say, metaphysics as well, which, as he there describes, permeates the whole realm of beings and defines each and every essence.

Later, in another work, he rises to the Good itself, the beginning and end of universal and intelligible being. And he accomplishes this ascent by using all the methods of negating; but, to put it briefly, as the power of dialectic is sought there again and again, he contemplates the cause of all intelligibles, separating it from all beings without neglecting any negation; and there he also adds negations to show that the first cause itself is above the intellect, above the intelligible, above truth, and above essence.

We therefore ask, 'Where in Plato's writings does the process of dialectic rise step by step through all negations and up to the first cause of all beings and intelligibles?'. For if it is not in this dialogue it is definitely nowhere. Therefore, since this dialogue is Plato's dialectic and since in his view dialectic is theology, anyone who denies that this dialogue is doctrinal is also denying that theology is doctrinal.

In this book, however, he does not proceed to the First by way of negations in the second hypothesis, where he affirms all things one by one. Nor again does he proceed in this way in the third hypothesis, where he does not negate all things but confirms many; but this is much less so in what follows.

Here, therefore, and in the first hypothesis, he fulfils his function by negating through dialectic all the properties of being in respect of the one principle of all intelligibles, the cause of universal being; and then he will never invalidate those things which Parmenides himself verified at all points in an indispensable sequence and which Aristotle, in his replies, often confirmed incontrovertibly: none of these things will he lightly call into doubt. This is why the majority of Plato's followers considered this to be the ultimate question of this hypothesis, and the reply to be, as it were, a general conclusion subsuming the individual negative conclusions.

For separate questions were asked as to whether the One Itself can be multiplicity or the whole or something that has form or the other things that follow. At each step the reply, accompanied by proof, was that this is not possible. Finally, and with attention only to the main point, everyone is summoned back into court to consider a single conclusion: Is it possible for these things – multiplicity, the whole, that which has form, and so on – to be around the One?

With attention only to the main point, the answer is finally given that even these possibilities do not seem to be around the One. With this reply all the preceding replies appear to be confirmed at a stroke. And this is right, for once you have posited a single principle of creation, no matter what you employ in addition, you will obtain such or such a nature in place of what is simple: in place of life, a particular life; in place of ideal equality, a particular equality; in place of the Good itself, a particular kind of good; and some particular one in place of the simple One Itself.

For this reason, once we have acquired the One Itself, we must not apply to it conditions of multiplicity, of the whole, of that which has form, or of anything else additional, so that there is purely the Absolute in its total simplicity and its universal nature, the first principle of all things equally.

For Plato, in his epistle to Dionysius, as we have explained elsewhere, says that those people who pursue something particular are making a serious mistake about the First.

From this it is clear that the second hypothesis does not treat of the First, for once it has posited the One it immediately applies to it a being that is multiple, whole, finite, and possessed of form, by which every individual thing is necessarily created.

It follows that the First is treated of in the first hypothesis, which drives all such things away from the One. Syrianus and Proclus are very thorough in rooting out these things, along with other things; and heeding Plato's every word at all points, they teach that a mystical sense lies hidden here, particularly when the words are *about the One itself*, for they say that when we read *de ipso uno* (*with respect to the*

One Itself) there is one meaning, and when we read *circa ipsum unum* (*about the One Itself*) there is a different meaning.

This is because gifted people can easily conduct inquiries *with respect to the One*, whether it be to affirm or to negate, although it is safer to negate. But about the One Itself no one affirms anything in any way and no one exactly negates anything. For if anyone were to meditate about the One Itself, he would pursue it and attain it. This, indeed, is what happens to no one.

Therefore Plato is justified when he says in his letter to Dionysius that about the King himself there is nothing that is related to us. But the soul declares what comes after him. Of course, if the mystery which we alluded to earlier seems to be concealed from the soul, when it utters the word *One* it is not expressing the simple One Itself, but it is proclaiming a particular one that belongs to itself and is implanted within itself and is putting forward its own concept of that One; yet it is not speaking about the Self, but is speaking with respect to the Self.

For the Self is in no way expressed by us, as Parmenides says a little earlier than this and as Plato says in his Epistle to the Syracusans. And Timaeus, too, attests that the Maker of the world cannot be openly portrayed in words, and this applies much more strongly to the Father of the Maker.

Therefore, after Parmenides has stripped us of all affirmations about the One and has then brought negations to our notice as being more probable, and wishing finally to prevent anyone from considering that the One Itself could be followed exactly by means of these negations, he asks Aristotle, 'Do you therefore think it is possible for these things to exist in this way about the One Itself?'.

Thus he suggests to him that things are not exactly like this and that we do not fully attain the Self through this method of negating. Hence the young man, now better prepared, replies, 'Not exactly in this way, as it seems to me.'

Now in his *Mystical Theology* Dionysius the Areopagite, the supreme defender of this book, negates with respect to the First the levels of beings given in a long sequence. And after he has removed the affirmations for being discordant, he completely removes the negations, too, for not being entirely concordant, and he enjoins silence on reason and on intelligence: on reason, because reason is restless, and on intelligence, because intelligence is manifold.

To enable us in our darkness to reach the light of lights Parmenides seems to impose this kind of silence upon us. After saying that the First cannot be known or declared, he not only forbids us, for that reason, to affirm anything with respect to the First but also directs us to place less value on negations; for both by affirming and by negating we are saying that that cannot in any way be declared.

Moreover, anyone who openly denies is secretly affirming. For to negate something with respect to the First is to distinguish this from something else; but we cannot distinguish *this* from *that* unless we first give a shape to *this* as it is within itself and to *that*. Therefore, if affirmations, which delimit the limitless, are disallowed, then by no means is any approval given to negations, which partake of affirmations.

For this reason Parmenides is right to advise us to put our trust not in negations so much as in a silence that is peaceful, divine, and loving. Indeed, this undoubtedly meets with the full approval of all the followers of Plato, together with Hermes and Apollonius of Tyana. The prophet David, too, says, 'Silence praises Thee, O God.'

But if anyone were obstinate enough to insist, through a final question and answer, that the directions given above be put in doubt, we should answer, with the consensus of many of the followers of Plato, that there is nothing here that has been put in doubt. For most of the points have been necessarily proved and have been indisputably conceded. But if there be some paradox, especially at the end, it is merely that a young man is being called in question by a feigning and dissembling old man and challenged to take up the gauntlet for the sport that will follow, just as if the old man is saying to the young man, 'Since what has already been said arouses your suspicions and since it is unlawful to speak of the unknown and the ineffable, let us now take this opportunity to resume our inquiry with respect to the One, and let us speak henceforth of a one which is intelligible to us and which can be spoken of because it accords with us in the very order of beings.'

But that which is above essence and intellect and speech let us commit to the celestial contemplators, with devout and respectful silence, until we ourselves, if not by our own ability yet by divine inspiration, are able one day to contemplate it in the same way.

We have travelled thus far along these roads, indeed through places where there are no roads, with Proclus and Syrianus as our guides or at least as sign-posts for us. But beyond this, where there is no one to guide us, we must move forward with God as our guide and trust henceforth in inspiration alone.

Chapter 80:
The aim of the second hypothesis

WHEN SOCRATES, in the sixth book of the *Republic*, had arrived at the Good Itself, the principle of the universe, he exclaimed, 'Let us for the time being leave this Father, who is quite unknown to our present level of contemplation and beyond words, and let us proceed towards the Son.'

Now his hearers were very willing to take up the contemplation of the Son, hoping that it would also reveal the Father in some other way. Socrates therefore went outwardly to the sun, the offspring of the Good Itself through reflection. But he went inwardly to the intellect and the first intelligible, the offspring of God through nature and, as the followers of Plato say, the firstborn, in whom that supreme Father established this entire world from eternity through Ideas. This is why they called the world intelligible.

We have said that Plato wrote to Hermias concerning this Father and this Son, and so it is of this Son, the intelligible world, knowable at times through intelligence and yet ineffable, that the second hypothesis treats, acknowledging within it, on account of its dignity, those things which, being the properties of universal being, he had negated in the first hypothesis with respect to the First on account of its pre-eminent simplicity.

But in all this you should understand that in the writings of the followers of Plato the intelligible world is the name given not only to this intellect but also to the host of all noble minds, while the soul is considered a goddess; for the celestial and universal souls which convey universal providence they call the gods which belong in some measure to the host of intelligibles. Remember that the affirmations of the second hypothesis therefore pertain to all these things and that all such intellects are named gods on account of the wonderfully transcendent unity of each one.

In short, everything concerning the one universal being, in which transcendent unity is conjoined with essence, is here treated of throughout. But, as I was saying, the one being is expressed as the whole order of intelligibles and intellects, but particularly the first intellect together with the first intelligible, and subsequently all others of this order.

Therefore, since the first conclusion, under this name of the one being, concerns the highest intellect in particular, it is right that the final conclusion, which is in this second hypothesis at the level of intellectuals which now participates in time, should concern the universal souls, in which time is first, so that the second hypothesis may be linked to the third, which will treat of the order of individual souls. It is also probable that through the central conclusions certain middle orders of intelligibles are denoted, yet specific ones are not designated by specific conclusions.

As if confirming these things, Dionysius the Areopagite, in his book *On the Divine Names*, which we have recently translated, argues that the common names of God as used by the prophets tell us nothing about the actual nature of God but indicate certain effects and properties and gifts which by the will of God move towards the intelligible and intellectual nature. And so he often calls those names intelligible gifts and intelligible titles, and he affirms them with respect to the highest beings in creation and the intellectual orders, but negates them with respect to the Creator, except insofar as they may indicate that He is the cause of these.

But next I shall speak briefly of the consequences of this hypothesis. For if you understand the reason and significance of negating all things one by one with respect to the First, you will understand why they have been affirmed with respect to the second, as we have endeavoured to suggest in all those things which have come before the consequences, especially if in this hypothesis various divine powers are denoted, the properties which are brought in for the good of all and which, although they are universally suited to all, nevertheless suit some with a particular sense and at a particular level and suit others with a different sense and at a different level, as was agreed by all the followers of Plato before Syrianus.

Sameness, stillness, likeness, and equality flourish in the higher realm, while their opposites thrive in the lower realm and have a moderate significance in the middle realm. Generation, time, and movement have one meaning when imparted to the things that are first, and another meaning when imparted to all things subsequent.

But we have no intention of introducing as many divine powers as there are chapters of conclusions, lest we join Proclus in saying that eight gods exist within time: 'is', 'becomes', 'was', 'has been', 'was becoming', 'will be', 'will become', and 'will have become'.

Chapter 81:
In the one being there is the principle of the One and there is also the principle of being. The whole has parts and infinite multiplicity

WHEN, AT the beginning of the first hypothesis, there was the proposition 'If there is the One and all else', it quickly became necessary to practise forbearance with these words, for words cannot fully satisfy intelligence. Perhaps one should have said, 'If the One exists', provided that by 'existing' we understand nothing more than the pure act of the One Itself, just as if we were to say, 'If One, then One and all else'. By this form of words, then, multiplicity, together with all that follows from it, is, of course, immediately negated with respect to the One.

But the first proposition in the second hypothesis does not accept the simple One but accepts the One together with essence. Thus Parmenides' words here are of great significance. But now our proposition is not 'If One, One', but 'If One is'. With these words, when he says 'But now', he is telling us that he has dealt with the first hypothesis, which concerns the simple One, and he is going through the second hypothesis, which concerns the One together with essence.

That the principle of the One and the principle of essence are different is clearly shown both in the first hypothesis and in the second, and we have demonstrated the same in other places. Now, too, we are briefly confirming this with an inference, albeit an inference that does not carry great weight.

It may perhaps be that the mass or the essence or the substance of something is increased through some addition, but the unity does not thereby increase and may, in fact, diminish. The thing can gradually wear away, yet the unity is not impaired but appears to be perhaps greater. The thing can be divided to some extent, but the unity is not divided: rather is it enhanced.

Therefore, since the principle of the One is different from the principle of essence, and since being comes through essence, just as living comes through life, it follows that if the One is, properly speaking, through essence, which is different from it, and if the One in some way partakes of essence or is composite, then, in the same way, essence partakes of the One, through which it is one. But since they are both very closely related and full of fertility, they must both come together into a single form of the whole.

Of this whole, I say, which is posited as one and which exists as one, both the One and essence can be predicated as parts. But since it would be childish to predicate being of being, or the One of the One, Parmenides does not say that the One can be particularly predicated of the one being, or that being can be particularly predicated of the one being, but he says that the One can be spoken of in respect of the being one, and that being can be spoken of in respect of the one being.

The conclusion, therefore, is that, just as the whole and the parts were negated from the beginning with respect to the One that is above being, so now both are rightly being affirmed with respect to the one being; and that for this reason it contains multiplicity, which he had from the beginning negated with respect to the simple One Itself.

Moreover, whichever of the four elements you take, even if it be perfectly mixed with fluids, it will contain the remaining elements within it. In the same way, and much more so within the one being, where the One is primarily unifying and where the being is unifiable, the state of the One is so fused with the state of the being that neither of them can ever, in fact, be separated from the other. Thus you will never find the One by itself.

It is the same with a line: the continuation of the line always coincides with the point in such a way that whenever the continuation of the line encounters change the point simultaneously encounters the same change. Now the continuation of the line represents being, while the point represents the One. Therefore the one being, just like a line, can be imagined as an infinite multiplicity, although not infinite in action or in effect.

What is the purpose of all this? It is that you may understand that this is the nature of anything intelligible and the nature of the divine substance, so that if there are a thousand – or a thousand times countless thousands – different parts or powers or principles or forms within this nature, they are all, to some extent, present within each individual nature.

And so, do not oppose nature herself or the thought that such things recur on countless occasions within oneself. For within the divine a wonderful unity coincides with an amazing fertility; and with the mind of the observer there is a free forward movement. But remember that, although this one intelligible is said to partake of essence, it is never-theless more important and, to some extent, higher than essence.

In the same way, although the one being is called the whole, it is nevertheless indivisible. Again, although it is said to have those parts which are not separate, since the whole is within every part, imagine that a force, which is in other respects perhaps stable, is being produced or is going into motion: unity into duality, point into line, the One into essence. Consider that time is born from the development of force into movement; that number is born from the movement or develop-ment of unity into duality; that continuity is born from the extension of a point into a line; and that being is born from the development of the One into essence. And just as those elements of the One exist in equal measure everywhere within time, within number, and within continuity, so the One and essence rule equally within being: within being, I say, within any intellectual and divine substance.

Remember that among these some are higher and others are lower; within some there are particular functions that prevail; within others there are other prevailing functions; but within them all the One and essence are equally apportioned.

Again, all kinds and all Ideas are within the first intellect and within every other intellect; but although they are all, to some extent, within all things individually, some – such as sameness, stillness, change, and movement – flourish more in some things than do others, while the One and essence combine in equal measure in every kind and in every Idea.

Meanwhile, remember that Parmenides often comprehends essence under the name of 'being'. This essence is absolutely nothing but the bringing forth or unfolding of the One through which being takes root. But now the elements, as it were, of being are equally the essential One and the one essence. When these two are fused together by God, a complete form, as I might call it, arises, which on a concrete principle we call a being and which on an abstract principle we can call an entity, so that the entity may be understood as the formal principle of the being.

Chapter 82:
Within the one being all the numbers
are held by means of two and three.
The numbers are prior to the development
of the one being into many beings

JUST AS there is one principle of the point, a principle prior to that of continuity, so there is a different principle of the One, a principle which is prior to that of essence. Therefore it is right to truly consider the principle of the One in isolation from the principle of essence and at least to imagine the principle of essence in isolation from the principle of the One. This is why the One is one, but essence is other.

Indeed, in the hierarchy of beings anything that is other than something else is obliged to be other on account of change, just as something is hot on account of heat. But since the principle of change is not exactly the same as the principle of essence or the principle of the One, there must exist, within being itself, not two – the One and essence – but three, with change as the third.

A triad arises on a different principle: from the union of essence and the One, the union of essence and change, and the union of the One and change. But in any union we are considering two items which do not manifest haphazardly but which are brought together in some third form, and this is how we normally name them both.

Thus the numbers two and three are within being. Within the number two, the first of the even numbers, are all the even numbers. In the same way, within the number three, the first of the odd numbers, are all the odd numbers.

There are all the different types of number: even, odd, evenly even, oddly odd, oddly even, evenly odd. Two is even, but three is odd. Four is evenly even, for two doubled produces it; but nine is oddly odd, for three tripled produces it. Six, on the other hand, when produced from three doubled, is called oddly even; but six produced from two tripled is called evenly odd.

What is the purpose of all this? The purpose is, of course, that you may understand that by means of the numbers, which subdue their diverse nature within the first being, the essential numbers of all beings in the hierarchy of the creation are ordered, together with the myriads of types and powers, as well as the diversification within each and every type. Thus you will not suppose that the formal differences of beings, by which the whole single hierarchy of creation is produced, arise from formless matter either through some random chance or through the sporadic ramifications of certain agencies.

In company with Plotinus, we have shown previously – and we briefly confirm the same now – that number is prior to all beings. In the first being there is the principle of the One and the principle of essence, but this One is prior to this essence. Two, therefore, seems to find its fulfilment with the principle of essence. From this principle of essence, together with the principle of the One, is constituted the being or the entity which is, as it were, the form of the whole. Now this form finds completion after the number two together with the number three.

Next, this one being is drawn into beings through the power of the number two and the number three. Of course, prior to all beings, all the numbers are contained within these two numbers. For it is by means of these numbers, which are prior, that the beings which follow can be distinguished and counted.

Chapter 83:
How essence, together with the One, is distributed in the intelligible world, and how multiplicity is either limited or unlimited

ON THE subject of the first intellect and the intelligible world in particular many words are spoken at various points.

When the first, single, universal number arises with the first, single, universal being, it is by means of this essential number that the one being is spread into many beings, that is, into kinds and Ideas. There number partakes of essence, and essence, in turn, is composed of number. But since an undefined power and manifold nature and a condition that is going to move forward are inherent both in being and in number, they can both be called unlimited in some way, that is, they can be called undefined.

But on the other hand, since each partakes of the One and of limit, each is considered limited, for there is a definite number of Ideas which differ one from another both absolutely and in form. Hence the types of divine things and of natural things are limited.

Each is also unlimited, since that divine intellect relates a unique special Idea within itself to each one of the countless objects that are going to partake of it in various ways, at various times, and in various places. But since multiplicity, albeit unlimited in its power and in its effects, is limited in its performance, Parmenides, shortly after saying that it is unlimited in some respects, wisely adds, as if correcting himself and reminding us, that in other respects it is as limited as may be.

In short, when he says that essence has been divided into very many parts by means of number, do not understand him to mean that it has been cut into many substances, but understand that the one common essence is wondrously propagated and distributed into very many essential forms, powers, and modes.

As we have said, on the principle by which essence is multiplied, the One, when united with essence, is also multiplied. Essence is multiplied, and the One is united with essence. Therefore, just as every single Idea exists, just as every essence exists, and just as every essential principle exists, so is there something which is unequivocal and One.

When it is said in this discussion that the One is wholly within all individual things, but is divided, take care not to think that within that totally indivisible substance that One, which is naturally indivisible and which resembles a point or a reflection in a mirror, is augmented when it appears divided. Take care, I say, not to think that the One is being cut into pieces like something with length, but understand that manifold powers are inherent in the universal One. These powers are not all included simultaneously within any particular Idea, but are distributed here and there among the Ideas.

Finally, just as essence is multiplied there, so the One, too, is multiplied there.

Chapter 84:
Within the intelligible world
the multiplicity of parts is subsumed
in a double form of the whole;
it has limits and a mean, as well as forms

SINCE THE first being is most fully one, inasmuch as it is closest to the simple One, the multiplicity within it – however great that multiplicity may be, or of whatever kind – is reduced to the single form of the whole.

The whole form within those things which are produced from various causes and which depend solely on that which is external to them normally follows the numerous parts of the same thing. But within the first being, which is born from the One and yet in some way exists of itself, the whole form is necessarily double.

The first form is prior to the multiplicity of its parts, and the second form comes after this multiplicity or, rather, accompanies it. The first is called the super-essential unity and goodness, the pinnacle of that intelligible world. The second is called beauty, that is, a coherence and order and a succession of Ideas; but as I am mentioning divine beauty at this point, it is right to recall our beloved fellow Platonist, Francesco Diacetto, a man who each day of his life writes many words full of beauty about this very beauty, a man whom nature and his own spirit undoubtedly seem to have moulded in conformity with Platonic wisdom. But let us return to the main theme.

This ideal beauty is reflected, like glory, from that unity which we have just mentioned, as if from light, and by means of Ideas, which are like numerous rays of light.

The first form is the uppermost limit of the intelligible world, while the second form is its final limit, and in the mean position are the essential One and the one essence, the limited and the unlimited, as well as substance, life, and intellect, with, moreover, the five kinds of things, followed immediately by the type-Ideas, and finally by the multifarious manners of types. Thus the whole of this multiplicity, even if it be imagined to be limitless in every respect, emerges meanwhile as limited insofar as it is embraced on both sides by the double form of the whole.

In this discussion remember that, when we are considering the first limit and the final limit within nature, we are thinking of those limits as opposite and dissimilar. But since the final limit ultimately proceeds from the first, while the first, through its natural action, must create things similar to itself before it creates things dissimilar to itself, we must, of course, put something in the mean position between those two extremes.

Indeed, nature herself, eager for union before anything else, suffers a vacuum nowhere, not even in the lowest parts of creation. But unless something more similar is brought in among separate individual things which are clearly dissimilar one from another, something which will restore unity through the wonderful nature of similarity, some sort of vacuum will occur between the levels of creation, so that, however great the multiplicity may be in the divine world, it is nevertheless between the beginning and the end.

If these two are present, then the mean is present too. But gradually and in due order, just as he begins, so he affirms of this one being those things which, in the first hypothesis, he had negated with respect to the simple One Itself. And so, after the parts and the whole and the multiplicity and the limits and the mean, he later affirms the straight line and the circular shape, and likewise their mean and everything else.

Indeed, in the intelligible world there are initially shapes, that is, the principles of shapes – figuratively, a threefold shape governed by a movement of some things from other things. Thus from fertile essence proceeds life, and from life proceeds intelligence. Between essence and intelligence the mean is life, which stands at an equal distance from both. For life is equally akin to both essence and intelligence; and it is permissible to consider all other developments in the same way.

But the first intellect describes a circular shape as it turns towards the Father from whom it was born; and it describes the mean shape as it attends to itself. Indeed, that self-attention depends partly on the very nature of the first intellect, and thus follows the circle; but it also depends partly on the Father, and so until it returns to the Father it does not complete the circle but, turning back from the Father, it describes a wave motion, the mean between a straight line and a circle.

Chapter 85:
The one being is within itself and within something other than itself

THE ONE being is all of its parts and it is also a whole, that is, if I may express it like this, a whole form. Therefore, since all the parts are within the whole, it follows that the one being is within itself; but, on a different principle, it will follow that it is also within something other than itself. Of course, no particular part and no particular parts can contain the whole. That none of the parts, taken individually, contains the whole is evident. That the parts taken all together do not contain the whole is now to be briefly demonstrated.

For the time being I pass over any natural wholeness which is composed of varied and even mutually opposed parts and whose very form in its totality necessarily depends on the efficient and ideal cause rather than on its own elements.

It is true that the first form of that first whole being is prior to the differentiation of any of its parts and powers, just as the root is prior to the branches and the shoots, and as the light is prior to the rays and the brilliance. However, it does not depend on these but solely on the simple One Itself, I mean, on that surpassing power granted to all its parts by the One Itself. Indeed, it is clear that all the parts together are not able to contain that power from which they issue forth.

What, then, shall we say? Shall we say that the whole of this form and this surpassing power are deep within nothing, so that they are not contained, or that they are limited by something? They are certainly not within all of their parts in this way; and, furthermore, that which exists does not exist of itself. For although this totality is full of diversity, it is obliged to issue forth from that which is utterly simple, especially since every Idea within it is something finite which is distinct from all the others. And so the universal is obliged to become finite on countless occasions.

On this reckoning, therefore, this is the totality, and the multifarious necessarily consists in something other, that is, in a principle which issues forth but, at the same time, also contains. For this reason, if you were to consider all the parts within the one being, while seeing them within the whole, you would deem them to remain within it, provided that the whole itself were all the parts taken together and not something different beyond the parts. For perhaps there is nothing else at the level of number or matter, although there is something else at the level of form and power; and, on this basis, it is contained not by its parts or even by itself, but rather by its Creator.

Chapter 53, on the first hypothesis, dealt with the way this intelligible world is within itself and at the same time within something other than itself.

Chapter 86:
The one being is always unmoving, and yet it moves

IN EVERY compound there is unity and multiplicity. And so, as long as unity prevails over multiplicity and thus holds it fast, the compound endures and suffers no dissolution. For this reason, where unity always prevails and holds fast, the compound endures, forever indissoluble.

First of such compounds is that intellectual world, from whose singularity and totality of form all its multiplicity is inwardly discharged. And for this reason it remains inherent within it and is contained by it as by its cause and not merely by some object.

Moreover, every compound is like this within every intellectual nature. For within the whole of this the manifold diversity of its powers and forms flows forth from singularity and is contained by it. But more on this topic elsewhere. Let us return to the main subject.

That intellectual world is, in some way, all of its parts together, that is, all its powers and forms together; and therefore, while this universal multiplicity is within the total form, that world is said to be within itself. But this multiplicity is continually within that form, for that is its cause and preserver. Thus that world exists continually for itself; it abides permanently within each unchanging aspect of itself; and it therefore stands fast for ever.

But if you contemplate things in a different way and do not, moreover, compare that multiplicity to what I have called its whole, but rather compare the whole, that is, the singularity and the total form, to the supernal principle of the universe, you will see that a world of this kind is not within itself – is not contained within itself – but is

168

instead within its higher cause, which is its directly efficient cause and the cause of its preservation; and you will therefore see this world moving rather than resting. In fact, those parts will have come to rest within their whole as within their cause; yet the whole does not rest within itself but moves around the higher cause.

But how does this come about? It is, of course, because it turns to its cause instead of looking within. It seems to wander here and there, since it alternately falls and rises. Its fall is proportionate to its movement away from its cause, and its rise is proportionate to the degree it turns towards it through some innate prompting.

Yet it continually moves away and continually turns back, and so it is in continual motion. Indeed, it moves forward to the extent to which it is brought forth from its cause. Yet it is not brought forth just once but for as long as it is maintained, which is undoubtedly for ever.

But its Creator brings it forth from Himself before there is anything here within Himself, for if it were otherwise it would not exist in conformity with the whole essence of the Creator. It seems, therefore, that in some way it has gone forth into essence from nothing; and if it is not continually brought forth from there and does not move forwards from there, it will at once fall back into nothing. And so, that it cease not to be, it never refrains from moving in this way.

Chapter 87:
The one being is the same as itself and different from itself. Again, it is the same as other things and different from them

THE WHOLE is necessarily related to the part, and likewise the part is related to the whole. Without the part the whole is not truly the whole, while the part, separated from the whole, no longer exists as a part.

Therefore, if they are compared with each other, neither can be said to be truly the same or truly different: not the same, because the whole is greater than its part; and not something different, because neither the whole nor the part exists by itself in isolation, although we think that all those things that we usually describe as different from each other can exist in isolation.

But anything in the hierarchy of beings that is compared with something whose self is neither part nor whole can be said to be either the same as it or different and divergent from it.

What shall we say, therefore, about the one being, which is neither a part of itself nor the whole? We shall say, of course, that in general terms it is either the same as itself or different from itself. We shall also say, in company with Parmenides, that the same and the different exist; that the same is undoubtedly with itself. For since the one being is not something other than the one being and it endures for ever in the same condition, it is certainly the same as itself and the same for ever; but, on the other hand, and on a different principle, it will be said to be different from itself, for, as we have said, it is within itself and also within something other than itself.

Moreover, as we have demonstrated, it is both still and in movement. Such principles, however, are mutually opposed: being within oneself and being in something other than oneself; or being both still and moving.

Therefore, if the one being, crammed with opposing principles, is compared to itself, it will, of course, seem one thing on one principle and something other on another principle.

Thus far we have compared the one being to itself. If we now compare it to all other beings, it turns out initially to be different, since the one first being, the whole, is very different from every other being, which is neither first, nor truly one, nor universal being. Thus, on some wonderful principle, let it turn out to be in some way the same as other beings, provided we prove that there is no difference of any kind in any place or at any time.

Indeed, since all things are endowed with infinite goodness by the simple One Itself, and are preserved and held by it, and are turned back by the unity predominant in everything, then sameness is supreme. Therefore difference can nowhere be supreme and cannot in any way exist, since it is obliged in all places to be mixed with a degree of sameness. Thus, since there is no unalloyed difference within the first being, or within anything else, the first being cannot be deemed to be wholly different or totally divergent from other things. Therefore it is the same in some way, if not through its own nature then at least through the sharing of some similarity and characteristic.

But this characteristic, part-way between the model and its images, together with a sharing of any kind, goes right down to the generative processes and the things that can be generated, and we are not dealing with these at present. For here the first essence is being compared, not to generative processes, but to essences, that is, the first and most divine intellect is being compared to all divine intellects everywhere, which consider themselves to have exactly as much sameness and union with the first as lines with their centre or as the light of the stars with the light of the sun.

If you imagine that there is multifarious difference in some place, you will be obliged to imagine that it exists for some length of time, for movement and time have a wonderful relationship with change, especially any major change, just as stillness and eternity have a wonderful relationship with sameness.

For this reason, while that change lasts for a length of time that is subject to division, there is no doubt that throughout all the parts of this period of time it will remain within the same, that is, within its own unchanging tenor and vibrancy and within the same movement, time, or subject. Thus it will have some degree of sameness commingled with itself, and it will no longer be the multifarious change that you were imagining.

As Parmenides hones the young man's mind ever more keenly, he often proceeds by way of enigmas and mysteries; and he frequently deduces lines of reasoning from points that are dissimilar and sometimes mutually opposed. Being thus forewarned, move on to what follows.

Just as the first One can nowhere be partaken of by any one, so the first being is partaken of by no being, and the first intellect by no intellect, since within any hierarchy the nature that is pre-eminent and cannot be partaken of precedes the nature that can be partaken of. The latter, however, perfects all things that partake of it.

For this reason, if you compare the single first being with beings, they do not partake of it, but, rather, are copies of it. If, therefore, they do not have within themselves that first being or one of its natural qualities, they do not possess within themselves that first essential part which pertains to it, but perhaps something that is in all respects similar to it. For otherwise – if they had that very part – they would likewise embrace the one being itself within themselves.

Much less does it seem that that being can be compared to them, either as part or as whole. It has been shown above that these are not directly different. Therefore, since they are not related to each other as whole or part, and since they are not strongly different, it follows that they are to some extent the same, just as we said a little while ago.

Chapter 88:
The one being is similar to itself and to others; it is also dissimilar to itself and to others

IN THE *Philebus* it is shown that within all things subsequent to the First there are simultaneously the One and multiplicity. It follows that within all things there are the same and the different, the convergent and the divergent, and therefore similarity together with dissimilarity.

For this reason every *same* is mixed with a *different*, and the converse is also true; every *similar* is mixed with some *dissimilar* and vice versa. But the main reason is that the realm of the Self to some extent commingles all things with the One. The power of such a mixture, however, is so great that the two ingredients take it in turn to follow each other, but with this distinction, of course: by virtue of difference a thing follows its own nature in particular, so that all things are different from each other and therefore dissimilar.

Moreover, by some law common to created things some sameness and some similarity arise by means of difference; and likewise, by means of sameness and its principle it comes about that all things are the same as each other and similar to each other. By their general condition, on the other hand, it comes about that all things seem different and dissimilar.

Granted, therefore, that *this* is different from *that*, then by the same and similar difference and in exactly the same and similar way that *this* is different from *that*, so *that* is different from *this*. Thus, as long as they are subject to the same and similar fate, they are reckoned to be the same and similar.

Again, given that *this* and *that* are to some extent the same, a certain logician will first reason that sameness is opposite to difference and effects the opposite. Hence, if some similarity has recourse to the presence of difference, then dissimilarity likewise also takes hold of present sameness.

Next, the philosopher will perhaps give the following demonstration: While you are comparing two natures with each other, you will realise that they are two different items if you declare that the same two are similar on account of some common condition; and furthermore, you will learn that they are different and dissimilar, provided that the natures are two specifics and not one, and also provided that the specifics have not assumed sameness and similarity. For in this way, and on account of different methods of this sort, these things will perhaps be seen as dissimilar.

For these reasons, if the one being is compared to other beings, it is the same as other beings and different from them, and as a consequence it is both similar to them and dissimilar to them.

Through sameness it will first have similarity and then dissimilarity; while through difference it will first have dissimilarity and, at the next stage, similarity. And when the one being is compared to itself, it will experience, in relation to itself, both the same and the different, as well as both similarity and dissimilarity.

Chapter 89:
How the one being touches and is touched; but it neither touches nor is touched insofar as it belongs to itself and to other things

FROM SIMILARITY itself Parmenides moves, quite rightly, to touch, a word with very extensive meanings in this context. For those things which are similar to each other are ready and willing to meet each other – I mean, to approach each other – to move and be moved, to feel sympathy, to be perceived and to enjoy.

This, at any rate, is why the more the one being is within itself and within all other beings, the more it meets both itself and others; but since touching has one principle and being touched has a different principle, the one being can be said to be simultaneously touching itself and being touched by itself, so far as it accepts different principles within itself. For since it is not the first principle of the universe, it may be manifold to some extent.

But if touching and being touched are considered to differ from each other, like two essences or two natures, the first simple essence certainly cannot in any way touch itself as though by means of a different substance; but can it touch other things in any way? If we consider that other things within the hierarchy of beings are similar in any way whatever to the first being, then it indubitably touches them and is touched by them with a metaphorical contact such as we have indicated earlier.

But if we view the principle of the one being as hidden within itself and at the same time consider that the principle of multiplicity is within itself we shall be fabricating a separate multitude, a limitlessness of total confusion, a power subject to diversification which can be manipulated extraneously and which, of itself, is not the formal One, does not partake of the formal One, and does not have a measure delimited by precise unities. And so, as long as they fail to reach the one being, the first form which formally delimits all things, they are not touched by it and they do not touch it.

If you compare a point to a line, you will likewise be able to investigate whether it touches the line or is touched. And you will be right both to deny and to affirm. You will deny that it simply touches or is touched, for the point is not actually touched by the line, or the line by the point, for if it were otherwise either the point would be divisible or the line would be absolutely indivisible; but you will perhaps affirm, and rightly so, that the point devised by you touches a point of the line and is in turn touched by a point of the line.

In the same way, the one being neither touches the multiplicity of beings nor is touched by it, inasmuch as the one being is already one, while this sheer multitude is not yet a formal one, but, being unlimited, it touches the unlimited, in a manner of speaking, and is touched in turn, inasmuch as this multitude has now become something that is a formal one, for the One does not touch and is not touched except through the One.

Here Parmenides is repeating in some way what he had partly said earlier, namely, that multiplicity, which is not the One, does not partake of the One; but now he adds 'insofar as it is multiplicity, it is totally other than the One.' Concerning the number of things touching and touched he declares what is obvious to anyone considering the matter: 'For who does not see that if two fingers touch one another, the number of fingers is two, but there is one central contact? If you add another finger, there will be three fingers but two contacts. If you add yet one more finger, there will now be four fingers, but three contacts. And so the series would continue.'

Chapter 90:
The one being is both equal to itself and unequal to itself; it is also equal to others and unequal to others

IF THE masses of the elements and the natures of fluids can be severally distinguished, and if any pure quality can be found in nature, much
more readily can the formal principles of creation, which are simpler
and loftier than their own nature, be severally distinguished, so that
they remain pure within themselves and so that any truthful intellect
is enabled to contemplate each of the principles within its own quality
in isolation from the others, because, clearly, that first intellect has,
from the beginning, perceived them as distinct, and within the intelligible itself one principle is quite different from another.

But if we now perceive the forms of creation within the mutual
inter-communication of things, we shall certainly perceive all things as
being to some extent within all things, which is what Anaxagoras perceived. Again, if through very precise perception we view them as being
highly abstract within their own formal, lofty principles, we shall
admit, again in company with Anaxagoras, that the intellect itself is the
discriminator of everything.

Now anyone who does not know how to make use of such rigorous exercises is not a follower of Plato and never uses the intellect. This
is why Parmenides, when preparing to train the mind of the noble
young man along these lines, obliges him repeatedly, by means of the
tightest constraints, either to withdraw from the false or else to make
use of these abstractions, in which, as the man whom you know also
says, there is no falsehood.

Moreover, as we have indicated from the outset, he conducts the
whole discussion as an exercise in logic. But in this form of dialectic
he often commingles mystical teachings too, not in a continuous
unbroken sequence but sporadically, as befits an exercise in logic. At
all points, however, he tackles difficulties and examines paradoxes, thus
testing the mind to the full.

But let us now proceed with what remains. There is the principle
of the One Itself, and there is a different principle for everything else.
There is a principle of largeness, a principle of smallness, and a
principle of equality.

Therefore neither the One, nor anything other than the One, is larger or smaller or equal through its own principle. But it is larger when largeness itself is added to its nature; smaller through smallness; and equal through equality.

However, ideal largeness or ideal smallness or ideal equality cannot be present in anything by virtue of any physical state; for if that were the case, many absurd conclusions would now be drawn. For if smallness were present in some object, it would, of course, be present either in the whole or in a part. If it were present throughout the whole, it would be present either inwardly or outwardly. Therefore, if it were present inwardly, it would certainly be equal to it. If it were present outwardly, it would be larger than it. But this is absurd. For in this way smallness would usurp the authority of equality and of largeness.

On the other hand, if smallness were posited merely in a part of the object, it would be either equal to it or larger than it, and the same errors would arise.

The other conclusion is that nothing would be larger or smaller unless ideal largeness or ideal smallness were able to be present through some non-physical authority. It certainly cannot exist through some physical circumstance, and so it will not be present in anything. But perhaps some things can be declared equal simply on account of the absence of this kind of inequality.

It should be noted, moreover, that if, on the one hand, the principles of largeness, of smallness, or of equality are posited, while on the other hand the principles of all other things are considered, the former will not be contained in the latter, and the latter will not be contained in the former. For this reason these, when considered within their natural context of speech, cannot yet be declared large or small or equal. But after the ideal principles of those things they arrive at these things.

Parmenides tacitly reminds us of these things, partly instructing the mind of the young man by means of some logical stratagem and partly sowing some hidden teaching here and there. But we have described elsewhere how the one being is within itself. On this principle, therefore, it can be declared larger than itself and smaller than itself, so that it includes something within itself and indeed is itself included in something other, that is, as an effect within its cause. It is also within other things as a cause is within its effects; and other things are within it as effects are within their causes.

Therefore, because these things are within it they are smaller than it, that is, they are less in their degree of power. On the other hand, because it is also, as it happens, within them, it is in some way smaller than they are: I mean, it has less diversity in its composition. For these things are collections of the many and the multifarious, while the quality of that, first and foremost, is simplicity.

But consider, if you will, what that means to itself: whatever is is somewhere or in something. Consider that this statement does not apply to what is higher than being, but it does apply to all being. Yet all being is within something, and each and every being is within something by virtue of some affinity, since the first being is within something and within everything, for even in its presence something is within something else. Again, it itself is within its cause, and it is also within beings, as a model is within its images.

Chapter 91:
The one being, in relation to itself and to all else, is numerically the same. It is also both more and less

FROM DIMENSION he proceeds to number, for number is frequently produced by continual division, and continuous division is generally measured by means of numbers.

For this reason, whatever is equal in dimension to something else also has the same number of parts; whatever is larger has more; and whatever is smaller has fewer. Therefore, the one being, insofar as it is wholly equal to the whole of itself, through its universal power, is also equal to itself through the number of its various powers.

Moreover, if any Ideas are superior, they, being greater in creativity and in number, have the power to do more; while the lower Ideas, being fewer, are less effective.

Thus the one being, in relation to itself and to all else, is said to be the same, as well as both more and less. For that intelligible world seems to some extent equal to the whole of its work, insofar as this single work accords with the single Craftsman. It also seems equal in number, if we believe Timaeus when he says that the intellect produces in this world forms as numerous as the Ideas which the Craftsman perceives; and that that archetypal world contains within itself as many living intelligibles as the sensory beings which it embraces here. In addition, just as that world is more powerful than this world, so to the same extent is it deemed to have a greater number of powers.

Finally, just as that world has less multiplicity and collectivity than this world, so it is exceeded by it, to some extent, in number. For the number of all the events in the world, the countless number of contingencies that occur in any one moment, exceeds the number of Ideas and the power of Ideals.

Chapter 92:
How the one being, in relation both to itself and to everything else, may be described as older and younger and of the same age

PARMENIDES rightly moves down from number to time. For where the first number originates is also the birthplace of movement and time, since within the first being, simultaneously with a determinate number of forms and powers and actions, movement is initiated, by means of which one thing comes forth from another, and this is also the beginning of time, by means of which one thing starts before or later than another.

But movement and time are necessarily within the first being and also within every being, since essence is like a movement forth from the One, while the One, of course, seems to be drawn forth into essence, as a point is produced into a line. Essence, in turn, moves forward into being, like a line into a surface; being into life, like a surface into depth; life into mind, like the depth resolving itself into form and figure. Finally, mind turns back through attention to itself, just as the first figure of the first depth is taken in its totality and rolled into a sphere.

But to return briefly to our subject: movement is necessary within being, and time is necessary provided that infinity, movement and change are present as elements and provided that the Idea of movement and time is also present. But always remember that movement and time, being fully enveloped and encased and sustained within the intellect and the intelligible in some form of eternity, quickly move into the soul and are there further expanded and made more explicit by means of some circulation; and remember that this kind of movement is action when within the soul, but becomes passion when in the body.

Remember, too, as we have advised you to do from the beginning, that Parmenides is here taking up the divine soul, in addition to the intellectual nature and the animate nature. But when he defines being as a participation of essence together with the present time, note that there is first a confirmation of what is often generally said, namely, that being itself is the action of essence, just as shining is the action of light and heating is the action of heat. Secondly, the present time is very extensive, so that it is not within the body alone but is also within the soul and the intellect, even the highest intellect. Similarly, what is spoken of here as 'was' and 'will be' is the past and the future, but it is in the One, too, on account of its nature and excellence.

We have dealt with many such matters concerning movement and time in the first hypothesis, and so at this point we shall briefly run through the subject and show that the one being – especially when it is considered within the soul, even the divine soul – can be called older and younger and, as we have said, of the same age, in relation to itself and to other things.

But how may this be said in relation to itself?

Whatever be the nature of the flow or movement within it, whether close to the intellect or to the divine soul, this flow or movement is certainly continuous. Therefore, while we consider it as extended step by step into a lengthy process, we call it older; I mean, it becomes older in relation to the process and is also older in relation to the present moment which has now been perceived. However, when it is in continuous contact, it is always judged to become older and to be older; yet, since 'older' is necessarily related to 'younger', it is at the same time judged to be younger, too. And again, when the whole of itself is briefly compared to the whole of itself, it is neither older nor younger than itself and is rightly judged to be of the same age as itself.

Subsequently, when he is comparing one to many, he repeatedly states that this one being that is under consideration is not the simple One Itself, because he confirms what he also said earlier, namely, that it has parts and a multiple nature, that it is in process of becoming, that it has become, and that it therefore depends on something higher.

But now he compares it to a host of beings which are not so much external as internal; and he makes this even clearer when he lists its parts in his comparison: by parts I mean its powers, its forms, and its actions. Keep in mind, or in your divine soul, that, as we have also said earlier, the total unity is, if I may express it like this, double.

The first unity is prior to the internal multiplicity, while the second unity follows it. The first is deemed older than the many, the second younger than the many. Thus one is considered both older and younger in relation to the many. But when it is compared to the inner multitude of Ideas, it seems as if it is being compared, in some measure, to external forms, which are the images of Ideas, for one is prior to the multiplicity which has now expanded more extensively. Since one is found in every kind of number and has the lowest inner number at its first level, it is rightly deemed older, especially as it is the origin of the expanded multiplicity.

But the one that at that very moment is reflected from the multiplicity – that is, the glory and the universal beauty of the Ideas – is not incorrectly described as younger than the multiplicity, especially since it comes to fulfilment after the creation of individual things.

But meanwhile, like the point, which is both first and last when compared to the parts of a line and yet is within every part of the line, that intelligible one is not only therefore that which is first, and hence the most remote of the Ideas, but it also completely fills every single Idea. For any one of the many is necessarily a one and is filled with the power of the first one and seems to accord with the final one.

Therefore, while the one makes multiplicity fully equal to itself, it is thought to be of the same age as multiplicity.

It is also legitimate to compare that intellectual or living world, especially the one within itself, to the universal multiplicity of the perceptible world. Thus that one is more ancient than this multiplicity, being its creator and model. It is also younger, for, since it is in constant flux and has been in flux every day, that eternal world, almost like a survivor, follows this as its junior.

In the same way, while it resides within itself, it is considered to precede, as its senior, the world that is, as it were, going to be re-born every day; but the extent to which that world acts is the extent to which this world depends on it, and so it seems to have the same age.

Chapter 93:
How older becoming is distinguished from younger becoming, and also how older being is distinguished from younger being. Concluding words on the one being

IN THIS discussion, notice how Parmenides, at times when philosophic tenets are being torn to shreds, trains the young man to be careful in his replies and judicious in his discrimination.

Thus, in his recondite discussion of older and younger, he seems to be keenly looking for a logical distinction of the following kind from the young man. Suppose Socrates is ten today, and suppose Plato is five. How much older than Plato is Socrates? The arithmetician will answer, 'Five', for he always answers in numbers. The geometrician will answer, 'Twice', for he considers the proportions within the measures. Each is speaking the truth.

Now allow at least five more years to elapse, so that Socrates is fifteen and Plato ten. What is now the difference in age? The arithmetician will answer, 'Five', as before. And, on this basis, Socrates was once older than Plato, while Plato was younger than Socrates; but henceforth neither ever becomes older or younger than the other, since, as long as they continue to live, they are separated from each other by the same number.

The geometrician, on the other hand, will answer, perhaps in company with the musician, that Socrates was previously twice as old as Plato, for between ten and five there is a factor of two, whereas now Socrates is older by not so much difference but by a smaller difference, since between fifteen and ten there is a factor of one and a half. Fifteen, therefore, exceeds ten by a proportion smaller than that by which ten exceeds five, for ten exceeds five by a half of itself, while fifteen exceeds ten by a third of itself; and every day from now on the factor by which Socrates is older than Plato will appear to grow ever smaller, until it reaches the stage where the one who was once older by a long gap seems to be older by an ever decreasing gap. Thus Socrates may be said to be growing younger to some extent in relation to Plato, while Plato seems to be growing older in relation to Socrates. Finally, let us conclude that, although one seems older or younger, yet they are never older or younger in relation to each other than they were at the outset.

In this discussion, when he openly calls what he is dealing with 'the one being', but calls all other things 'beings', he is confirming what we have said, namely, that he is dealing here not with the simple One Itself, but with the one being.

In brief, the conclusion is that the one being, considered either within the intellect and the intelligible or within some divine soul, has within it both movement and some time and some differentiations of time. Hence it could be said to become in some way, that is, to expand more fully within itself and to be fashioned or to act in different ways according to circumstances. A change of this kind, however, develops more noticeably within the soul. Therefore, since a being of this kind has some connection with intellect of any kind, it can be cognised and named and, by means of its images, it can be perceived by the more penetrating of the senses.

Chapter 94:
A summary or review of the second hypothesis. On distinguishing the divinities

WHILE I AM hastening on towards the third hypothesis, it occurs to me that it would be worthwhile to first make a summary, or rather, a review, of the second hypothesis from the beginning once more.

The followers of Plato think that the Trinity, which we have often described as impossible to reckon by any order of priority, is the Good itself, the intellect itself, and the soul of the world. Indeed, they frequently describe the Good as the Father, the intellect as the Son, and the soul of the world as the Spirit. The Spirit nourishes inwardly. If they mean that the substance of this Trinity is the same, they are like the Catholic Christians. If they mean that there are three substances, they are like the Arians.

They call the first intellect the intelligible world, and they all think that between it and the perceptible world there are many orders of divinities, that is, of sublime intellects. I, for my part, think that there are many, as I have shown in the *Theology*. If perchance they are in some way distinguished in the writings of Syrianus and Proclus, it is weari-some for you to read what it is certainly irksome for me to write.

For the present, it is enough to make this rough distinction: some of the supra-mundane divinities or angels – for they are the same – are closer to the intellectual world, others are as close as possible to the perceptible world, and others are intermediate.

Syrianus and Proclus call the first group intelligible, the last group intellectual, and the middle group both intelligible and intellectual. We, for our part, prefer to call them higher, lower, and intermediate; but they are all above the mundane divinities.

We also consider the mundane divinities to be of three orders: higher, lower, and intermediate. In the first order are the souls of the great spheres; in the middle group are the souls of the stars; and in the last group the invisible spirits have their positions within the spheres.

But for the time being I pass over the remaining distinctions between the supra-mundane and the mundane, especially such distinctions as were brought in by Syrianus and Proclus, who try to prove that Parmenides brings in exactly as many orders of divinities as there are propositions posited in his first and second hypotheses. But, as I have said elsewhere, I approve neither of this inquisitiveness nor of such distinctions among the divine orders, distinctions which they pursue with more effort than usefulness. It is acceptable, as I was saying just now, to make a rough distinction.

It is also acceptable that Parmenides should use the name of the One now in one way and now in another; and that from time to time he should touch upon various orders of divinities, inasmuch as what he is dealing with pertains more to this order than to that order, although to some extent it belongs to them all.

For this reason, therefore, all the propositions of the second hypothesis discuss the divine intellects, giving reasons why they are divinities. Now they are divinities because, as we have said elsewhere, they have the super-essential one within their essences. Thus whenever the one being is discussed, the divinities are discussed in the same measure. And whenever it is acceptable to change the meaning and application of this name – that is, of the one being – let it also be acceptable for the significance of the divinities to be affected. But, meanwhile, you are not to account for specific divinities with specific formulae.

Chapter 95:
The distinctions made in this summary or review.
On the one being; on multiplicity; on limitless
number; and on the orders of the divinities

AMONG THE principles of the second hypothesis, he first goes to
the intelligible world and later to all the divinities, even those that
transcend the world. He posits two of these principles quite openly:
the One and being. A third he tacitly hints at: a power midway between
the first two, a power which is the reciprocity between the One and
being; through which there is the One of being and also the being of
the One; through which this super-essential unity, which is called
existence, produces an essence that is conjoined to it; through which
and from which this essence is generated and is turned towards the
unity and is connected to it.

Now this power is like the effective movement and development of
unity into essence, since there is no other means by which this one,
which is going to have essence as its partner, can proceed from the
simple One Itself. Through the power that is naturally deep within it,
this one moves forward into essence, just as essence, through the life
within it, moves into mind. Indeed, the life between essence and intellect is of the same quality as the power between one and essence.

Certain powers, therefore, which are subsequent to essences, are
within created things, and, more than that, within the divinities – if I
may speak in the manner of Plato – there are powers which are mirac-
ulous. Some of these powers are prior to essences and maintain a totally
unbroken succession with their own unities and divinities; it is through
them, therefore, that the gods are considered capable of making
essences, which, in fact, could never be made by any powers subsequent to essences.

But Parmenides proceeds methodically, putting the more general
before the less general. He locates a more general and earlier multiplicity within the first parts; for all parts are multiplicity, but each multiplicity, though kindred, is not parts. From the parts he quickly
constructs a whole which is nevertheless related to the parts, and thus
he comes to limitlessness. All limitlessness is in some way the whole,
but the converse is not true.

After limitless multiplicity he moves down to limitless number, since multiplicity is more extensive than number. All number is multiplicity, but the converse does not hold. For multiplicity of parts, unless it be discrete on occasion, is not, in fact, automatically called number; for true number is not any multiplicity, but discrete multiplicity.

The followers of Syrianus give this as a reason for the extended levels, followed by the more restricted levels, which they have in their propositions, at the same time introducing similar levels for the gods; and since they differentiate the intelligibles from the intellectuals, as higher from lower, and elsewhere do the same through substances, they certainly attribute this, which is called the whole and a virtually unbroken multiplicity, to intelligible substance, but ascribe discrete multiplicity to intellectual substance.

For our part, we are at one with them in thinking that the former pertain more to the higher deities, and the subsequent ones more to those that follow; but to some extent in relation to them both we differentiate intelligible nature from intellectual nature not so much by substance as by reason.

In any divine intellect, therefore, whether it be first or subsequent, we put its intelligible and essential nature before its intellectual force, and in both we locate the multiplicity of its parts or powers or forms. But since such multiplicity is astonishingly inherent in the intelligible level, and since different things are inherent in different levels, and since the whole is contained within everything through a wondrous union, and since this multiplicity therefore seems virtually unbroken, we agree with the followers of Syrianus not to call such multiplicity number as yet.

But since the aforesaid multiplicity is now more extensively and more particularly unfolded within the intellectual level by means of the intelligence which differentiates all things, and since different things are perceived by different agencies, so that something may be seen in isolation from something else, we grant here that number has a more obvious origin; and hence it comes about that in all places manifold differentiation of forms, rather than differentiation *ad infinitum*, is related to the mind, that is, to the rays of intelligence which in their purity perceive all individual things. Hence, too, visible light, as the image of intelligence itself, everywhere differentiates things that are commingled. But the intelligible itself is already constituted by means of essence, substance, nature, light, and motive power; and within it, therefore, all things are connected through their nature, for all things are naturally related to each other.

But precise differentiation comes about through intelligence as though through a radiant eye, most precisely distinguishing one object from another, even though they be related. This is why Anaxagoras attributes the power of discrimination to the intellect, which he does when he is going to grant developed number to the intellect.

Let us, therefore, grant the manifold nature of things both within the intelligible, which precedes, and within its intellect, which immediately follows; but in the former like lines at the centre of a circle or like rays in the central light of the sun, and in the latter like lines on the surface of a sphere or like rays on the periphery of the sun. Hence it comes about that the proper action of any intelligence is like some form of differentiation, and many intellects frequently merge into one in the presence of the intelligible.

But the question at this point is: How does limitless multiplicity appear there? Although we have already explained this, we shall state it clearly once more. Infinity is not put there by quantity or by number, for there is no quantity there, and infinity is incompatible with number that is now reduced to types and pertains to measure. And in matters divine, which are close to the One Itself, a limitless host, which is totally different from the One, cannot hold sway. For there multiplicity is directly contained by the One. There infinity means, therefore, a universality which embraces all but is not itself embraced by any other universality: a universality which has moved so far forward through the intelligibles that it cannot move any further and cannot be overtaken by anything else.

But now that multiplicity matches the first infinity, just as union or limitation within multiplicity echoes the first limitation. Therefore, just as the first infinity is not called limitless in terms of number, but limitless in terms of power, a power that is perhaps not only manifold but perhaps also, as Syrianus would have it, capable of multiplying and advancing, so the intelligible multiplicity, which is the first multiplicity, and the intellectual multiplicity, which is like its consort, are said to be infinite, both because multiplicity, as such, is not limited and, indeed, echoes infinity and also because, being the first, it particularly relates to the first infinity, and finally because through the generative power of all beings, together with their adaptability, it unfolds within itself the universal multiplicity of unities and of intelligible beings right down to the least of the intelligibles as such, both individual and universal, insofar as they are capable of development at that point.

Therefore, since it is not any multiplicity, but is the first multiplicity and the universal multiplicity, and cannot be embraced by any other multiplicity, but embraces them all, it is rightly called infinite. And just as the first One is the primal limit, so the first multiplicity after infinity is called the first infinite – infinite, I say, especially for us, since its nature, power, and extent cannot be fully understood by our intellect or by any individual intellect. Hence, when all is said and done, it happens that we are unable to understand the whole outworking of number and we are continually overcome by its limitlessness. In short, we should speak more truly of the infinite if we said that multiplicity were limitless rather than limitlessness.

But that within the divine mind there is manifold power as well as the numbers which it allots to individual natures is demonstrated by the marvellous arrangement of natural things and by the constant appearance of numbers within things that are wholly subject to change. This is why the Magi, who took heed of solar and lunar numbers and applied them to these matters and to those matters, were often able to attract solar or lunar qualities towards these matters and those matters and to reconcile, through an astonishing power, things which are mutually compatible.

Proclus writes that, in order to accomplish special sacred offices, the priests in ancient times frequently made use of numbers possessed of indescribable power, and he would have seen these things. Plato, of course, declares that the life-spans of souls and of states are fulfilled by their own numbers and that the universal orbit of the world is indeed contained by number. Following Pythagoras, he postulates two principles of number: paternal and maternal, unity and duality, limit and limitlessness. But he has it that the first number is three, a composite of limit and limitlessness. Unity he calls the simple One Itself, and duality he calls essence, while trinity is both being and the first intelligible.

Moreover, within unity and duality all the numbers are held in perfection; and thus all the numbers are brought forth from there: the even numbers through duality, the odd numbers through unity, which is lord of duality. And so all things are arranged in sequence through these numbers. Through the even numbers in particular are ordered processes, divisions, and dissoluble compounds. Through the odd numbers are ordered the simpler and nobler qualities, whatever is indissoluble, and all that is gathered together into one.

But let us briefly return to the distinctions of the supra-mundane orders. Although whatever is enumerated in this hypothesis belongs, to some extent, both to them all and to their head, which is the first intellect, yet, as we have said, some things belong more to some, and others to others. Abiding within oneself, being identical to oneself, being similar to oneself, being equal to oneself, being contiguous with oneself, and similar conditions; again, being different from other things, being dissimilar to them, being unequal to them, not touching them, not being touched by them, and other things of this ilk: all these belong more to higher things. But their opposites can be attributed to lower things.

Take note here that when any of the divinities is said to be identical to others, the same as others, and equal to others, if comparison is then made with perceptible things, it can be demonstrated quite fittingly that God Himself is present to all things and that, in relation to Himself, He is present as whole, as same, as similar, and as equal, and He is present in a way that is same, similar, and equal, although other things, by contrast, do not receive from there in a way that is same, similar, or equal.

Now Parmenides seems to indicate the final order of intellectuals when he says, 'It touches others and is in turn touched.' Similar to this is the statement in the *Republic* that the goddess Necessity touches the spheres of the world with her knees, and the Fates touch them with their hands. Again, it is said in *Cratylus* that Proserpina and Pluto, the underworld divinities, lay their hands on transient nature. For those who are closest to the perceptible world and to the world-divinities seem to turn aside from a more general providence to a providence that is more particular and distinct and to impinge upon physical things as if from some intimate disposition.

But, at the same time, none of the divinities touches himself or other things. He does not touch himself, because when he has a head that is undivided there is no need for contact; he does not touch other things, because while he is ordering individual things he does not turn aside from his stillness and purity.

However, he does touch himself insofar as he has many parts within himself and insofar as these parts, touching each other, also touch the whole; and he does touch other things insofar as, when dealing with them very closely and effectually, he seems to make some vestigial imprint on the work.

However, when Parmenides finally moves down to movement and time and age, he moves from the intellectual divinities to the divinities of life and of the world, and he seems to be very appropriately anticipating the subsequent discussion concerning the soul.

The Third Hypothesis – Chapter 1:
The aim of the hypothesis. How the soul may be called being and also non-being. On movement and time within the soul. On its eternal quality. How it manifests all things through some change in itself

THE THIRD hypothesis, treating of the soul, does not start with any particular soul but begins with the whole, fully divine soul. It is divine, I say: not a goddess in substance, yet having an express likeness to the gods.

It has three orders. The first is that held by the souls of the greater spheres. The second is that held by the souls of the stars. The third is that held by the souls of the invisible divine powers which furnish universal providence within the spheres.

The third hypothesis discusses all these, presenting the world divinities arranged in three orders. If I have by chance said something different elsewhere about the purpose of this hypothesis, it would have been the view of others.

Here is our interpretation: this hypothesis is very conveniently arranged according to the five mean positions of the soul. As we have shown in the *Theology*, the soul holds the mean position in the five levels of creation and is suited to the body, which is universally five-fold, being composed of the qualities of the four elements and then filled with some celestial power. The followers of Plato, however, think that the body is also fit for celestial souls.

Moreover, just as the soul consists of opposites, as we have shown in the *Timaeus*, so the third hypothesis, which examines the soul, is a mixture of affirmations and negations. And, very fittingly, it moves down at once, right from the outset, into time. For when we speak aright we locate the first movement and time within the soul.

This one is also spoken of immediately, because the soul is understood to have become – and at the same time not to have become – one living being. For in any fluctuation that passes through earlier and later, non-being is mixed with being. This is why it was said long ago that this one which is under discussion is in some way to be located beneath being, like something temporal located beneath the eternal.

Indeed, just as the one moves forward into being and falls into the not-one, so pure being, by some forward movement, falls outside itself and into non-being, that is, into some being which is henceforth mixed, to some extent, with non-being. And just as within the first being, that is, within the intellectual being, there has so far been some natural order of priority, if I may call it thus, through which, according to some beginning or some ordering, there is, in relation to it, something earlier or something later; so within the second being, that is, within the living being, which grows through expansion and differentiation, a temporal order of priority (if I may so call it) occurs, as does an identical order of what follows.

Again, where there is priority certain levels of nature are in order, and at the level where something is first the second is not yet ready to arise immediately in like fashion. Thus where there is temporal priority there is now something which is earlier and much more clearly defined, while anything that is going to emerge later is not yet on the same basis.

But within the soul change and movement at an earlier or later time is still divine, and, as the whole Platonic school agrees, even within the reason and intellect of the soul there is some exceedingly quick temporal movement, since movement and time come together naturally and primarily within the soul: within the whole soul, therefore, and within all the powers of any soul.

For this reason, within the intellect of the soul, if any action has been undertaken insofar as it corresponds with the pure intellect, a temporal movement nevertheless accompanies it there, just as wind and darkness accompany a lightning flash. Now some change occurs with the soul, even the divine soul, in its fundamental quickening power, insofar as some seed-causes flourish – or rather, rule – at some times, while others develop at other times, and this is necessarily so in its sensual – or rather, its conceptual – part, which particularly influences some images of creation at one time and other images at another time. It also occurs with the rational power itself, which reveals particular causes and forms of creation at particular circuits of the years. Finally, it happens within its mind, which beholds the Ideas and wonders of the deities with a gaze that, although very swift, is variable and sequential.

While such changes occur within our soul, they do not seem so pertinent to essence. For they are not so uniform, so constant in impulse, so effective in disposition or action, and the forms, powers, and actions of the soul are not so close to our essence as they are to the essence of divine souls.

For these reasons, while Parmenides saw that sublime souls change inwardly in this way, he dared to declare here that such changes belong, to some extent, to the very being of those souls and also to essence itself, just as Proteus changes form with such authority that he seems to have come into being in one form and to perish and immediately to be re-born. At the same time, however, since the sublime souls possess not only vital and intellectual force but also some divine element, totally indivisible and eternal, and, for the reason given earlier, are also perhaps in some way changed in eternity if they are compared to that, they do not move, they are not subject to temporal phenomena, and they do not at any time take up, as if by nature, any stillness that is in opposition to movement.

Therefore, while temporal and transient phenomena are affirmed of the divine souls for the reason given earlier, they are, at the same time and for the reason I was just mentioning, equally negated. For the celestial soul is exactly like a celestial sphere. Now in a sphere the centre is indivisible and steadfast, while everything moving around the centre is unsteadfast and manifold. In the soul, therefore, there is a similar centre and a similar movement around the centre.

But perhaps Parmenides was particularly eager to put before our eyes the imitative nature of the soul as part of the whole. For since it is the mean of the creation and the beginning of universal motion, it imitates all others very easily and shrewdly, and by the differentiation of its manifold movement it reflects the varied nature of all actions.

Now above the soul is the intelligible world, while below the soul is the perceptible world, and each has its respective appearance. The former always has more, and the latter always does more. But between them the soul – the mean – conforms to both extremes, like the mean element of the elements or the mean quality of the qualities, and, indeed, like a tiny nimble creature, portrays within itself the appearances of them both. For if a chameleon can, with its skin, portray, as in a mirror, the form, the colour, and the movement of a body or any object, much more can the soul, imitating the inward rather than the outward, directly portray the features of both worlds, features which are presented to its innermost recesses and are naturally imparted to it, so that through its varied and powerfully effected imitation of diverse things it is not to be wondered at that the soul, if only it can look inwards, seems to become some things at some times and other things at other times, especially if its vegetative nature is discerned, any power and action of which is not an image but, rather, a natural quality, both a particular nature and nature itself. Therefore, while it reveals different features and images at different times, it seems to be changing its own nature continuously.

Plotinus thinks that the actions and forms of the higher powers, too, are so essential that if the soul acts sequentially through its various powers and forms, which are all the soul itself, the soul can be said to be fully constituted now in this way and now in that way and, at times, to possess a different life and nature. Thus you will not be surprised if Parmenides says that the soul comes into being and also perishes.

But in the meantime you have realised that what changes is not the actual essence of the soul or the first type of soul but its features, image, and character; that the soul is not constrained or driven by some external force; but that it continuously transforms itself by its own nature and of its own volition. For they do not say *changed in form like Proteus* but *changing forms like Proteus*. In the same way, the fewer the different faces, forms, and masks assumed by a skilful person, the more is he himself stripped clean.

You should not shudder, therefore, when you hear that divine, that is, celestial, souls expand and diminish, become rarified and compressed, are born and perish, provided that you remember at the same time that these statements are taken on a metaphorical basis; that the very movements which are caused within bodies, especially the lower bodies, by an external agency and are merely phenomena are accomplished within and by those souls especially; that actions occur and that souls themselves are, as it were, perfected by perpetual vicissitudes of this kind and certainly delight in them and rejoice in their future form and diversity as much as in their past form and diversity, just as the heaven which they thus continuously revolve is perfected by the diversity of its revolutions and configurations and finds stillness in movement, and while it seems to come to a stop it begins once more, returns by passing away and is re-born by perishing.

Hence it first possesses matter through itself, so that, admitting all the forms of all things, then losing them, and once more receiving them, it rejoices in all situations alike, and it appears to constantly come into being and to perish, to increase and then to decrease, while, like the celestial soul and the heaven, it always remains the same.

The Third Hypothesis – Chapter 2:
Why the celestial soul moves and makes an orbit around the steadfast mind. How many movements of the soul there are. The number of movements and the stillness within time. Concerning the mean between movements

THE DIVINE MIND, as we have shown in the *Theology* and the *Timaeus*, continuously conceives all the forms of all things with a single steadfast act, gives birth inwardly, and observes. We have shown in the same works that the divine soul begins its journey from there, being heavy with all the forms and, like a rival of the divine mind, it also cherishes a similar conception, birth, and observation.

But the more divided it is within itself, as it were, the less efficacious it becomes. And so, since, unlike the mind, it cannot attend to all things at one and the same time, it strives to at least comprehend them sequentially within itself through multiple acts of time. For this reason it manifests certain forms and powers at certain times, and other forms and powers at other times; it increases the number of actions in due progression; and little by little it reveals its multiform seed-like offspring.

Hence the statement by Boethius: 'It encircles the deep mind and, by a similar likeness, it turns the heavens'. That this encircling is needful for it we briefly confirm, for it is the first movement in the soul, and especially in the celestial soul, and the first time is undoubtedly a movement which is whole and everlasting in the soul.

If it proceeds perpetually through the forms, the particular forms of things are defined by number. Eventually it goes beyond them all and is obliged to stop, unless it goes back to the same things and starts all over again. But since it is unable to come to rest, being mobile by nature and inclination, it is not surprising that it makes its orbit of its own will as much as of necessity.

By a similar necessity the heavens revolve, as we have shown in the *Theology* and in Plotinus. In the heavens the moon equals one revolution of the sun with twelve of its own revolutions, and the sun, too, likewise equals one revolution of Jupiter with exactly twelve of its own. From this it is clear that just as Phoebus is a friend to Jupiter, so

Phoebe is as much a friend to Phoebus. But we have dealt with this subject in the books *On the Sun* and *On Light* and in the *Book of Life*. In the same way, among the celestial souls the supreme soul, with a single universal revolution of forms and actions, accomplishes what the souls that follow it effect with many repetitions and round-about journeys.

But to return to the paradoxes of Parmenides: How does the soul come into being? How does it perish? Indeed, while it adopts a definite set of forms, principles, and actions, then the soul is said to come into being or to be produced in this way. But when it casts this off, then it is said to perish or to cease. Such is its constitution. And so, just like the phoenix, it everlastingly perishes into itself and is re-born from itself, but to a much more excellent state.

Again, how does the soul become rarefied? How does it become compressed? It seems to compress itself insofar as it gathers various elements together into one, either by taking action or by observing. It seems to become rarefied, on the other hand, when it differentiates and expands the one into many.

The soul also enlarges itself as it perceives greater expansions and arranges them within itself. But it diminishes when it brings forth and differentiates things subject to greater limitations. In these ways it seems to become larger or smaller.

But it is considered to be made equal inasmuch as it deals with things that are equal and, at that time, it is thought to be, as it were, in balance.

But the aforesaid movements seem to belong, in some measure, to substance and quantity. What, therefore, is change within the soul as far as quality in particular is concerned? It is, perhaps, a changeable disposition which at one time gives more attention to some things, and at another time gives more attention to other things. For a changeable disposition changes attitude, and attitude changes quality.

Are there any local movements within the soul? Indeed there are. For all movements are within the first movement by virtue of its power and its position as model. The soul, therefore, rises to causes and comes down again to effects. It moves to the right and it moves to the left, pondering the connections. It goes forwards and it goes backwards, balancing the earlier against the later.

Finally, it moves in a straight line, continually taking something from something else; and it also moves sideways, still observing itself. Lastly, it moves in a circle when it eventually brings the revolutions from the forms back to the same forms; when, having moved forward from causes to effects, it once more returns to the causes; and also when, through its disposition and contemplation, it turns back to its parents, from whom it went forth.

When describing the movements, Parmenides frequently uses an active verb, *metaballein*. By using this verb he is indicating that the soul is not changed by some external agency, but that it changes itself and goes from stillness into movement and from movement back to stillness, from one extreme to the other; that in the midst of all these extremes it preserves something which is eternal and indivisible and in which it experiences neither of the two extremes.

But when we refer to the indivisible, it is useful to take some evidence from the natural philosophers. They show immediately that one point is kept apart from another point by something divisible. Otherwise, if a point is placed as closely as possible to another point, we might be obliged to admit that what is divisible and continuous is composed of indivisibles, and that the indivisible is divisible.

For if one point touches another point, it may be asked whether one point is deeply embedded within the other or whether they touch each other externally through their outer limits. If the first answer is given, nothing continuous is composed therefrom; if the second is granted, each of the two points becomes divisible.

After this they conclude that the movement of bodies, too, when it has become continuous, necessarily continues in an unbroken state, as anything that is similarly in motion separates, by its motion, one moment from another. For otherwise there would follow the absurd conclusion that the things in movement are the things without interval. But since time is an occurrence, the same movements are adduced with regard to all moments of time.

They are also quick to assert that no movement occurs within an indivisible moment. For since movement is always a continuously enacted going forth from one thing to another, it would not be move-ment unless it crossed a defined space in a particular lapse of time.

Now imagine, for example, that a movement on foot is being made, in a moment, across space. Once this movement has been suggested, a quicker movement can be discovered. This quicker movement will undoubtedly cover the same space more quickly; and if more quickly, then that moment which has just been conceived of as undivided will be divided.

In brief, something moving through space initially touches the first part of the space and later touches the following part. Hence time, even that moment in which it has been accepted that there is movement, is divided. Hence, therefore, they conclude that all the movements of bodies occur within a time that is divisible. But since stillness is the opposite of movement and occurs at the same point, and since, in the same way, there can be stillness in any time-measure in which movement takes place, and vice versa, they also draw the conclusion that stillness occurs not in a moment but in time.

They also reason that, among all the mutually opposed movements, there is some mean in which the moveable suffers neither of the movements, for, if there were no mean, it would come about that opposite movements would be a single movement and, at the same time, something whole would be disturbed by certain opposite movements.

The natural philosophers think that the mean which is inserted into the midst of these movements is perhaps some period of time. Since there may be stillness, and since stillness occurs through time, just as if it interrupted a purely indivisible moment, they will be afraid, as I think, of being obliged to say that a moment has maximum proximity to other moments.

Parmenides, however, is speaking of the movements not of bodies but of the soul, which is circumscribed by laws that are in no way similar. For what objection is there to the proposition that, just as the soul consists of indivisibles, so the movement and time of the soul are also composed of indivisibles? Or that, within the soul, these are more akin to numbers than to measures? Or that the mean, placed here between two movements or between movement and stillness, is totally indivisible? Especially as those movements in the soul are not the same as those in the body, and since this indivisible movement that is undertaken is not so much temporal as eternal, as well as being, as it happens, more exalted, since the celestial soul, through its unity, which is the supreme aspect of its essence, and in accordance with the indivisible, which is always the same, and with the steadfast moment, enjoys the simple One Itself.

And at this level it is, in all respects, above all the phenomena of opposites, just as the One Itself stands wonderfully high above the opposites. Such a level, as I have also indicated previously, Parmenides calls the mean between the opposites, as it is neither of the opposites and is like the centre and pivot by which any repercussions between states of opposition are justly regulated.

But Parmenides accepts what the natural philosophers demonstrate:

that movement and stillness are always brought to conclusion within a certain period of time, and that that which supports the opposites abides not within the same time but within another.

The Third Hypothesis – Chapter 3:
A summary of the third hypothesis; or concluding words on the One, multiplicity, being, non-being, movement, stillness, moment, time, and oppositeness. The movement towards movement and towards stillness

IT REMAINS to look briefly at the coherent nature of this hypothesis. For the one being is not simply one, but one something, both one and many. It is therefore one and not one, for, being many, it is not one and the same.

Again, since that one, after the intellectual level, undergoes fluctuations and time at the vital level, it can be called not only being but non-being as well. If this is its condition, it partakes of essence and does not partake of essence. If this is so, the effect is that when it receives essence it comes into being, and when it loses essence it perishes.

And since it cannot bear these opposites simultaneously, it follows that it bears one at one time, and the other at another time. For the array and the appearance of the forms and actions which it now brings forth within itself it does not project shortly afterwards in the same form, or even in a closely similar form, but in a different form; so that one thing now exists in a certain measure, and later there will be something different.

In some of its configurations and actions it betakes itself rather forcefully to unity, limit, sameness, stillness, simplicity, and the single form that is common to many things, as if laying aside multiplicity, ceasing to be many, and beginning to be one. The converse is often true, too, as when it turns quite strongly towards the opposites of those things which have been mentioned and seems to be divided into many, and to cease being the one which it was previously, and to become many.

In the first case it seems to concentrate, and in the second to dissipate. It often becomes dissimilar to itself, as when it changes its pristine condition, and it becomes similar again whenever it resumes this long-abandoned condition. It becomes larger of itself when it conceives larger things, and smaller when it conceives smaller things. It remains equal when it looks around and brings forth what is equal. In these ways it seems to grow larger or smaller or to remain equal.

Thus far it seems to have experienced movements that are mutually opposed, but it is considered to experience, in all places, different things at different times. And in any pair of opposites there is always some mean that is sublime and totally free from obligation to either of the opposites.

But what does Parmenides mean when he says that this living being, of which we have been speaking for a long time, that is, the divine soul, passes from stillness to movement and from movement to stillness? For my part, I think that this soul is to be considered to be in stillness rather than in movement all the time that it is looking attentively upon, striving ardently after, and effectively expressing, the things which are eternal and intelligible and the principles which are related to stillness; and that it is in movement rather than in stillness whenever it betakes itself to all that is opposite. It does these things according to the changing fortune of the other.

But in those changes of fortune the soul is the mean, as we have said: not merely an indivisible moment of time – lest opposing states become a single state, or the soul be influenced simultaneously by opposite states – but also, and much more importantly, a divine mean, if I may express it thus, a moment which we have said transcends eternity. As it is true in that moment of time, so it is much truer in this moment that it experiences none of the opposites.

Parmenides rightly says that there is no time in which a thing neither moves nor is at rest. For at every point of time, at every temporal pause, anything temporal must be either moving or at rest, the direct opposite of movement. There is, however, something which is completely indivisible and which is either around time or within eternity or even higher, and within which anything that is particularly divine does not actually move or experience stillness, the opposite of movement.

He deems that between these two the change experienced in a moment is effected by one opposite upon the other. But he does not think that movement itself, which is bound to time and space, is enacted in a moment. Moreover, whatever moves cannot, by virtue of its movement, be simultaneously at rest; and the converse holds true as well. Therefore it does these things at different times. And while it is at rest it strives, by virtue of being at rest, after stillness. Likewise, while it is moving it strives after movement. And so, while it is still it does not change to movement, and while it is moving it does not change to stillness.

Some change, however, is necessary, by which there is a transference from one thing to another and which is necessarily in the moment that is the mean of them both. This mean is needed between two opposites, to prevent them from being kept in unity against their nature.

If it happens that some natural philosophers maintain that this mean is divisible, this has nothing to do with Parmenides, who intends living movements, rather than bodily movements, to be understood here. He concludes that at this token-point between stillness and movement the soul does not move, for movement requires space, and, indeed within the one which is indivisible and eternal, the divine itself, it does not find rest, which is the opposite of this movement and which is going to endure for a time.

The living one is not to be called non-being [*non esse*], for it exists there above fluctuations; and it is not to be given the other name for non-being [*non ens*], for it exists there above essence and close to the simple One Itself. At this level it does not yet undergo stillness or movement, sameness or change, for these have no place near the One Itself. However, it does experience them at the second or third level.

He concludes, at last, that within the indivisible which is around time no movement of opposites occurs. For movements do not take place in a moment; and if there happen to be any opposite movements there, that is where the movements are produced at the same time. The implicit conclusion, as we have often said before, is that the one which, to its own advantage, has been taken within the divine soul above essence does not directly support opposing movements, or other opposites, within itself.

The Fourth Hypothesis – Chapter 1:
The aim of the fourth hypothesis.
The whole before the parts. The whole after
the parts. Divine matters. Natural matters.
The relation of the parts to the whole

THE THREE previous hypotheses, as we have said elsewhere, contemplate the One Itself rather than all else, and they relate the One to itself first of all, and then relate it to all else.

But two of the following five hypotheses, on the contrary, consider all else rather than the One and give a threefold reason for relating them. Indeed, they relate every one of those parts to the One, partly to itself, and partly to other things.

And so the fourth hypothesis, which we are now confronting, looks at other things in three different ways. For as soon as it has posited that the one being exists beneath the simple One Itself (since it is seeking to trace the one being from its origin), it at once demonstrates that other things are neither this simple One Itself nor the one being that is very close to the One, but that they partake of the One. In this way, therefore, it relates other things to the One. It also relates each of these other things to itself when it reasons that it is multiple by nature, that it has parts, that it is a complete unified entity, and so on.

On the other hand, the hypothesis relates it to other things when it reasons that *this* is similar or dissimilar to *that*, and so on. It would be worth recalling what we have also said elsewhere: under the appellation *other things* the fourth hypothesis considers the natural things and types which, at the next level, follow the souls.

Furthermore, as we have explained elsewhere, since all intellectual and rational substances (among which our souls are numbered) start from the eternal principle – indeed, from eternity itself and, above all, from the One – they are so fully endowed by this that some eternal unity within them rises high above multiplicity and movement and is prior to any point of origin.

It is in this way, therefore, that from the inner unity of those things very many powers flow forth and then turn back to themselves and to their cause and are distinct from matter and are considered distinguishable from matter. Moreover, the substantial forms and the types in particular seem to portray, at least within this One, a similar gift of divinity in natural things, because the form of substance and type is the origin of their multiple properties. For example, the fire-type has brought with it light, heat, dryness, keenness, lightness, and nimbleness. But from *that* it slips down into *this*, as we have shown in our *Theology*.

Unlike the higher substances, they do not possess their own being and existence within their essence, but they gather them into a compound. For this reason, if we consider such a compound as one complete being, if I may express it like that, arising from form and matter together, we say that this whole depends on the parts and that this one depends on multiplicity, through the unifying function of the higher cause.

For this reason, therefore, even those things which appear as simple bodies are compounded, and what appears as a uniform continuum is composed of many parts in succession, and what seems to be a mixture of elements is ultimately resolved, in some way, from the former multiplicity into a single form of the whole.

And so the fourth hypothesis considers these forms, these continuums, these mixtures, and such like, in which the whole depends on the parts, and the one depends on multiplicity, by virtue of a higher cause, and finally the first principles depend on power.

Just as art, bringing its work from many to a perfect conclusion, produces, beyond the many, a single design, form and force, much more does nature, the everlasting instrument of divine unity, in achieving the aim of its Mover, produce one from the many, beyond the many, so that the limit of generation coincides with the unity of the Mover and so that there is the single work made by the single craftsman, and, finally, so that there is the single action of the single work.

But to put it briefly, when we relate natural works to the simple One Itself, we irrefutably judge a work of this kind to be not the One, since it is something other than the One Itself: that is, we judge it to be something multiple and manifold, and, as it is dependent on the One which works mightily in all things, to become a partaker of the One.

For the same reason we consider it to be one, not torn asunder or imperfectly assembled, but engendered from its parts through the power of the One Itself and from the perfect fusion of its parts. Such parts are related to such a whole. It is not a whole unless it consists of parts; and they are not truly parts unless they are parts of a whole.

But when we say *whole*, we understand either a new form that transcends the number of its parts or simply the number of the parts, but we consider this number to be whole. If we take the first way of understanding *whole* and relate the parts, as parts, to this One Itself, we are in accord with Parmenides. But if we take the second way we depart further and further from Parmenides every time we try to relate a particular part to this kind of whole.

For imagine that four is the number of parts in this kind of whole. Let me take the first part. I ask whether this first part should be called part of the whole: Is it part of the universal assemblage? If it is said to be so, it will follow that it is a part of every one that can be reckoned within the assemblage. For it is not right to refer it to anything except these four. Once this is conceded, nothing at all is the whole except the assemblage of parts.

And so it will follow, as I was saying just now, that once any part has been taken, if it is a part of the whole assemblage, it exists as a part of every one. Any part will therefore be a part of itself and a part of every part, which is plainly absurd. Thus for us to depart from the untrue and be able to truly relate the part to the whole, we must admit that in addition to the assemblage of the four parts there exists a single complete form. But of this one, which is common to all alike, any parts are declared multiple in relation to it.

Now this form of the whole beyond the parts is so essential within things that are not separate that the followers of Plato consider it vital within numbers, too, clearly thinking that the trinity-type exists in the number three in addition to its particular unities, a type that partakes of the general unity.

It is a similar situation in all else. He affirms not only that any whole partakes of one but also that the individual parts are composed of unity, because they partake of the general unity within the whole and also because any part is distinct from any other and different from the whole. Any part, therefore, is rightly said to be every part, that is, a certain one differing from another in its particular quality, a difference that necessarily belongs to unity.

The Fourth Hypothesis – Chapter 2:
On multiplicity and its relation to the One.
On the unlimited and on limit. On the elements of
beings. On other things that are mutually opposed

IF YOU CAN imagine a multiplicity totally devoid of the One, it will be, as we have frequently shown, a multiplicity whole and unlimited; each part and each particle of each part will be equally unlimited throughout the unlimited.

But is it permissible to imagine multiplicity in this way? It is perhaps permissible for Parmenides when he is considering with the most precise reasoning that the very principle of the One is different from the principle of multiplicity, since the principle of the One is necessarily followed by union, limit, stillness, sameness, equality, and similarity, while the principle of multiplicity is followed by the opposite: division, limitlessness, movement, change, inequality, dissimilarity, and others of this kind.

But when he is considering multiplicity in isolation from the One, he is not considering this multiplicity or that multiplicity; or a multiplicity of unities or of other things that are in any way fixed; or a multiplicity that behaves in this way or in that way; but he is considering simple multiplicity itself and perhaps a power that is capable of indefinite multiplication and of being formed in any way whatever by an external agency, always behaving without distinction to assume this or that multiplicity, and the multiple ways and limits through these or those forms or movements.

Therefore, while Parmenides conjectures an indefinite and very unstable assemblage which of itself is very different from the One and does not yet partake of the One, he rightly has a limitless view of this assemblage as limitless. But since what is below the One is given effective shape and strong limits, he predicts that this, too, will soon be subject to forms and limits, and that in this way what is produced as a compound is a commingling of the limitless and of limit. Indeed, this is the nature of all things except the First.

But in natural things, which he is now relating to the First, limitlessness especially prevails, together with the conditions consequent upon limitlessness. Hence it comes about that all natural things are alike in this at least, that they are individually produced from limitlessness and limit. They are alike, I say, through the conjoining of these two. For this conjoining is in all things.

But, on the other hand, since these two are mutually opposed, the types sustain the same phenomenon, whether it be limitlessness or limit. Yet since these two are opposed each to the other, they impart to things a diversity through which each individual thing experiences some dissimilarity within itself, partly in relation to the limit put upon limitlessness and partly in relation to the limit put upon those things that are subsequent; and through which, on the other hand, each thing is also different from other things, since it holds within itself the conjoining of different elements. For this is how discords arise, and different things partake in different ways of limitlessness and limit.

But to put it briefly: from this conjoining of limitlessness and limit, which are the first elements of all beings, the other conjoinings of opposites take place sporadically. I mean the conjoinings of dissimilars: sameness and change, similarity and dissimilarity, stillness and movement, equality and inequality, parity and imparity, and such like. Some of the opposites accompany limitlessness, and others accompany limit. But such conjoinings of divergent elements have either a discordant concord or a concordant discord, as Empedocles proclaims: thus they are not the One Itself, but are beneath the One and partake of the One.

The Fifth Hypothesis – Chapter 1:
The aim of the fifth hypothesis. On the One. On things separate from the One. Whether the One is in accord with them. On omniform being. On formless matter

FIRSTLY, WE NEED to remind ourselves of what we said initially when treating of the one being and of matter, especially in this fifth hypothesis. And while some things are related here to the one being, others with the same name signify the first matter, which, in spite of being single, is treated as if plural by being named not only *something else* but also *other things*, for its formative power extends to all. Its location, however, is to be confirmed by logical ingenuity.

The result is that he discusses the One or the others, as he will, provided that he is teaching, by these means, the consequences of such reasonings. And so, if he happens here to touch upon the simple One Itself as well as upon all other things, it is true that what is currently designated the One Itself has nothing in common with everything else. If this were not the case, it would not be the first and utterly single Absolute. It is also true that the One Itself has no parts and is not immanent, either wholly or partially, in other things. Then, according to the present analysis, other things follow logically.

There is an underlying mystery here, too, by which we understand that primal matter is compared to the one being, to itself, and to other things. In this context, understand the one being as principally the intelligible world, the first uniform and omniform form. To this compare matter, which is utterly without form. Although these two are in harmony inasmuch as they both, in their respective ways, partake of the simple One Itself, they are not in harmony inasmuch as there is no common element that can be imparted to them both. For the Absolute stands supreme. Although they seem to be in harmony insofar as they both depend, through their own unity, on the simple One Itself and reflect the simple One Itself according to their respective powers, yet, putting aside the impress of that source, which is, as I might say, extraneous to them both, consider each with its own specific nature: the former fully omniform, the latter quite lacking in form. You will see that they are mutually opposite in all respects and so divergent that nothing of the first is in the second, and nothing of the second is in the first.

Again, the two fail to meet in any common being which is intelligible and endowed with a form. With respect to the former, all forms are predicated, together with all that potentially has a form. But with respect to the latter, all such predications are rightly withheld.

Now consider Parmenides' statement that there is nothing beside one and others. If, as I was suggesting, you take *one* as the divine, omniform world, and if you take *others* as the material world, it is true that there is nothing beside these in any hierarchy of beings. But if you perceive *others* as formless matter, there is nothing apart from these in which they could meet within any particular form.

Now consider the statement that one does not have parts. If you wish that to be a statement about the one being, it should be said that, just as the simple One Itself simply has no parts, so the one being has no essential parts on account of which it could be said to contain within itself numerous essences or an essence which can be separated from itself within various Ideas.

In short, however, it is said to have no parts, that you may understand that when the intelligible world, either as creator or as model, is considered to form matter, it neither subjects itself wholly to matter nor imparts anything of its own nature to matter, but rather does it impart images and shadows.

You may therefore conclude that, when *others* are said neither to be one nor to possess any one within themselves, matter is not the formal one and does not naturally possess any manifestation of the formal one itself.

The Fifth Hypothesis – Chapter 2:
Confirmation of the above, and how matter has no formal conditions within itself. Also, where it comes from, how it is formed, and how it moves

BUT TAKING UP these things once more, let us then move on to what remains. If we consider, on the one hand, the One Itself in its sublime simplicity and, on the other hand, matter in its pure primal state, we shall see that matter, being wholly dependent on the One, possesses something of the One or receives something from the One. For each is unitary and simple. Of each all things are negated, but it is an excess-negation for the One and a deficiency-negation for matter. Between these two – between the highest and the lowest – all things are encompassed.

But if we now reflect that the One in some way comes down from its pre-eminence and simplicity and forthwith becomes omniform, which is what the followers of Plato call the one being, and if we also compare matter to this one, we shall undoubtedly discern that matter, being completely formless, has within itself nothing of that which is omniform and does not depend on it initially, provided that the dominion of the simple One Itself is not more extensive than the power of the one being. But if matter which has not yet assumed any forms depends on the one being in some way, such dependence, as we have said elsewhere, certainly seems due to the fact that it is one rather than to the fact that it is a being.

Matter, therefore, is not a formal one, and is therefore not a formal 'many'. It is not a whole, for a whole is a form. It does not have parts of a whole, and it is not a formal part of a whole which is formal, for it naturally has nothing formal within it. I make but passing reference to what Plotinus says: that matter is not, in truth, a part of any compound, but is everywhere the basis of images, rather like a mirror. It has no specific number within itself, for number is founded on formal discrimination.

Besides, since similarity and dissimilarity relate to forms and qualities, matter which is not yet formed is not deemed to be similar or dissimilar to the one being or to any being. Again, it is not equal or unequal if it has not yet received quantity, which is other than itself. It is not the same and it is not different, for formal sameness and difference are differentiations of the one being which matter does not undergo unless it is first formed therefrom.

For this reason it is neither still nor moving, since stillness and movement are formal properties of being, while matter, which naturally has neither one nor the other, is beyond their mutually opposed actions. If, then, it has no movement itself, it certainly cannot move from non-being, or vice versa. For this reason it is not born and does not die.

In short, it does not naturally possess any of the opposites, either simultaneously or sequentially. It does not possess them simultaneously because opposites cannot occur simultaneously within something quite indivisible and basic which cannot reconcile them. It does not naturally possess opposites sequentially because it is immutable in itself and it does not admit formal conditions or differences in its first state. It does not, moreover, possess numbers or numerical differences because these are all formal.

In brief, matter by its very nature (if any nature is merely to be mentioned) has no unity, no form, no movement. But it is allotted unity from the simple One Itself as it comes forth from it. Then it is allotted forms from the one being. Thirdly and lastly, it is allotted movements from the soul.

But if the first mind and the soul of the world impart unity and existence to matter, and yet they do so not as mind or as soul but as one which is simply an instrument, they consider that matter is brought forth formless, being derived from the One through the limitlessness which, within the intelligible world or even within the world of soul, is analogous to matter. It is also said that the One produces matter from limitlessness. These are the statements that would be made on the view of the general school of those who follow Plato.

The Sixth Hypothesis – Chapter 1:
The aim of the sixth hypothesis.
In what way Parmenides is poetical.
More on being and non-being

PARMENIDES not only expounded the mysteries of philosophy as a philosopher but also sang them in verse as a divine poet. And in this dialogue, too, he plays the part of the poet.

For, like a poet, he cultivates the number nine, which, as it is said, is sacred to the Muses. By means of nine hypotheses, which are like the nine Muses, the guides to knowledge, he leads us to truth and to Apollo; for while he is moving towards the simple One Itself he seems to be advancing towards Apollo, the name by which the followers of Pythagoras mystically designate the simple One Itself; for Apollo, as Plato and his followers teach, signifies the simple Absolute devoid of multiplicity.

At the same time, to play the part of the poet with some precision, he varies the meanings of the names. Using the name *One* in different ways at different times and in different places, he experiences it in different ways. On a similar basis, being versatile in many other things, he sometimes imagines it as a poet would. For not only does he affirm the things that are but he also frequently fashions things that are not and, indeed, those things that cannot be.

In fact, through poetic licence he often employs paradoxes. He often conceals things under the names of other things. He takes frequent delight in metaphors, through which he graphically transposes strange things onto others. For who but a poet would invest indivisible nature with form, or eternal nature with motion? Only a poet would call his awareness a sphere.

And so, most of his words require an allegorical interpretation. This is why Plato was right to warn us in *Theaetetus* to take care not to be deluded by his art in this dialogue and not to take matters and words otherwise than in the way he intends and declares. But what dealings does a dialectician have with a poet? Clearly, the closest possible dealings. For together and separately they deal, as they say, with their own concepts and their own devices; both are considered divine; and both have an element of the ecstatic.

But let us now proceed with our theme. So far he has gone through five hypotheses that assume the One to be. But from this point onwards he adds four hypotheses that assume the One not to be. Thus, in the earlier hypotheses he introduced this word *One* in many ways, like a poet, and discussed it first of all by saying that if the One exists above being, then no being really exists. And he cherished that talent within himself as something worthy of respect. For it is preferable for light to exist outside colours than to be inherent in colours.

Secondly, he showed that if the One is within being it is all beings. Thirdly, he pointed out that if the One is not only within being but also beneath being, then all things are and equally are not. In the fourth and fifth hypotheses he compared other things to the One which stands above being and the One which is within being, but particularly to the One which is within being.

After these five, as if thinking that poets have full licence, he not only imagines the non-existence of that One which he thinks necessarily exists, but also, after he has imagined that it is not, he wants to know exactly what happens to that One, as if something could happen to that which is not. But, at the same time, his attempts are never absurd.

Moreover, since he is not ignorant of the fact that opposites revolve about that which is the same, when he comes to this sixth hypothesis, and likewise the seventh and eighth and ninth, and is going to imagine that the One is not, he does not go back to that simple One to which being does not belong, for that One is far more sublime than essence; but rather does he go back to that subsequent one which being already reaches and concerning which it is more acceptable to imagine the opposite, that is, to imagine non-being. Here, therefore, as well as subsequently, he particularly wishes to know what follows if that one is not, that one which is within beings, that is, within intellectual and divine substances.

But, as I have said, he did not venture to do away with the first One.

For he had more freedom to imagine that a second one, coming from a source outside itself and therefore by no means self-existent, does not in any way exist; and, if it does not in any way exist, to import something lower which is nevertheless dependent on the First.

But it would have been very awkward to negate the First, which is the very bedrock of existence, or, if the First were somehow negated, to dream up something further. It was in this way, therefore, that he denied that his hyperbolical fiction was inept.

Finally, in this sixth hypothesis, he imagines the one being, the intellectual nature, not to be; but in such a way that it partly is and partly is not. But in the seventh hypothesis he is more at liberty to imagine that it absolutely is not, for he is clearly in a position to understand the absurd conclusions that arise from both propositions.

The Sixth Hypothesis – Chapter 2:
How the One, while called non-being, may also in some way be understood as being. How this kind of non-being is recognised. Concerning the soul

A LOGICIAN posits a subject and a predicate within a proposition. In fact, in the proposition 'One is not' *One* is, as it were, the subject, while *is not* is the predicate; as if being dissolves into non-being and as if One is called non-being.

Therefore compose a different proposition, such as 'The non-One is not'. This seems the opposite of the earlier proposition. Firstly, in the former proposition the subject is the One Itself, but now it is the non-One; and so they are opposite or mutually contradictory. Secondly, the meanings of the two propositions are in opposition, for the former in some way does away with the One, while the latter completely restores it.

Let us now compare, not the propositions in their entirety, but the subjects *the One* with *the non-One*. The second subject is certainly the opposite of the first. For when we say *One*, we have not yet removed it from the universal nature of things. But when we say *non-One*, we have now cast it out.

The One, therefore, has not yet been removed by the subject of the first proposition and is not directly considered to be indefinite, but is considered as a principle that is different from non-being, since we have not yet added non-being to it. And when we do add it, we add it as something different.

Indeed, it is truer to say that we introduce the One Itself as something different. Similarly, when we say *If magnitude is not*, we are referring to magnitude itself as something other than the One and as something other than non-being. And in both cases, while we are making our conditional statements by saying *If One is not* and *If magnitude is not*, we are declaring that One, or magnitude, is other than non-being.

Perhaps, therefore, we shall seem here to be making an affirmation by recognising the very principle of the One Itself as something different from all others and from non-being. The very principle of the One, therefore, is something unique to itself and may be thought of as distinct from all else and from non-being.

For the principle of the One exists of itself before there is added to it the principle of being or the principle of non-being or of any other kind of being. And while we are joining non-being to it, we can understand what that is within itself of which we are predicating non-being, and how it differs from non-being and from all else.

Therefore, since by saying *If One is not* we are certainly saying and understanding something, we seem at the same time to have some knowledge of the One Itself, of non-being itself, and of the condition that has now been proposed. For this reason, if the One is not, but in such a way that it also to some extent is, and in such a way that it furnishes us with a clear-cut principle of itself, there is certainly some knowledge of it.

It is worth observing that if the simple One Itself ever becomes the one being it also immediately becomes the intelligible and the intellect. Again, if this one intelligible and intellectual being degenerates in some way into non-being, while experiencing the first movement and the first time, it is transformed into soul.

Through this change, therefore, while the soul rules in place of the intellect and the supreme intelligible which has now been replaced, all things in the universe would henceforth be subject to motion. Nowhere beneath the soul would things be stable, for the soul, acting naturally through movement, produces moving things everywhere. But of this, if it is appropriate, we shall speak subsequently.

On the other hand, if the one being is totally changed into non-being and the soul now perishes, all that is subject to motion will henceforth cease to be. But similar words on this subject will be held over until later.

For the present it is enough to recall that in the sixth hypothesis Parmenides, while detailing in some way the many conditions of the one being and of non-being, is detailing the conditions of the soul. But how the soul mingles within itself both non-being and being we seem to have expounded at sufficient length in the third hypothesis. There he introduced the eternal and the temporal parts of the soul equally, while here he leans more towards the temporal.

But in this part also, where non-being seems to degenerate towards flux, he shows that it still has absolutely all the conditions of being, such is the excellence of the first movement and of the first time and so intermingled is the nature of opposites within the soul.

In this hypothesis, therefore, he mingles opposites with opposites, as befits the soul, and he investigates movement; and he partly affirms and partly negates, just as he did in the third hypothesis.

The Sixth Hypothesis – Chapter 3:
How the One which is called non-being is the nature of the soul; why it is subject to movement; knowledge concerns this non-being; to it belong change, multiplicity, and characteristic features.

WHILE YOU are investigating the mysteries hidden throughout this hypothesis, and likewise throughout the other hypotheses, discover at the same time the very clever way in which the conclusions are wonderfully interwoven and in which every point is confirmed not only by things related to it but also by things opposed to it.

Individual things are distinguished with the greatest precision. The whole is fittingly discovered within the individual, so that, as

Anaxagoras had said earlier, almost anything can be produced from anything else. So always be shrewd and adroit: be logical as well as philosophical. Thus advised, proceed with what remains.

One aspect of the truth about this living non-being lies in universal nature itself and in formal principles. Change is inherent in nature and also inherent in non-being insofar as non-being is fluid. Through such change non-being is different from all other things, and its type of movement and time is different from that of other things. Unless they add some qualification, the followers of Plato always speak of the two kinds of being [ens, esse] on the understanding that they are constant and eternal.

Here, therefore, while being is negated with respect to nature and the inconstant action of the soul, understand that it is eternal being that is negated, rather than particular being. However, although on this principle true and eternal being is not inherent in it, yet temporal being is found to be intermingled with some kind of non-being.

For in this temporal and changeable situation we are considering two things: changeability itself on the one hand, and on the other hand the unchanging force and everlasting steadfastness by which it is governed. Insofar as it belongs to this kind of steadfastness mingled with movement, it can be called both being and non-being; but insofar as it is related to flux, it is more aptly called non-being. For being can belong to it on account of the principle of flux itself.

On the basis of this principle, however, it can rightly be called multiple. For, in a way, one is many, and multiplicity is, in a way, single. On this principle it is permissible to call this some kind of one and some kind of multiplicity; of it and for it, flux is the being.

And since nothing is negated with respect to this one, except that being alone which is eternal and true, there is nothing to prevent many other things from belonging to it. If this were not the case, it would not be spoken of or thought of as one or as multiple or as moving, and we should be unable to speak of it.

The Sixth Hypothesis – Chapter 4:
Around this non-being One stand dissimilarity, similarity, inequality, equality, largeness, smallness, and, in some measure, essence.
Also concerning the soul

WE AFFIRM that this changeability within the soul is truly quite different from other things: different, indeed, from other things which are totally constant, because movement is opposed to stillness; and different, too, from other things which are changeable, because the soul is changeable of itself, while other things are moved by external agencies.

We therefore rightly deem that changeability to be dissimilar to others by virtue of a dissimilarity which is compatible with that kind of changeability. But that principle by which it is distinguished from all others is that property by which it is compatible with itself and similar to itself. If this were not the case, it would be devoid of its very own property.

He subsequently negates equality, and rightly so. For the changeability of the soul is not equal by the standard of true equality, that is, totally unvarying and eternal equality. It is not equal to other things, that is, to absolutely eternal substances, which are, in fact, deemed equal because they are always constituted equally. Otherwise, if the changeability of the soul possessed true equality it would truly be and would possess true similarity. Again, it is not at all equal to other temporal things, for it is by nature considerably superior.

Therefore, since the basis on which changeability is deemed different is the basis on which it is unequal, it is no wonder that, on account of its inequality, it is called both larger and smaller. And since the larger and the smaller are very far apart on account of their being in opposition, they require a mean, that is, a certain equality, and, of course, as the changeable nature grows or diminishes it seems at some point to encounter some kind of equality: I do not mean true everlasting equality, but a fluid equality comparable to some kind of flux or to part of the flux.

For this reason the following are compatible with this one living, or flowing, non-being: inequality, equality, smallness, largeness, similarity, dissimilarity, change.

Essence is also, to some extent, compatible with it, and rightly so, for the things we were enumerating are deemed differences of being.

Moreover, when we attribute non-being, and the other things enumerated previously, to this changeable one, we are thinking and speaking the truth, if it is the case that the truth is what is, for truth and being are inter-changeable. And so this one is truly non-being, and this truth is within universal nature and with formal principles, that is, this one non-being, this perfect non-being.

Therefore this one is non-being in such a way that it partakes to some extent in some kind of essence. Otherwise, if you remove this very truth, this very being, by which it is called non-being, we shall certainly speak untruly when we say that one is not.

Therefore, when non-being is predicated of this one, this is a true assertion. It is being itself, but in such a way that it is non-being. For the confirmatory basis of being is that it is not non-being. But the confirmatory basis of non-being is that it is non-being. The bond, therefore, by which non-being is joined to one is some sort of being. If this be the whole being, it will not join one with non-being, but with perfect being. Yet if it in no way is, it will join nothing and will predicate nothing.

There is, therefore, some plastic being which allows non-being to be predicated of the one. This being which partakes of non-being, and, on the other hand, this non-being which is composed of being are, as we have said, the very nature of the soul, in which stillness is commingled with movement, and movement with stillness. And what is within it is the one that is subject to movement: on account of its fluidity it is described as partly non-being, and on account of its steadiness, which in turn is likewise restored within movement, it is rightly described as partly being.

The Sixth Hypothesis – Chapter 5:
Around this non-being One exist being and non-being, movement, change, and annihilation, together with their opposites.
More on the soul

IN THE MOVEMENT of the soul, such as we have described it else-where, the past and the future are in mutual opposition, so that they cannot be together at the same time. The present, for its part, has nothing of the past or of the future.

In this movement and time the soul, as we have said earlier, goes through a range of attitudes within itself. These attitudes cannot all be together at the same time. And when one of them is present, a second is past, and a third is yet to come.

For this reason, therefore, the soul, in some way, alternately is and is not, through perpetual alternation. And it is necessary for this one that is subject to movement, that is and is not by turns, to bear these two conditions with patience and, for that reason, to move. For it seems unable to move for any other reason, since it cannot change. For this one that is subject to movement, and is therefore fluid, has no place within the order of beings, for all these are steadfast.

Therefore it cannot be changed from one being to another, from one eternal to another. By this stipulation, therefore, it does not change, and by this proposition it does not move. Yet it is not only straight movement of this kind that is negated: circular movement is also negated. For the perfect circle is compatible with pure intellect, and it turns within that identity. But that very identity, belonging to perfect steady being, is not compatible with this living flux. Nor is change compatible, when the change is so great that it diverges from its very nature and quality.

For the earlier reasons, it seems to move: for the later reasons, it seems to be at rest. And each is true, in accordance with its own set of conditions.

Finally, the principle by which it endures, remaining the same within its own nature and not changing from it, is the principle by which it moves certain attitudes and alternates them, and the same is changed in attitude. Thus dispensing with the earlier attitudes and adopting the later ones, it seems to die and to be reborn; but, on the other hand, not previously assuming or ever abandoning the property natural to it, it never comes into being and never perishes.

However, if anyone supposes the One partly to be and partly not to be, he will understand that the being that remains as a result of this supposition would not be alive, just as he explains that non-perceptible being does not change, does not die, and is not born; clearly, since the matter within even perceptible things is everlasting, he follows us in his exposition of everything else. We, however, consider the exposition already given to be more fitting.

The Seventh Hypothesis:
The aim of the seventh hypothesis.
Concerning the levels of the One, of being, and of non-being. How all things are negated with respect to the One and with respect to non-being

WHEN WE SPEAK of the simple One Itself we are proclaiming the limitless by saying that it is not multiple, not composite, not circumscribed, not conjoined. But when we affirm the one being we are appreciating the One Itself as limited by the very form of essence: a form, however, that is pure and quite universal.

Again, when we contemplate the one being within an essence that is to some extent subject to movement – movement, however, that is generated through itself – we now have a being which is commingled to some extent with non-being, and thus we obtain henceforth the intellectual soul in place of the pure intellect.

Moreover, when we consider the One in a condition that is liable to be moved by an external agency, we now have the minimum of being together with the maximum of non-being.

Lastly, when we completely remove all movement and all admixture, we seem to view non-being as a dream and perhaps as having two possibilities: either it is nothing, since it is lower than any being whatsoever and is also deprived of the One; or it is the simple One Itself, since it is higher than all beings, however exalted they may be.

For this reason, in the seventh hypothesis we consider the one being not only to have fallen of itself into a soul subject to movement, and

217

not only to have been cast into a flux that is dependent on something external, but also to have been finally released into total non-being; strictly speaking, to have fallen into nothingness, but metaphorically to have been restored, as I might say, to the simple One Itself.

The seventh hypothesis seems to discuss this One Itself, insofar as it negates, with respect to this simple non-being, properties which are rightly negated through default with respect to nothing and through excess with respect to the simple One Itself. Here someone might understand the One, which in no way is, as formless matter also, which indeed in no way is, so that of itself it has no formal essence. In truth, the One exists by partaking of the One; but more on this later if there is an opportunity.

Parmenides, however, both in these four hypotheses and also in the previous ones often comes to opposite conclusions about the same thing. For my part, I strive as far as I can to harmonise individual items and to deduce probabilities, so that, when he makes suppositions, his suppositions do not seem rash.

For your part, learn to understand the reasonings on both sides in any subject and to distinguish the two meanings, and thus avoid being obliged to admit impossibilities.

Now in these four hypotheses he adduces opposing proofs about the same thing, not only to make you adept through the process of reasoning but also to enable you to discern the great number of absurd and self-contradictory points that have to be made if the One is imagined to be non-existent.

The Eighth Hypothesis – Chapter 1:
The aim of the eighth hypothesis.
If mind is removed and soul remains, soul will be deceptive and will abide in the realm of shadows

THE EIGHTH hypothesis compares other future possibilities. If the one being is imagined not to be, but in such a way that it partly is and partly is not, that is, if all pure, intelligible, and intellectual substance be removed – the substance that purely and simply is – immediately there rules in its place that soul in which, as we have said, the one being is commingled through flux with non-being.

Now the soul, being illumined and strengthened by the intelligible substance, has true cognition and brings forth natural forms. But if deserted by the intellect, it would engage in false imagination, bring forth likenesses and shadows instead of natural forms, and devise scenarios that are nothing but empty dreams. If these manifest outside the soul, they will have no substance, formal distinction, or unity.

Moreover, since within the soul, which under present conditions that profoundly unified intellectual substance has abandoned, unity itself has henceforth degenerated to such an extent that multiplicity will overpower unity within the soul itself, any assemblage will much more readily and fully absorb the unity within those things which are devised or expressed by the soul, so that unity will no longer prevail in these things, unless there can in any way be an assemblage that is made manifold by unity; but in such an assemblage unity, overcome now by non-action, cannot re-assemble those things which have been scattered; it is as if unity were not present anywhere.

Yet perhaps it is not merely that unity does not act in these things, but the fact is that there will be no unity; for since unity has totally disintegrated in the soul which, as we have supposed, is destitute, it seems probable that unity will be absent from the machinations of the soul; but when unity is lost, is it proper to conceive of multiplicity? Perhaps it is proper to conceive of it once and for a moment, for multiplicity is other than unity, division is other than union, change other than sameness, and flux other than stillness. But it is not proper to prolong this conception, since multiplicity is the repetition of unity, or some forward movement of unity.

It is also probable that just as unity stands above multiplicity in the upward movement through the levels of creation, so unity stands beneath multiplicity in the downward movement through these levels; at all events, however it may be conceived, multiplicity is more fitting than unity for things that are quite empty and shadowy.

Therefore, if Parmenides had held that the One in no way is, he could not then in any way conceive other things to be, since all things necessarily depend on the One. But since he has conceived it in some way to be and also not to be, it was proper for him to grant that other things in some way are, but that their being is much less than that of the One.

Moreover, if the pure intellect be removed, it is permissible to consider the soul to be living and creating images and perceiving, but in a false way; for every true cognition depends on the first intellectual cognition, and if it is granted that this has been removed, then no true imagination remains, and there is no true perception anywhere. There will thus remain deceptive perceptions, deceptive imagination, and false percepts.

Perhaps there will also appear, as in a mirror, images or reflections, which do not exist so much as seem to exist; or rather, whatever they are, they will not be beyond the concepts of the soul, but will be some machinations of the soul itself. And these machinations are false, for Parmenides calls them apparitions, figments, dreams. If they go forth, they will be emptier than insubstantial shadows, which no sooner appear and show their position than they vanish away.

But to sum up: people who are delirious and befuddled with dreams and for whom the eyes create images, often believe their internal conceptions to be external perceptions. Perhaps the soul is affected in the same way, being demented when, as we have supposed, the mind has been removed from the universe.

The Eighth Hypothesis – Chapter 2:
If you remove the One, all things will cease; they will be shadowy multitudes; the inconceivably infinite will merge with their opposites about the same; and faltering imagination will be ever deceitful

NOW FIRSTLY, other things are imagined in some way to be; then they are imagined to be different; and thirdly, the question is asked: From what are these things different?

They are not different from the true One Itself, for they cannot be compared to the true One Itself, that is, to the one true being, when we have imagined this not to be. And they cannot easily be compared to the one soul; for if there were not the one intellect, there would not be the one soul, because oneness has to be transferred from there to the soul.

The multitudes of things will therefore be compared with each other. But what sort of multitudes? First of all, those that are shadowy;

secondly, those that are countless. Each multitude, moreover, will be infinitely limitless; it will not be such as the imaginer imagines.

But how will they differ one from another? Once the One Itself has been removed, the difference will not be that *this* is a particular multitude, while *that* is a different multitude. We have often shown elsewhere that if any multitude is devoid of the One, not only is that multitude a countless totality but it will also be a part and even a detail, an incalculable percept, of the infinite. For if an indivisible one is nowhere to be found, it will be permissible to split it into many in countless different ways.

These and similar consequences arise once the One has been removed. But to concede these things – the removal of unity from individual creatures and the denial of the One Itself to the whole of creation – is as foolish as it is wicked.

Moreover, whatever multitude may occur to the imaginers in a moment as one, the One will not then appear. It will appear as number; and number will not come next. Indeed, since both unity and measure are missing, it will necessarily appear simultaneously as precisely the smallest and precisely the greatest; as the smallest within a given part, and as the greatest and the greatest possible within the tiny parts proceeding from it and, in fact, immediately flowing together.

Some multitudes will seem to be equal to others, since any multitude may appear now as smaller, now as larger, and on occasions perhaps as equal. However, there will not be any equality if unity, the well-spring of equality, is missing. When many multitudes arise, one of them will seem to be beyond the bounds of another, and both, in turn, will seem to have a common boundary, and yet neither of them will have inner limits or a mean, for whatever you accept as a beginning will, being forever multiple, resolve itself into a different beginning and, in the same way, into an end that is forever different.

Anything encountered will be as the end, but because a mean is thought of as equidistant between these and since it is unendingly divisible into more and more parts, it will be forever possible to relate it to a different mean. When the one and undivided is absent, whatever you divide with your imagination will always recur as something to be divided again; firstly, the one will appear, and soon afterwards the limitless. Thus the same things will appear as one and as many, as limited and as unlimited, to those who are imagining or in some way perceiving.

To put it simply, while multitudes appear as one, within this one they will appear as similar or identical; but while they appear as being full of variety, they will seem dissimilar and then as contiguous multitudes, but they will not be confined anywhere by precise contiguity, since those things inherent in them which seem extremes are always further resolved into something, and thus they will seem to be something separate. They will appear to move, and yet not to move: to move, because one can always imagine a movement from one thing to another; yet not to move, because there is no other place to which the unlimited can move.

You will think that multitudes of that kind arise and perish as long as you see them as divisible and differentiated; but you will surmise that they are everlasting as long as you find neither beginning nor end within the unlimited itself, and as long as you deem its power to be unlimited. Into these and similar paradoxes or, rather, insanities will you be cast headlong if for any reason you cast the One out of the universe.

The Ninth Hypothesis:
The aim of the ninth hypothesis

FINALLY, THE NINTH hypothesis teaches that, if the one being does not in any way exist within the creation and within creatures, not only is intellect banished but so is the soul, which is reckoned to be partly within beings. And once the soul is removed, not only are all perceptible things destroyed but all adumbrations perish, together with all perceptions and imaginations; and once the One, which is necessary for multiplicity, is absent, there will be no further multitude of adumbrations.

There will be no naked matter, which cannot exist in isolation from forms, and there will be nothing to appear either as many or as one. For there will not be anything that can appear; no imagination or sense remains to which anything can in any way appear; and if one somehow imagined the survival of imagination, which Parmenides, in an earlier chapter, seems to have concealed under the name of intelligence, such imagination would not be able to make a true and lasting image of multiplicity without the One; but when we said that it is permissible to contemplate multiplicity without the One, we ourselves seem to have exceeded the bounds of imagination.

Indeed, something that in no way exists, and is in no way one, cannot rightly be contemplated or imagined. For whatever you imagine in any way, that figment is at all events conceived within you as a particular entity and as one; and the very movement springing from somewhere to imagine this is from something and from one, and is itself an entity and one.

After such words the conclusion of the whole book is reached. If the simple One Itself, from which arises the one being and from which comes each particular one everywhere, be removed from the universe, there will be absolutely nothing anywhere.

To this general conclusion, however, are subjoined others which are enunciated throughout the entire dialogue and which are introduced partly through the opposing truths spoken on both sides to express a variety of meanings, and partly so that he can exercise the mind of his listener on both sides of the argument (as we have often said before) and at the same time so that it can be more clearly appreciated just how many impossible consequences there would be if the One Itself were removed: the One, which is essential to all things as their maker, their preserver, and their end.

Here end the commentaries on *Parmenides*.

GLOSSARY
to Ficino's *Parmenides* Commentary

Translator's Introductory Notes

THIS GLOSSARY is intended to serve three functions:

1) To give key English words with their Latin originals;
2) To present what Ficino's commentary says about many of these key words;
3) To provide the reader with the opportunity of seeing some of the translated passages side by side with Ficino's Latin.

A degree of mental flexibility is required of the reader, for the 'definitions' are not always as definite or fixed as might be expected or required. This is the case, for example, with the word 'unum', which is central to the whole work. In his dedication to Niccolò Valori, Ficino gives a tantalising warning when he says, 'It should also be noted that when One is mentioned in this dialogue it can, as in the system of the Pythagoreans, indicate any single substance that is totally detached from matter, such as God, mind, and soul [Illud insuper advertendum est quod in hoc dialogo cum dicitur unum, Pythagoreorum more unaquaeque substantia a materia penitus absoluta significari potest, ut deus, mens, anima].' Much later, in Chapter 94, Ficino issues another warning to tread warily: 'It is also acceptable [Placet et] that Parmenides should use the name of the One now in one way and now in another [Parmenidem interdum ipso unius nomine aliter atque aliter uti].' The result is that the translator has sometimes been unsure whether to use 'One' or 'one'. The reader is invited to join in the game by deciding at each occurrence whether the capital is justified.

Again, Ficino refers on several occasions to poetical compositions produced by Parmenides, but it is not until the end of the book is approaching that Ficino spells out the implications of this poetical

225

nature. In his commentary to Chapter 1 of the Sixth Hypothesis, Ficino speaks of the fluidity in the language:

'At the same time [Interea], to play the part of the poet with some precision [ut exactius poetam agat], he varies the meanings of the names [nominum sensus variat]. Using the name 'One' in different ways at different times and in different places [Hoc nomen unum alibi aliter introducens ac passim], he experiences it in different ways [varia sentit]. On a similar basis, being versatile in many other things [in caeteris plerumque simili quadam ratione versutus], he sometimes imagines it as a poet would [fingit etiam nonnunquam ut poeta]. For not only does he affirm the things that are [Non enim sola quae sunt asserit] but he also frequently fashions things that are not [sed etiam quae non sunt saepe confingit] and, indeed, those things that cannot be [illa quinetiam quae esse non possunt]. In fact, through poetic licence he often employs paradoxes [Poetica sane licentia frequenter aggreditur paradoxa]. He often conceals things under the names of other things [Alia frequenter aliorum nominibus occulit]. He takes frequent delight in metaphors [Delectatur saepe metaphoris], through which he graphically transposes strange things on to others [quibus aliena significanter ad alia transfert]. For who but a poet would invest indivisible nature with form, or eternal nature with motion [Quis nam praeter poetam individuae naturae figuram dederit, aeternae motum]? And so, most of his words require an allegorical interpretation [Itaque ferme omnis verborum facies poscit allegoriam].'

GLOSSARY

absolute [absolutum]

'For the Absolute stands supreme [Extat enim supereminens absolutum].' (Hypothesis 5, Ch.1).

abstract [abstractum]

abstraction [abstractio]

accidental [accidentalis]

affirmation [affirmatio]

analogy [comparatio]

awareness [cognitio]

beauty [pulchritudo]

'This ideal beauty [Pulchritudo haec idealis] is reflected, like glory, from that unity which we have just mentioned, as if from light, and by means of Ideas, which are like numerous rays of light [ab illa quam modo diximus unitate, velut a luce, per ideas quasi per radios multos resultat, ut splendor].' (Ch.84).

being [ens/esse]

'The opposite of being is non-being [oppositum quidem entis est non ens], but the opposite of good is evil [oppositum vero boni malum]; yet evil and non-being are not exactly the same [sed malum non idem penitus atque non ens].' (Ch.47).

'The five kinds of being [Quinque genera entis] are dealt with in the *Sophist* [in sophiste tractantur], and we have dealt with them at some length in the *Philebus* and the *Timaeus* as well as in Plotinus [ac nos eadem in Philebo et Timaeo atque Plotino satius pertractavimus].' (Ch.66).

'But when he defines being as a participation of essence together with the present time [Ubi vero definit esse quasi quandam participationem essentiae una cum praesenti tempore], note that there is first a confirmation of what is often generally said [primo quidem adverte confirmari quod dici plerumque solet], namely, that being itself is the action of essence [ipsum esse actum essentiae], just as shining is the action of light and heating is the action of heat [ferme sicut lucere lucis et calere caloris est actus].' (Ch.92).

'For this one being [Unum ens enim] is not simply one [non est simpliciter unum], but one something [sed unum aliquid], both one and many [et unum atque multa]. It is therefore one and not one [Igitur est unum et non unum], for, being many [Qua enim ratione multa est], it is not one and the same [non eadem est et unum].' (Hypothesis 3, Ch.3).

'In this context, understand the one being as principally the intelligible world [Unum ens hic in primis accipe mundum intelligibilem], the first uniform and omniform form [formam primam uniformem et omniformem]. To this compare matter, which is utterly without form [Ad hunc materiam compara prorsus informem].' (Hypothesis 5, Ch.1).

'When we speak of the simple One Itself [Quando ipsum simpliciter unum vaticinamur] we are proclaiming the limitless [infinitum prorsus auguramur] by saying that it is not multiple, not composite, not circumscribed, not conjoined [quasi negando scilicet non multiplex, non compositum, non circumscriptum, non coniugatum]. But when we affirm the one being [Quando vero unum ens asserimus] we are appreciating the One Itself as limited by the very form of essence [iam ipsum unum sub ipsa essentiae forma comprehendimus definitum]: a form, however, that is pure and quite universal [sed mera illa quidem et penitus universa].' (Hypothesis 7).

cause [causa]

> **contingent causes** [contingentes causae]
>
> **efficient cause** [causa efficiens]
>
> **final cause** [finalis causa]
>
> **ideal causes** [ideales rationes]
>
> **model causes** [causae exemplares]
>
> **proximate causes** [causae propinquae]
>
> **seed causes** [rationes seminales]
>
> **type-causes** [speciales]
>
> **universal and absolute causes of creation** [comunes quaedam rerum absolutaeque rationes]

cognise [cognoscere]

concept [notio]

consciousness [cognitio]

> 'Essence is akin to stillness, and life to movement [Essentia quidem statui, vita vero motui similis]; again, life is akin to direct movement, and consciousness to reflected movement [item vita quidem motui recto, cognitio vero reflexo].' (Ch.46).
>
> 'Consciousness perceives things as they are within itself [Cognitio res quemadmodum sunt in ipsa percipit].' (Ch.46).

creator [conditor]

defender [adstipulator]

'Dionysius the Areopagite [Dionysius Areopagita], the supreme defender of this book [libri huius summus adstipulator].' (Ch.79).

dialectic [dialectica]

difference [alteritas]

'But remember [Sed memento] that difference is rightly described [alteritatem proprie dici] as a divisive factor [proprietatem quandam divisoriam] implanted within beings [entibus insitam] and directly opposed to the sameness brought about through unification [identitati per conciliationem advenienti prorsus oppositam].' (Ch.68).

differentiation [discretio]

dissimilarity [dissimilitudo]

effect [effectus]

element [elementum]

entity [entitas]

equality [aequalitas]

essence [essentia]

'Therefore essences and types are everywhere [ubique igitur essentiae speciesque sunt].' (Ch.24).

'Essence is akin to stillness, and life to movement [Essentia quidem statui, vita vero motui similis].' (Ch.46).

'Essence itself, as essence, does not increase or decrease [Essentia ipsa, qua ratione essentia est, magis minusve non suscipit].' (Ch.46).

'The first essence, life, and mind are identical [idem est prima essentia, vita, mens].' (Ch.57).

'Now it is a property of this intelligible essence [Est autem proprium intelligibilis huius essentiae] to be especially within the One [esse in primis in uno], since it is as close as possible to the One [siquidem est uni quam proxima] and it cleaves to it uninterruptedly and unwaveringly [ipsique indistanter et indeclinanter inhaeret].' (Ch.62).

'Remember that Parmenides often comprehends essence under the name of *being* [memineris Parmenidem saepe sub nomine entis essentiam intelligere]. This essence is absolutely nothing but the bringing forth or unfolding of the One through which being takes root [Quae quidem essentia ferme nihil aliud est quam unius productio vel processio quaedam, qua ens interim coalescit]. But now the elements, as it were, of being [Iam vero entis quasi elementa] are equally the essential One and the one essence [sunt essentiale unum, pariter et essentia una]. When these two are fused together by God [Quibus sane duobus invicem conflatis divinitus], a complete form, as I might call it, arises [totalis quaedam, ut ita dixerim, forma consurgit], which on a concrete principle we call a being [Quam et sub ratione concreta ens] and which on an abstract principle we can call an entity [et sub ratione abstracta entitatem possumus appellare], so that the entity may be understood as the formal principle of the being [ut entitas ratio formalis entis intelligatur].' (Ch.81).

'But movement and time [Iam vero motus et tempus] are necessarily within the first being [necessario est in ipso ente primo] and also within every being [et in quolibet ente], since essence is like a movement forth from the One [Siquidem essentia est quasi quidam processus ab uno], while the One, of course, seems to be drawn forth into essence, as a point is produced into a line [ubi sane unum in essentiam quasi signum in lineam produci videtur]. Essence, in turn [Essentia rursus], moves forward into being, like a line into a surface [velut linea in superficiem prodit in esse]; being into life, like a surface into depth [Item esse in vitam velut superficies in profundum]; life into mind, like the depth resolving itself into form and figure [vita pergit in mentem ceu profundum absolvitur in formam atque figuram]. Finally, mind turns back through attention to itself [Mens denique sui quadam animadversiónem reflectitur], just as the first figure of the first depth is taken in its totality and rolled into a sphere [sicut figura primi profundi prima consumatur volviturque in orbem].' (Ch.92).

evils [mala]

First [primus]

'When we name the First [Quando nominamus primum], we usually do so [solemus appellare] with some very common epithets of perfection [quibusdam perfectionibus communissimis], such as essence, life, mind, truth, and virtue [scilicet essentia, vita, mente, veritate, virtute].' (Ch.45).

'But the First is utterly single [Primum vero penitus unicum].' (Ch.49).

'This is why Plato in his letters [Plato igitur in epistolis] forbids us to inquire, in relation to the First of all [de ipso omnium primo quaerere] what it is or what its nature is [quale sit, vel quale quid sit], for any such terms undermine and restrict its universal pre-eminence [Conditiones enim eiusmodi eminentiam ubique diiciunt atque definiunt].' (Ch.56).

form [forma]

'The material form [forma materialis] is the most defective of forms [est imperfectissima forma].' (Ch.35).

'The first form [Prima quidem] is prior to the multiplicity of its parts [suam partium multitudinem antecedit], and the second form [Secunda vero] comes after this multiplicity [sequitur], or, rather, accompanies it [vel potius comitatur]. The first is called the super-essential unity [Illa quidem appellatur superessentialis unitas] and goodness [bonitasque], the pinnacle of that intelligible world [mundi illius intelligibilis apex]. The second is called beauty [Secunda vero pulchritudo], that is, a coherence and order and a succession of Ideas [id est, contextus quidam et ordo, ac series idearum].' (Ch.84).

'The first form [Illa quidem] is the uppermost limit of the intelligible world [summus est intelligibilis mundi terminus], while the second form [haec autem] is its final limit [terminus eiusdem ultimus], and in the mean position are [media vero sunt] the essential One and the one essence [essentiale unum et essentia una], the limited and the unlimited [item finitum, et infinitum], as well as substance, life, and intellect [rursus substantia, vita, intellectus], with, moreover [Praeterea], the five kinds of things [quinque rerum genera], followed immediately by the type-Ideas [subinde speciales ideae] and finally by the multifarious manners of types [denique multiformes specierum modi].' (Ch.84).

God [Deus]

'He defines God as the sole beginning of everything, totally simple and totally supreme [Deum principium omnium unicum, simplicissimum, eminentissimum esse designat].' (Ch.40).

'Unity, therefore, is the proper name of God [Unitas ergo proprium est Dei nomen], the unity that is completely above essence [unitas omnino super essentiam], God single and first [Deus unicus et primus]; while the pre-eminent unities within sublime essences are the numerous favourable gods [unitates in essentiis sublimibus eminentes dii multi sunt atque secundi].' (Ch. 50).

Good itself [bonum ipsum]

'The opposite of being is non-being [oppositum quidem entis est non ens], but the opposite of good is evil [oppositum vero boni malum].' (Ch.47).

'The opposite of the Good is the not-good [oppositum boni est non bonum], just as non-being is the opposite of being [sicut non ens entis oppositum].' (Ch. 47).

'The Good is what all beings seek [Bonum est quod omnia entia appetunt].' (Ch.47).

'Nothing is better than the Good itself, and so nothing is higher [nihil ipso bono melius, nihil ergo superius].' (Ch.56).

'But since there cannot be two principles [Cum vero duo principia esse nequeant], the One and the Good are the same in all respects [idem est penitus unum atque bonum]; yet, as we have said elsewhere, we call it the One on account of its uniqueness and surpassing simplicity [sed unum quidem, ut alibi diximus, propter singularitatem et excellentem simplicitatem], and we call it the Good on account of its abundance and all-pervasiveness [bonum vero propter foecunditatem communicationemque amplissimam nominamus].' (Ch.56).

goodness [bonitas]

Idea [idea]

'they come to the investigation of Ideas, in which the unities of all things consist [ad ideas investigandas perveniunt, in quibus rerum unitates consistunt]' (Dedication).

'For an Idea is a totally unmoving cause [Idea enim causa est prorsus immobilis].' (Ch.8).

Xenocrates' defintion of Ideas: 'Ideas are the model causes [Ideae sunt causae exemplares] of those things which always exist in accordance with nature [eorum quae secundum naturam semper consistunt].'

'God Himself is every Idea [quaelibet … idea est ipse Deus].' (Ch.13).

'Since an Idea exists within itself [cum in seipsa consistat], it can, through its presence [potest per praesentiam], be fully present at the same time in many disparate objects [tota simul multis inter se disiunctis adesse].' (Ch.18).

'It is clearly seen [plane constat] that Ideas are remote from all differentiation, all place, all movement, and all time [illas procul ab omni divisione, loco, motu, tempore esse], being indivisible, unmoving, eternal, and present everywhere [impartibiles, immobiles, aeternas, ubique praesentes]: so present that each quality of an Idea [ita praesentes ut cuiuslibet ideae proprietas quaedam] extends to the uttermost ends of creation [ad ultimas perveniat mundi formas].' (Ch.20).

'the Ideas themselves [ideas ipsas], which are the principal intelligible things [quae praecipua intelligibilia sunt].' (Ch.22).

'Now Ideas are distant intelligible things [ideae vero intelligibilia sunt remota] (Ch.22).

'Therefore, when we speak about Ideas [Quando igitur loquimur de ideis], we ought not to consider Ideas as intelligences or actions [non tanquam intelligentias scilicet actiones quasdam ideas excogitare debemus], but as subjects [sed tanquam objecta]], as the types and natural powers [et species viresque naturales] which accompany the essence of the primal intellect [intellectus primi essentiam comitantes] and upon which is focused the intelligence of that intellect [circa quas intellectus illius versetur intelligentia].' (Ch. 23).

'Ideas are intelligible things rather than intelligences [Ideae non tam intelligentiae quam intelligibilia sunt], and these intelligible things [atque haec] are prior to intelligences [intelligentias antecedunt].' (Ch.24).

'Ideas are not simple notions [Ideae non sunt simplices notiones] but natural types [sed species naturales] which possess model power and effective power [vim exemplarem efficientemque habentes].' (Ch.26).

'He puts forward a true and definite view of Ideas, saying [Veram certamque de ideis sententiam proferens ait] that they abide within nature as models [eas tanquam exemplaria in natura consistere], while all other things are made like them [caetera vero his similia fieri] and are nothing but the images of Ideas [nec esse aliud quam imagines idearum].' (Ch.26).

'Ideas and all things divine are separate from nature [ideae divinaque omnia et natura segregata sunt] and have a power [et virtutem habent] that can be imparted to everything [cunctis communicabilem].' (Ch.28).

'... the very great difficulty in being able to understand what Ideas are [difficillime comprehendi posse quid sint ideae], where they are initially [ubi primo sint], how they relate to themselves and to the things of our world [quomodo ad se et ad nostra se habent], and through what steps and what kinds of powers [per quos gradus et quales earum vires] they proceed to the things of our world [ad nostra procedant].' (Ch.28).

'Indeed, in Plato's view it is certainly reasonable for an Idea to have two properties [Oportet sane duas ideam apud Platonem proprietates habere]. The first is a distinctive substance [primam quidem substantiam eminentem], having no admixture or participation with nature and no tendency towards natural forms [videlicet neque commixtionem communionemque naturae neque inclinationem ullam ad naturales formas habentem]. The second is power and action [secundam vero virtutem actionemque] which can be imparted throughout the universe [per universum communicabilem], diffusing its own beneficial gifts in all directions [suaque passim munera, propria etiam, praesentia diffundentem].' (Ch.28).

'On the six orders of Ideas or forms [de sex ordinibus idearum vel formarum]':

1. 'If any Ideas exist in the first principle [si quae sunt in principio primo] ... they will in no way be intelligible to us or to any other beings [nullo modo vel nobis vel ullis intelligibiles], since they will exist beyond all the limits of intelligence itself [existentes videlicet super omnes ipsius intelligentiae terminos].'

2. 'Ideas which are now simply intelligible [ideae iam intelligibiles quidem simpliciter], yet comprehensible to us with difficulty and at long last [nobis autem vix et tandem intelligendae]. These are the causes of all things within the first intellect [Rationes scilicet rerum omnium in intellectu primo] – or, as our writers would say, within the first angelic level [ut nostri dicerent, angelo primo] – causes distinct one from another through absolute principles [absolutis iam rationibus inter se discretae].'

3. 'Thirdly, there are the intellectual Ideas [sunt tertio et intellectuales ideae] within the successive intellects [in sequentibus intellectibus] that have no dealings with bodily matters [a corporum commertio separatis].'

4. 'Fourthly, there are the living Ideas [Quarto sunt animales], implanted within the very minds and thoughts of divine, or even human, souls [ipsis animarum vel divinarum vel etiam humanarum mentibus insitae].'

5. 'Fifthly, there are the natural Ideas and types within quickening nature [Quinto naturales ideae speciesque sunt in vegetali natura], that is, the seed-causes of bodily forms within the nature of the natural soul [seminales videlicet formarum corporalium rationes in natura quidem et naturalis animae] and within the natures of the higher souls and of our souls [et in naturis animarum superiorum atque nostrarum].'

233

6. 'Sixthly, there are the forms within matter [Sexto formae sunt in materia], which, depending as it were upon all that is higher to them [quae quidem tanquam a superioribus omnibus dependentes], have something from each preceding world [aliquid e singulis habent]: from the divine world [a divinis] something mysterious and divine [occultum aliquid et divinum] as well as unity and goodness [et unitatem atque bonitatem]; from the intelligible world [ab intelligibilibus] a particular kind of eternality [aeternitatem specialem] and the distinctiveness necessary for living beings [distinctionemque necessariam animalibus] as well as a quite distinctive beauty [distinctiorem pulchritudinem] together with action and movement [et actionem atque motum]; from the natural world [a naturalibus] their point of manifestation [ortum] and their final differentiation [et divisionem ultimam].' (Ch.33).

image [imago]

'He puts forward a true and definite view of Ideas, saying [Veram certamque de ideis sententiam proferens ait] that they abide within nature as models [eas tanquam exemplaria in natura consistere], while all other things are made like them [caetera vero his similia fieri] and are nothing but the images of Ideas [nec esse aliud quam imagines idearum].' (Ch.26).

immobility [status]

immobile things [res stabiles]

incorporeal [incorporeus]

indissoluble [indissolubilis]

individual [singularis]

indivisible [impartibilis, indivisibilis]

inequality [inaequalitas]

intellect [intellectus]

'intellects are completely circular and pure [intellectus sane circuli quidam sunt atque mundi]' (Ch.5).

'Intellect is more eminent and closer to reality than is sense [intellectus praestantior et verior est quam sensus].' (Ch.22).

'Intelligence and intellect are not imparted to all things everywhere [non ubique intelligentia intellectusque omnibus distribuitur].' (Ch.24).

'Intellects are primarily intelligent souls [intellectus sunt particulariter intelligentes animae]: either daemons or angels [sive daemones, sive angeli].' (Ch.49).

'However, the one being, the first intellect, is everywhere [Unum vero ens, id est, intellectus primus, est ubique]. Firstly, it is within its cause, which is the Good itself, the begetter of intelligence [Primo quidem est in causa, id est ipso bono intelligentiae patre]. Secondly, it is within itself, where

234

there is intelligence within life, and life within essence [deinde etiam in seipso, penes quem est intelligentia in vita, haec in essentia]. Thirdly, it is within whatever follows, carefully regulating every individual thing, wherever it may be, and distributing in all places forms which are to some extent similar to their model [Est insuper in sequentibus, singula providenter ubique dispensans formasque quodammodo similes exemplari ubique disponens].' (Ch.62).

'Indeed, it is a property of the intellect itself [Proprium quidem est intellectus ipsius] that while it is within something else [dum in alio est] – its father [scilicet patre suo] – it nevertheless abides within itself [interim in se ipso manere], that is, it is turned back to itself through some perfect form of attention [id est, et ad se ipsum perfecta quadam animadversione reflecti], and it is not encompassed or influenced by anything that follows [et sequentibus nullis coerceri vel affici].' (Ch.62).

'We shall admit, again in company with Anaxagoras, that the intellect itself is the discriminator of everything [iterum cum Anaxagora, intellectum ipsum esse discretorem omnium confitebimur].' (Ch.90).

'The intellect produces in this world forms as numerous as the Ideas which the Craftsman perceives [quot ideas architectus inspicit, intellectus totidem in mundo formas effingit].' (Ch.91).

intellectual [intellectualis]

intelligence [intelligentia]

In Ch.23 Ficino says that Parmenides gives the name *notion* to true intelligence ['intelligentia vera, quam nunc nominat notionem'].

'Intelligence is really an action [Intelligentia quidem formaliter actio quaedam est] and a sort of movement [et quasi motus], while type is essence and power and aim [species autem essentia est, et virtus, et terminus]. Therefore intelligence is not identical with the first type [Non igitur idem intelligentia speciesque prima] which is perceived everywhere through intelligence [per intelligentiam ubique percepta].' (Ch.24).

'Intelligence and intellect are not imparted to all things everywhere [non ubique intelligentia intellectusque omnibus distribuitur].' (Ch.24).

'All intelligences are related to their respective intelligibles [ad sua intelligibilia intelligentiae quaelibet referuntur]: divine to divine [divinae ad divina], human to human [humanae ad humana], and so on [similiaque].' (Ch.31).

intelligible [intelligibilis]

'... those things, too, which are always the same and which are called the intelligible [intelligibilia], perceptible no longer by the senses but by mind alone [sola mente]' (Dedication)

'As intellect is more eminent and closer to reality than is sense [quanto intellectus praestantior et verior est quam sensus], so intelligible things are closer to perfection and reality than are perceptible things [tanto intelligibilia sensibilibus perfectiora sunt atque veriora].' (Ch.22).

'Now the intelligible things are those to which the intellect naturally turns whenever it is unencumbered [Intelligibilia vero sunt ad quae naturaliter convertitur intellectus quotiens est expeditus]. These are the universal and absolute causes of creation [Hae vero sunt communes quaedam rerum absolutaeque rationes].' (Ch.22).

'The true intelligible things, however [vera autem intelligibilia], are both unchangeable and prior to intelligence [et immutabilia sunt et intelligentiam antecedunt].' (Ch.22).

'Now Ideas are distant intelligible things [ideae vero intelligibilia sunt remota], while these intelligible things which are closest [proxima quidem haec intelligibilia], being nearer to perfection [tanquam perfectiora], are not gathered together by perceptible things, which are imperfect [a sensibilibus tanquam imperfectis collecta non sunt], but are imparted by the first intelligible things [sed a primis infusa].'

'Now the things that are intelligible [Intelligibilia vero] are the type-causes of all things [sunt speciales ipsae omnium]: they are universal, unchangeable, absolute [communes, immutabiles, absolutae].' (Ch.23).

'But in all this you should understand [Tu vero inter haec intellige] that in the writings of the Platonists the intelligible world is the name given not only to this intellect but also to the host of all noble minds [mundum intelligibilem non hunc tantum intellectum, sed omnium quoque sublimium mentium caetum apud Platonicos nominari].' (Ch.80).

knowledge [scientia]

'Within the primal intellect [In intellectu primo], ideal pure knowledge is nothing but intelligence and a sure understanding of itself and of all things [est idealis ipsa simpliciter scientia nihil aliud quam intelligentia certaque sui ipsius omniumque comprehensio]. Again, it is the ideal truth [est item idealis ipsa veritas], that is, the primal and complete essence and nature of the Good itself [id est, prima omnisque essentia naturaque ipsius boni], shining with light [lumine fulgens], the light by which intelligence looks at and discerns its own intelligibile [quo quidem lumine et intelligentia spectat et cernit intelligibile suum].' (Ch. 31).

life [vita]

'The first essence, life, and mind are identical [idem est prima essentia, vita, mens].' (Ch.57).

'Essence is akin to stillness, and life to movement [Essentia quidem statui, vita vero motui similis]; again, life is akin to direct movement, and consciousness to reflected movement [item vita quidem motui recto, cognitio vero reflexo].' (Ch.46).

limit [terminus/finis]

limitlessness [infinitas/infinitum]

'All limitlessness is in some way the whole, but the converse is not true [Omne quidem infinitum est quodammodo totum, neque contra].' (Ch.95).

'But to put it briefly [Summatim vero]: from this conjoining of limitlessness and limit [ex isto infinitatis terminique coniugio], which are the first elements of all beings [quae prima sunt entium elementa], the other conjoinings of opposites take place sporadically [caetera quoque oppositorum coniugia passim accidunt]. I mean the conjoinings of dissimilars [Coniugia inquam in dissidendo]: sameness and change [identitas, alteritas], similarity and dissimilarity [similitudo, dissimilitudo], stillness and movement [status, motus], equality and inequality [aequalitas, inaequalitas], parity and imparity [paritas, imparitas], and such like [caeteraque deinceps].' (Hypothesis 4, Ch.2).

matter [materia]

'Since the essence of matter is deformity [cum materiae ratio sit informitas]' (Ch.35).

'In this context, understand the one being as principally the intelligible world [Unum ens hic in primis accipe mundum intelligibilem], the first uniform and omniform form [formam primam uniformem et omniformem]. To this compare matter, which is utterly without form [Ad hunc materiam compara prorsus informem].' (Hypothesis 5, Ch.1).

'If we consider, on the one hand, the One Itself in its sublime simplicity [Si hinc quidem ipsum unum in ipsa sua eminentissima simplicitate consideremus], and, on the other hand, matter in its pure primal state [inde vero materiam in ipso mero primoque ipsius gradu], we shall see that matter, being wholly dependent on the One, possesses something of the One or receives something from the One [solum inde, id est ab uno pendentem videbimus hanc aliquid illius habere vel ab illo]. For each is unitary and simple [Utrumque enim et unicum et simplex]. Of each all things are negated [De utroque negantur omnia], but it is an excess-negation for the One [quamvis de illo quidem per excessum] and a deficiency-negation for matter [de hac autem per defectum]. Between these two – between the highest and the lowest – all things are encompassed [Inter utraque tanquam summum et infimum omnia coercentur].' (Hypothesis 5, Ch.2).

'In brief, matter by its very nature [Materia denique sua quidem natura], if any nature is merely to be mentioned [si qua modo natura dicenda est], has no unity, no form, no movement [nec unitatem habet neque formam neque motum]. But it is allotted unity from the simple One Itself as it comes forth from it [Sed ab ipso simpliciter uno, mox inde procedens, sortita est unitatem]. Then it is allotted forms from the one being [Deinde vero ab uno ente formas]. Thirdly and lastly, it is allotted movements from the soul [Tertio tandem ab anima motus].' (Hypothesis 5, Ch.2).

formless matter [informis materia]

237

mind [mens]

'The first essence, life, and mind are identical [idem est prima essentia, vita, mens].' (Ch.57).

'The divine mind [Divina mens], as we have shown in the *Theology* and the *Timaeus* [quemadmodum in Theologia Timaeoque probavimus], continuously conceives all the forms of all things with a single steadfast act [omnes omnium formas unico stabilique semper actu concipit], gives birth inwardly [paritque intus], and observes [et inspicit]. (Hypothesis 3, Ch.2).

model [exemplar]

'He puts forward a true and definite view of Ideas, saying [Veram certamque de ideis sententiam proferens ait] that they abide within nature as models [eas tanquam exemplaria in natura consistere].' (Ch.26).

ideal model [exemplar ideale]

movement [motus/processus]

moving things [res mobiles]

multiplicity [multitudo]

natural [naturalis]

nature [natura]

'Just as the first One [Quemadmodum primum unum] can nowhere be partaken of by any one [a nullo usquam uno participabile est], so the first being is partaken of by no being [ita ens primum a nullo ente], and the first intellect by no intellect [primus intellectus ab intellectu nullo], since within any hierarchy [Siquidem in quolibet ordine] the nature that is pre-eminent and cannot be partaken of [supereminens imparticipabilisque natura] precedes the nature that can be partaken of [participabilem antecedit]. The latter, however, perfects all things that partake of it [Participabilis autem omnia participantia perficit].' (Ch.87).

'Nature, the everlasting instrument of divine unity [natura tanquam unitatis divinae perpetuum instrumentum].' (Hypothesis 4, Ch.1).

enlivening nature [vegetalis natura]

negation [negatio]

notion [notio]

'True intelligence, which he now calls *notion* [intelligentia vera, quam nunc nominat notionem].' (Ch.23).

number [numerus]

'All number is multiplicity, but the converse does not hold [omnis numerus multitudo, neque vicissim].' (Ch.95).

One [unum]

'when One is mentioned in this dialogue it can ... indicate any single substance that is totally detached from matter, such as God, mind, and soul [in hoc dialogo cum dicitur unum ... unaquaeque substantia a materia penitus absoluta significari potest, ut Deus, mens, anima].' (Dedication)

'The simple One Itself [ipsum simpliciter unum] first creates the superior divine unities [unitates primo excellentes procreat et divinas], which are also known as gods [quae et dii vocantur]; then it creates the unities which are implanted within things [Deinde uniones rebus insitas], and then those which are related and specific to those things that are united [iamque cognatas et proprias unitorum]. The One Itself, however, differs from those unities [differt autem ipsum unum ab unitatibus illis], for it is absolutely free of all characteristics [quoniam ipsum ab omnibus proprietatibus est absolutum].' (Ch.52).

'The One Itself is totally indivisible [unum esse penitus impartibile].' (Ch.53).

'The One Itself [ipsum unum] is not multiplicity [neque multitudo est], and it has neither whole nor part [neque totum, neque partem habet]. Again, it has no beginning [Rursus nec habet principium], no middle, no end, no limit, no shape [nec medium, neque finem aliquem aut terminum, neque figuram]. It is not within another [nec est in alio] and not within itself [nec in seipso]. It neither stays nor moves [neque stat, neque movetur]. It is neither the same nor other [nec idem est, nec alterum]. It is neither similar nor dissimilar to itself or to others [vel sibimet, vel aliis, neque simile, neque dissimile]. It is neither equal nor unequal to itself or to others [nec aequale, nec inaequale]. It is neither greater nor less than itself or others [neque maius, neque minus]. Again, it is neither older nor younger [Item non senius, non iunius]. It does not partake of generation or of time or of what is said to be being [neque generationem participat, neque tempus, neque est particeps ipsius quod dicitur esse]. It cannot be named, spoken of, thought about, or known [nec est nominabile, nec effabile, nec opinabile, nec scibile].' (Ch.56).

'Finally, let us conclude, with the followers of Plato [Concludamus denique cum Platonicis], by saying that when Plato negates multiplicity with respect to the One [ubi Plato multitudinem negat uni], he merely means that nothing higher can be thought of [nihil aliud velle quam et ipsum supra quam cogitari possit]; that the One is utterly simple and unmanifest [simplicissimum secretissimumque esse]; and that from it the whole multiplicity of the form of things proceeds as numbers proceed from unity [et universum ab eo rerum multitudinem formae, sicut ab unitate numeros proficisci]. What Plato here calls the One [Quod autem hic unum nominat] that is above being [ente superius], in the *Republic* he calls the Good that is above essence [in Republica nominat bonum similiter super essentiam], but as we learn from the *Phaedo* and from *Parmenides* [ut autem accipimus ex Phaedone simulatque Parmenide], the One and the Good have the same property [idem est proprium unius atque boni] of perfecting all things, containing all things, and pervading all things [scilicet perficere omnia atque continere et pariter per omnia propagari].' (Ch.56).

'Nothing is simpler than the One, and so nothing is above the One [nihil etiam simplicius uno, nihil igitur super unum].' (Ch.56).

'But since there cannot be two principles [Cum vero duo principia esse nequeant], the One and the Good are the same in all respects [idem est penitus unum atque bonum]; yet, as we have said elsewhere, we call it the One on account of its uniqueness and surpassing simplicity [sed unum quidem, ut alibi diximus, propter singularitatem et excellentem simplicitatem], and we call it the Good on account of its abundance and all-pervasiveness [bonum vero propter foecunditatem communicationemque amplissimam nominamus]' (Ch.56).

'The most significant property of the One Itself is not to be within another in any way [ipsius unius maxime proprium est nec esse in alio ullo modo].' (Ch.62).

'When we speak of the simple One Itself [Quando ipsum simpliciter unum vaticinamur] we are proclaiming the limitless [infinitum prorsus auguramur] by saying that it is not multiple, not composite, not circumscribed, not conjoined [quasi negando scilicet non multiplex, non compositum, non circumscriptum, non coniugatum]. But when we affirm the one being [Quando vero unum ens asserimus] we are appreciating the One Itself as limited by the very form of essence [iam ipsum unum sub ipsa essentiae forma comprehendimus definitum]: a form, however, that is pure and quite universal [sed mera illa quidem et penitus universa].' (Hypothesis 6, Ch.5).

opinion [opinio]

perceptible [sensibilis]

'... those things which flow and are subject to the senses and are named the perceptible [sensibilia]' (Dedication)

power [vis, virtus]

effective power [vis efficiens]

model power [vis exemplaris]

principle [principium/ratio]

'There is the principle of the One Itself [Alia quidem ratio est ipsius unius], and there is a different principle for everything else [alia aliorum]. There is a principle of greatness, a principle of smallness, and a principle of equality [Alia magnitudinis, alia parvitatis, alia aequalitatis].' (Ch.90).

'Among the principles of the second hypothesis [Inter ipsa suppositionis secundae principia], he first goes to the intelligible world [mundum in primis attingit intelligibilem] and later to all the divinities [consequenter autem et deos omnes], even those that transcend the world [vel tramundanos]. He posits two of these principles quite openly: the One and being [In quibus duo quidem palam praecipua ponit, unum scilicet atque ens]. A third he tacitly hints at [Tertium vero clam innuit]: a power midway between the first two [Potentiam scilicet utriusque mediam], a power which is the reciprocity between the One and being [Quae quidem est mutua quaedam unius ad ens habitudo]; through which there is the One of being and also the being of the One [per quam et unum est entis et ens unius].' (Ch.95).

Providence [providentia]

ratio [ratio]

sameness [identitas]

'Since all things are endowed with infinite goodness by the simple One Itself [cum omnia ab ipso simpliciter uno infinita virtute praedita fiant], and are preserved and held by it [serventurque et contineantur], and are turned back by the unity predominant in everything [atque convertantur merito regnante in rebus unitate], then sameness is supreme [regnat identitas]. Therefore difference can nowhere be supreme and cannot in any way exist [Omnimodo igitur alteritas neque regnare usquam, neque quomodolibet esse potest], since it is obliged in all places to be mixed with a degree of sameness [cum ubique cogatur cum quadam identitate misceri].' (Ch.87).

similarity [similitudo]

skill [artificium]

soul [anima]

'It (the soul) has three orders [Huius vero tres sunt ordines]. The first is that held by the souls of the greater spheres [Primum quod tenent sphaerarum ampliorum animae]. The second is that held by the souls of the stars [Secundum vero stellarum animae]. The third is that held by the souls of the invisible divine powers which furnish universal providence within the spheres [tertium numinum invisibilium animae universalem providentiam in sphaeris agentium].' (Hypothesis 3, Ch.1).

'As we have shown in the *Theology*, the soul holds the mean position in the five levels of creation [Quae inter quinque rerum gradus, quemadmodum in Theologia probamus, tenet medium].' (Hypothesis 3, Ch.1).

'For the celestial soul is exactly like a celestial sphere [Caelestis enim anima ita ferme se habet ut sphaera caelestis].' (Hypothesis 3, Ch.1).

'Now above the soul is the intelligible world [Super animam quidem mundus extat intelligibilis], while below the soul is the perceptible world [Infra vero mundus ille sensibilis].' (Hypothesis 3, Ch.1).

'The divine mind [Divina mens], as we have shown in the *Theology* and the *Timaeus* [quemadmodum in Theologia Timaeoque probavimus], continuously conceives all the forms of all things with a single steadfast act [omnes omnium formas unico stabilique actu concipit], gives birth inwardly [paritque intus], and observes [et inspicit]. We have shown in the same works [Probavimus ibidem] that the divine soul begins its journey from there, being heavy with all the forms [divinam formam illinc formis cunctis gravidam proficisci] and, like a rival of the divine mind [Et tanquam illius aemulam], it also cherishes a similar conception, birth, and observation [similem quoque conceptum, et partum, et intuitum affectare].' (Hypothesis 3, Ch.2).

'For my part, I think [Opinor equidem] that this soul is considered to be in stillness rather than in movement [animam hanc in statu quidem esse potius iudicandum quam in motu] all the time that it is looking attentively upon, striving ardently after, and effectively expressing, the things which are eternal and intelligible and the principles which are related to stillness [dum aeterna, intelligibiliaque et rationes statui cognatiores attentius inspicit, ardentius affectat, efficacius exprimit]; and that it is in movement rather than in stillness [magis autem in motu versari] whenever it betakes itself to all that is opposite [quando se potius ad opposita transfert].' (Hypothesis 3, Ch.3).

'The soul, in some way, alternately is and is not, through perpetual alternation [anima vicissim est atque non est quodammodo, mutatione perpetua].' (Hypothesis 6, Ch.5).

'Now the soul [nunc quidem anima], being illumined and strengthened by the intelligible substance [per intelligibilem substantiam illustrata atque roborata], has true cognition [vere cognoscit] and brings forth natural forms [et formas efficit naturales]. But if deserted by the intellect [Tunc autem ab intellectu deserta], it would engage in false imagination [imaginaretur falso], bring forth likenesses and shadows instead of natural forms [et pro naturalibus formis simulachra quaedam et umbras effingeret], and devise scenarios that are nothing but empty dreams [et imaginamenta, velut somnia prorsus inania, secum ipsa confingeret].' (Hypothesis 8, Ch.1).

rational soul [rationalis anima]

'It has been handed down from the ancients that the substance of the rational soul is divine [animae rationalis substantiam esse divinam].' (Ch.32).

substance [materia, substantia]

'In the commentaries on Plotinus, whom I follow more gladly than I do Proclus, both here and in many other matters, we have often shown [Saepe probavimus in commentariis in Plotinum, quem in hoc, sicut et in pluribus, libentius quam Proclum sequor] that the intellect, the intelligible, the first being, the first essence, and the first life are in fact a single substance [intellectum, intelligibile, ens primum, essentiam, vitamque primam re ipsa unam esse substantiam], although within that substance they do differ in principle [haec autem ibi quadam ratione differre].' (Ch.56).

supercelestial [supercoelestis]

Supreme [summum]

theology [theologia]

'As Socrates discusses in the *Republic* [ut Socrates disputat in Republica], the art of discernment [ars discernendi] is theology itself [est ipsa Theologia].' (Ch.79).

time [tempus]

'Time, which is dependent on eternity [Tempus ab aeternitate dependens], possesses mostly its own nature [plurimum quidem habet sui], but also something of eternity [aeternitatis quoque nonnihil].' (Ch.76).

Trinity [Trinitas]

'The followers of Plato think that the Trinity, which we have often described as impossible to reckon by any order of priority, is the Good itself, the intellect itself, the soul of the world [Trinitatem, quam saepe diximus principiorum ordinibus nullis connumerabilem esse Platonici putant, ipsum bonum, ipsum intellectum, mundi animam]. Indeed, they frequently describe the Good as the Father [Bonum quidem saepe patrem nominant], the intellect as the Son [Intellectum vero filium], and the soul of the world as the Spirit [animam mundi spiritum].' (Ch.94).

truth [veritas]

'This universal intelligible [universum et hoc intelligibile], which we have called truth [quod appellavimus veritatem], offers itself to the intelligence and penetrates it in order to be thoroughly understood [seipsum offert et insert ipsi intelligentiae penitus compraehendendum].' (Ch.31).

type [species]

'The first types of creation [Primae rerum species], which are also the principal subjects of the intellect [quae etiam sunt principalia intellectus objecta], are prior to the intelligences [intelligentias antecedunt].' (Ch.23).

'Therefore the first types are not actually intelligences [Non igitur primae species formaliter intelligentiae sunt], but intelligible things [sed intelligibilia quaedam], that is [id est], the essential, actual, and true causes of all things [essentiales formalesque et verae rationes omnium], the models and efficient powers of all things [exemplares atque virtutes omnium effectrices].' (Ch.24).

'Type is essence and power and aim [species autem essentia est, et virtus, et terminus].' (Ch.24).

natural types [species naturales]

'Therefore essences and types are everywhere [ubique igitur essentiae speciesque sunt].' (Ch.24).

type-causes [speciales]

'Now the things that are intelligible [Intelligibilia vero] are the type-causes of all things [sunt speciales ipsae omnium].' (Ch.23).

unchangeable [immutabilis]

union [unio]

unity [unitas/unio]

'Unity, therefore, is the proper name of God [Unitas ergo proprium est Dei nomen], the unity that is completely above essence [unitas omnino super essentiam], God single and first [Deus unicus et primus]; while the pre-eminent unities within sublime essences are the numerous favourable gods [unitates in essentiis sublimibus eminentes dii multi sunt atque secundi].' (Ch.50).

'The simple One Itself [ipsum simpliciter unum] first creates the superior divine unities [unitates primo excellentes procreat et divinas], which are also known as gods [quae et dii vocantur]; then it creates the unities which are implanted within things [Deinde uniones rebus insitas], and then those which are related and specific to those things that are united [iamque cognatas et proprias unitorum]. The One Itself, however, differs from those unities [differt autem ipsum unum ab unitatibus illis], for it is absolutely free of all characteristics [quoniam ipsum ab omnibus proprietatibus est absolutum].' (Ch.52).

virtue [virtus]

    civil virtues [civiles virtutes]

    moral virtues [morales virtutes]

visible [visibilis]

world [mundus]

    physical world [mundus corporeus]

    world-soul [mundi anima]

NAME INDEX

The Letters of Marsilio Ficino

Translated from the Latin by members of the Language Department of the School of Economic Science, London

'With philosophy as its guide the soul gradually comes to comprehend with its intelligence the nature of all things'

MARSILIO FICINO of Florence (1433-99) was one of the most influential thinkers of the Renaissance. He put before society a new ideal of human nature, emphasising its divine potential. As teacher and guide to a remarkable circle of men, he made a vital contribution to changes that were taking place in European thought. For Ficino, the writings of Plato provided the key to the most important knowledge for mankind, knowledge of God and the soul. It was the absorption of this knowledge that proved so important to Ficino, to his circle, and to later writers and artists.

'From every point of view it is a pleasure to read this perfect introduction to one of the most attractive and influential figures of the Italian Renaissance'
Daily Telegraph

'[Ficino] was at the very fountainhead of some of the most characteristic and influential aspects of the Italian Renaissance' The Times Literary Supplement

'All that we regard as the norm of Western European art – Botticelli's paintings, Monteverdi's music, Shakespeare's philosophical lovers, Berowne and Lorenzo, Jacques and Portia – has flowered from Ficino's Florence' The Times

'Undoubtedly these letters comprise one of the "spiritual classics" of the past thousand years' The Spectator

'...so well translated, so well annotated and so beautifully produced it is a pleasure to read and possess' Heythrop Journal

To date seven volumes have been published and may be purchased individually or as a set. Volume 8 is scheduled for publication in 2009.

ISBN for the set 978-0-85683-199-7 £140

Marcus Aurelius: The Dialogues

Alan Stedall

'In this delightful and well-written book, Alan Stedall ... has done an enormous service in making some of Marcus Aurelius's reflections very accessible to the modern reader'
Faith and Freedom

'The Dialogues are eminently readable and immediate ... in places irresistible'
The Philosopher

'I was drawn deeper and deeper into the simple solid reasoning ... Stedall's imagined dialogue had me fully in the present'
Midwest Book Review

'I knew within a few lines this was going to be a treasure ... Stedall is a word master ... Bravo!'
The Smoking Poet

Marcus Aurelius, one of the greatest Roman emperors, is remembered less for his military exploits than for his private reflections, *Meditations,* as they became known – the pen is mightier than the sword.

Seeking an alternative to faith-based religion, Alan Stedall came across the book and found rational answers to questions about the meaning and purpose of life that had been troubling him. Here too were answers to his concern that, in the absence of moral beliefs based on religion, we risk creating a world where relativism, the rejection of any sense of absolute right or wrong, prevails. In such a society any moral position is considered subjective and amoral behaviour is unchallengeable.

Because the *Meditations* were jotted down in spare moments during a busy life ruling and defending a huge empire, they lack order and sequence. Inspired by the wisdom of Marcus Aurelius, Stedall sought to present the contents in a more contemporary and digestible way.

To achieve this, he employed the Greek philosophical technique of dialogue to create a fictional conversation between five historical figures who met at Aquileia on the Adriatic coast in AD 168. Apart from Marcus, they were his brother and co-emperor, Lucius, the famous Hellenic surgeon of antiquity, Galen, an Egyptian high priest of Isis, Harnouphis, and Bassaeus Rufus, Prefect of the Praetorian Guard.

The Dialogues afford Marcus and his guests the opportunity to express their views on such topics as the brevity of life and the need to seek meaning; the pursuit of purpose; the supreme good and the pursuit of a virtuous life – issues as relevant today as they were in antiquity. By a gentle process of question and answer, Marcus shows up the weakness of his guests' arguments and reveals how a virtuous life may be lived without the threat of eternal damnation or promise of salvation to enforce compliance. Virtue is its own reward.

112pp   ISBN 978-0-85683-236-9   £9.95 hb